THE OFFBEAT RADICALS

Also by Geoffrey Ashe available from Methuen

Kings & Queens of Early Britain

Mythology of the British Isles

THE OFFBEAT RADICALS

THE BRITISH TRADITION OF ALTERNATIVE DISSENT

GEOFFREY ASHE

Methuen

Published by Methuen, 2007

1 3 5 7 9 10 8 6 4 2

Methuen & Co. Ltd
11–12 Buckingham Gate
London SW1E 6LB

www.methuen.co.uk

Methuen & Co. Ltd Reg. No. 5278590

ISBN 10: 0-413-77460-0
ISBN 13: 978-0-413-77460-6

A CIP catalogue record for this book is available from the British Library.

Typeset in 11 on 15pt Sabon, by FiSH Books, Enfield, Middlesex.
Printed and bound in Great Britain by MPG Books, Bodmin, Cornwall

Author's Note

My special and supreme thanks are due to my wife Patricia, whose contribution to the making of this book was phenomenal. She took on alarming tasks of transcription, revision, inquiry, and compilation, and made many valuable comments and suggestions. These things were all done in superlative style, and with a sustained and wonderful outpouring of enthusiasm.

Contents

List of Illustrations

Introduction

The greatest event of the nineteenth century in England was the revolution which did not happen.[†]

Readers of G. K. Chesterton (there are still plenty of them) will recognise the voice in that statement. I found it quoted, with approval, in the writings of Jawaharlal Nehru, the first prime minister of independent India. It may seem strange to find Chesterton in the company of Indian nationalists, but he has every right to be there. The reason is one of the surprises that come to light when this dictum about the non-revolution is unpacked.

Why was there no revolution in nineteenth-century England, or, to be more accurate, Britain? The short answer is that while the nation harboured immense poverty and injustice, those in power forestalled an explosion by giving way at critical moments: for instance, by granting the Reform Bill of 1832, and by broadening the franchise at other times. But that is not the whole answer. The original reason why there was no revolution in Britain – a reason prior to all others – was that there had been one in France.

Its well-wishers on this side of the Channel hailed the French Revolution as a magnificent step forward. Then the Reign of Terror and the Napoleonic sequel brought disillusionment.

† Nehru, Jawaharlal. *Glimpses of World History*. London, Lindsay Drummond, 1942.

Twenty-two years of almost uninterrupted war with France, first republican and then Bonapartist, produced a thoroughness of hostile reaction, and an unwillingness to sympathise or imitate, that had no real equivalent in other countries. The revulsion was so general and prolonged that the Government could easily clamp down on the rebellious few who refused to share in it.

Some of the Revolution's former enthusiasts, such as William Wordsworth, lapsed into patriotic conservatism. But the reaction left an ideological loose end for others. Some of the ex-enthusiasts, such as William Blake, concurred in disavowing the Revolution, yet remained revolutionary in outlook themselves, and were as vehement as anyone against the evils of the time. They had no obvious, ready-made position to take. What did they say, what did they do?

I became aware of this issue when examining certain British traditions in my book *Camelot and the Vision of Albion*. Moreover, much the same problem presented itself in a variety of settings long after the reverberations of France had died down. During the nineteenth century, and even after, a series of articulate people called for a transformation of society, yet had no use for revolutionary violence as a means of achieving it, and explored paths of their own instead. For these individuals, I have coined the term 'Offbeat Radicals'. This is of course to take a liberty. Most of them were so different from one another that they would probably have objected to being classified, as if they were members of a party. But when they are passed in review together, with all their interrelations, a certain consistency appears, and it becomes fair to speak of a succession that embraces such seemingly improbable bedfellows as Blake and Chesterton.

Dissenting from left-wing and right-wing orthodoxies, the Offbeat Radicals, in one way and another, talked about 'something else': an alternative, a transformation. This might be social or economic; it might be cultural or religious; it might be a different way of living; it might even be an alternative revolution. But their unanimous theme was a clear-cut break with what existed. They did not envisage 'progress' within that context, they envisioned a transition into something fundamentally 'other', something better. This was not a passing ideological fashion. While this study concentrates on figures from the eighteenth century on, the roots of their aspiration can be traced centuries earlier, in a recognised mindset with an origin and a history. My first, prefatory chapter aims to show the long-term perspective without which their radicalism is much less comprehensible.

These studies are not biographies, and they could not be. They are snapshots, taken with one particular aspect in mind. But I find the Offbeat Radicals interesting – and often more than interesting – as human beings.

1

Antecedents

Offbeat Radicalism has an ancestry. Its roots are medieval, in a prophetic system which Norman Cohn has called 'the most influential one known to Europe until the appearance of Marxism'.[†] The system's inventor planted a new concept in European minds. It was hailed, denounced, exaggerated, distorted; after many provocative years, it seemed to vanish; but even in apparent eclipse, it turned out to be inextinguishable.

The man behind this system is known to history as Joachim of Fiore. Late in the twelfth century, while England's absentee monarch Richard I was dazzling foreigners, Joachim was quietly doing a great thing that could never be undone. He was making room in the thinking of his contemporaries, and those who came after, for optimism about the earthly future. In doing so, he was not discoursing vaguely of a vague uplift. He had a definite notion of the way a change for the better would happen. The Offbeat Radicals were the eventual inheritors of Joachim's legacy, though few understood its nature, and some did odd things with it.

What exactly was his achievement?

† Cohn, Norman. *The Pursuit of the Millennium*, p. 108.

The Christians of Joachim's day assumed that while this world had its good times and bad, it was essentially a fallen world and could never be fundamentally improved. It would simply jog on, and sooner or later God would put an end to it. The jeremiads of priests, and other disseminators of gloom, were apt to give the impression that the end might as well come quickly. Then Christ would return in glory, and that was really the only thing to look forward to. The righteous would enjoy a blissful eternity, the damned would be dismissed with no hope at all, and both would have left this present life behind.

Given the habitual thinking of the time, this attitude could only be changed by something in the nature of prophecy: not irresponsible soothsaying, but a reinterpretation of Christian ideas about the future, acceptable as inspired in the eyes of a Christendom that believed in inspiration. This was what Joachim provided. It could not have been provided before – not because Christendom had no prophetic tradition, but because the tradition itself had severe limitations.

The basis of Christian prophecy was the Apocalypse or Revelation of St John, the final book of the New Testament, with its spectacular scenario leading up to the end of the world, the consummation aforesaid. The early Church produced a few would-be prophets, who enlarged on the visions of the Apocalyptist, but still trod in his footsteps. They composed stories that elaborated his imagery of looming disasters, divine judgement on sinners, the Second Coming, the End itself. They added characters to the story, including the arch-persecutor Antichrist – already hinted at in scripture – and a last earthly ruler who would triumph over pagan powers and prepare the way of the Lord.

But they confined their anticipations to the original theme – the End and how it would happen. They chose not to speculate about events unrelated to that, events in the unknown interval between their own time and the End's approach. Admittedly, there was a stubborn delusion that this interval would be cut short, so that there might not be much point in projecting unrelated events into it. Long or short, however, it was not a field for prophecy. The nearer future was left to seers and astrologers in the unhallowed backwaters of Christendom. And since it was forbidden to take such charlatans seriously, there was no way in which a hope for the nearer future could take shape, no way in which it could modify the usual negation.

Then, quite suddenly, the possibilities broadened out, and a fresh appraisal of the future became conceivable. The main reason was strange, even accidental. The prerequisite of Joachim's system was more literary than religious. A Christian people existed near the edge of Europe who rejected the normal prophetic limitations: namely, the Welsh. They had their own inspired bards, and they expected the return of their legendary hero, King Arthur, which would surely happen before the world's last days; after all, it would be pointless if it didn't happen until history was over. Conspicuous in these traditions was Merlin, famous as a prophet long before he was famous as a magician.

In the 1130s an Oxford scholar from the Welsh borderlands, Geoffrey of Monmouth, wrote a highly imaginative 'history' of Britain. So far as a book could become a bestseller before printing, this one did. It introduced both Arthur and Merlin to an international public, starting repercussions that are still with us. Among much else, Geoffrey gave his readers what he alleged were Merlin's prophecies, dozens of them. They foretold future happenings in cryptic language. Some of the comprehensible ones were political, such as a Welsh resurgence; others were topographic, such as a narrowing of the English Channel until people could have conversations across it. Most were more obscure, and it was hard to be sure whether any had been fulfilled. But they fascinated readers in several countries, who tried to make sense of them, launching a flood of commentaries that went on for centuries. It was an uphill task. Still, the enthusiasts liked to think that if the sense was elusive, it was their own fault rather than Merlin's.

And here we come to the crucial point. The 'Prophecies of Merlin', unlike previous Christian prophesying, were not about the Last Days. They spread over a long stretch of time, and broke off in an indefinite future, with upheavals in earth and sky but no conclusion. Their religious content was slight, but Geoffrey, their promulgator (and probably the real author of most of them), was a learned cleric in good standing. His work convinced others besides the would-be interpreters that it was legitimate to range over the future in general, between the twelfth century and the End. Things would happen in that future, and it might be possible to foresee and foretell them without making use of forbidden arts. After all, Merlin had! According to Geoffrey he spoke under the influence of a controlling spirit, but nothing suggested that the spirit was evil. The Apocalypse itself had passages that *could* refer to the same period. They had always been ambiguous, and now it was easier to read them in that sense, and perhaps combine them with other predictions.

What followed was not, of course, due to the impact of the one *tour de force* of myth-making. But Geoffrey's continental vogue created a new atmosphere, a new readiness to discuss these matters, a new willingness to listen when others did. Hildegard of Bingen (1098–1179), the most brilliant and versatile woman of her day, had visions herself of the newly-opened nearer future and, through her writings and discussions, was the chief agent in making prophecy about it acceptable in the Christian context. But the most significant prophet was yet to appear. His name was Joachim.

*

Joachim of Fiore (the place name is often given inaccurately as 'Flora' or 'Floris') was born in the south of Italy around 1135.

Very little is on record about his early life, except that he made a pilgrimage to the Holy Land. He joined the Cistercians, the order responsible for Fountains Abbey and other great foundations in England. Presently he became abbot of Curazzo in Calabria, near Italy's southern tip. He was well known for his biblical erudition and his rare comprehension of mysterious topics. When the government of the monastery interfered too much with his studies, he left to stay at the sister house of Casamari as a guest of its own abbot, who gave him freedom to work and secretarial assistance.

Recognition came at the highest level in 1184, when he met Pope Lucius III at Veroli. Probably to test his reputed talents, the Pope asked him what he thought of a prediction of trouble for Rome, found among some papers left by a cardinal. Joachim was not greatly interested, but his comments satisfied Lucius, disposing him to listen when the visitor spoke further. What Joachim wanted was papal approval for a project of his own, a study of the relation between the Old and New Testaments. It was, and still is, a mainstream Christian belief that the Old Testament can only be fully understood in the light of the New, because the Old foreshadows the New, prophetically, symbolically and otherwise. The Pope was persuaded, and commissioned Joachim to proceed with his book.

The abbot's thought had been maturing for some time, and now, with the papal blessing, ideas began to pour out. He left Casamari and went away to live by himself, but he was acquiring disciples, and they followed him. Another pope, Celestine III (the Roman pontiffs were always friendly), authorised him to form a congregation of his own, San Giovanni in Fiore. It went on to survive its founder, but without him it had only a mediocre career, and was eventually reabsorbed into the Cistercian Order.

The book on the Testaments remains Joachim's major work, but he wrote more, developing the same themes in a highly distinctive way, and inferring a hitherto unimagined future. It is hard to be sure about his sources. He had a thorough knowledge of Scripture and the works of the Fathers of the Church. His southerly location may have opened his mind to currents of thought in the Mediterranean region. He shows traces of Jewish influence; a hostile critic described him, improbably, as a converted Jew.

Joachim was a scholar rather than a mystic or visionary, but he had moments of illumination like Hildegard of Bingen, and they played a part in moulding his theories. When contemporaries credited him with a gift of prophecy, he was willing to indulge the notion, at least to humour important inquirers. King Richard I, Coeur de Lion, in Sicily on his way to the Third Crusade, invited him over from Calabria. It is not certain what Joachim told the king. He is supposed to have assured Richard that he would be successful, and that his arch-enemy Saladin would be slain. He is also reputed to have foretold the early manifestation of Antichrist. If he really said these things, he hardly shone as a short-term prognosticator. But he never laid much stress on such activities. Essentially, he was a biblical expert who found hidden meanings by what was widely thought to be more-than-mortal insight. It was by enlarging on these that he created his prophetic system. He completed it only in the last part of his life, after the meeting with Lucius.

Its keystone, in its final, revolutionary form, was the Christian doctrine of the Trinity – Father, Son and Holy Spirit, three coequal Persons in one God. Joachim's unprecedented idea was to relate this doctrine to the movement of time. He contended that each of the three Persons, in turn, presided over a phase of history. That meant the history of the people to whom God had been revealed: the biblical patriarchs and their kinsfolk, the ancient Israelites, the Jews, and the Christians with their Church centred on Rome. This was the history that mattered, the sacred history which Joachim interpreted. To be fair, knowledge of the world beyond Christendom's horizon was so imperfect that interpretation would not have been feasible. Nations outside the sacred history could be related to it: Egyptians, for instance, as oppressors of the Chosen

People, Romans as persecutors who repented and turned to Christ. But it was through the sacred history, which was central to everything, that the human career as a whole became intelligible.

Joachim is often said to have divided history into three ages, corresponding to the three Persons of the Trinity. In itself, the word 'age' sounds too hard-and-fast, too rigid. It suggests that the Father handed over to the Son, and the Son handed over to the Spirit. Actually, God is not divided in Joachim's system, but each Person has a time of ascendancy, giving an epoch its character. 'Age' is a proper word to use, so long as we think only of dominant characteristics at one stage or another.

There was an Age of the Father, a time of law and fear, authority and obedience, corresponding roughly to the Old Testament. With the Incarnation of Christ came the Age of the Son, a time of grace and faith and the Gospel. In this era Christ founded the Church, headed at first by the apostle Peter, and subsequently by the popes, Peter's successors. The Age of the Son was still a time of authority, but a different kind of authority, and it was still in being when Joachim wrote. The Church taught that the second age would continue until the end of the world when Christ returned. Nothing new would happen.

But why stop there? Joachim, with impeccable logic, took a further step. If the Trinity's first and second Persons had presided in turn over two ages, the third Person must surely preside over another, which was yet to come. He predicted an impending break-up, a spell of apostasy and trouble, perhaps an onslaught by Antichrist himself. But it would pass fairly quickly, a corner would be turned, and the third age would dawn: the Age of the Holy Spirit. Long prepared, it would become manifest by way of a clear transition, creating a transformed world.

However bold Joachim's prophecies might seem, however subversive in their implications, he was not mounting a challenge to the Church in which he was an abbot. He accepted that Christ had founded it and its claims were valid. Christianity would go on. In the Age of the Holy Spirit, however, it would acquire new dimensions, bringing in the Jews, for instance, not as converts but as partners. The Church would still exist, but it would be changed utterly. Its head would still be a successor of Peter – who might be called the Pope – but the Age of the Spirit would be more expressive of the 'beloved disciple' John, the John of the Fourth Gospel and the Epistles ascribed to him. Two new religious orders, untainted by power and wealth, would lead the way into it. There would be far less hierarchy, far more community. It would be a golden age of contemplative wisdom, of love and liberty, peace and universal enlightenment.

Joachim was imaginative and ingenious. He made some of his points with number-symbolism and diagrams. He drew parallels between characters in different parts of the Bible, making them shed light on each other and on his whole system. Moreover, while there had been pre-Christian myths that described the world and humanity passing through a series of stages, he revolutionised the idea in Christian terms. Greek and Hindu mythology, for instance, asserted a four-age sequence, but pictured the world as in a relentless decline; there was some leeway for temporary reversals, but the trend was downhill and each age was worse than the one before it. Joachim probably had no direct knowledge of these myths, but, consciously or otherwise, he reversed them, presenting a history that still passed through stages but moved in the opposite direction. He did this not by merely concocting an alternative myth, but by applying his Trinitarian logic. When the Age of the Father was succeeded by the Age of the Son, the Age of the Son was a step upward. When the Trinity completed its unfolding in history, the Age of the coequal Spirit could only be a further step upward.

Joachim never questioned the orthodox expectation that the End would arrive – some day. But, once again, he achieved something tremendous: he gave a place in Christendom for optimism about the earthly future, in the indefinite interval between the present and the End, when the Holy Spirit would be in the ascendant. This optimism was not founded on anything like 'progress'. The idea of progress, in the sense of a general and gradual improvement, never occurred to anyone until the eighteenth century. The hope that Joachim held out was for a non-violent but clearly-marked transition – a quantum leap, we might say – to a different and better state of society. This pattern of expectation was to reappear again and again far into the future, sometimes in a religious form, sometimes not.

It was new, it was exciting, but – a crucial question in his time – was it heretical?

Joachim died around 1202, without ever having been in trouble with higher authority. As his views became better known, they drew some posthumous enmity. Opponents insinuated that he had, by implication, split the indivisible Trinity into three separate gods, one for each of his ages. The charge was mistaken, and too abstract to disturb people whose imagination he had stirred. A century after his death he received an unequivocal tribute in Dante's *Divine Comedy*. The poet places Joachim in Heaven among the wisest men, and speaks of him as truly gifted with the prophetic spirit. Some of the poem's imagery may have taken a hint from his diagrams. Dante's endorsement is almost proof in itself that the abbot was not outside the boundaries of the Faith. Rome, in fact, never condemned his system, and loyal members of the Catholic Church were at liberty to agree with it.

*

Nevertheless, deviations and eccentricities began to creep in. Ironically, these did more to keep Joachim's ideas alive than the authentic version: later generations were to discover him partly through the medium of a falsification.

His system was always revolutionary, but it was only in the decades after his death that its revolutionary content began to be pointed up and emphasised. Enthusiasts steered it along sensational paths that led to trouble. Some of them were trying to push things ahead. This was partly the abbot's own fault. In one of his less inspired moments, he had come perilously close to fixing a date for the beginning of the transformation: namely, 1260. This created a sense of urgency, even immediacy.

A potent factor was the fulfilment of one of his chief predictions – that two new religious orders would come into being, not corrupted by wealth and power. The subsequent establishment of the Dominican and Franciscan orders could be seen, in his terms, as initiating the change. The Franciscans fitted particularly well. St Francis founded his Order in 1210. His humility, dedication to poverty, and love towards all creatures, seemed to be foreshadowing the Age of the Spirit. Francis's death in 1226 was followed by dissension. His successor, Brother Elias, modified the rigours of the original Rule in the interests of practicality. Some zealots revolted, insisting on the original ideals, and calling themselves Spirituals. These, and sympathisers with their protest, adopted Joachim's system and distorted it, with much publicity and scandalous consequences.

In 1254 a too-enterprising Franciscan, Gerard of Borgo San Donnino, produced a book entitled the *Eternal Evangel* or *Everlasting Gospel.* (The title refers to *Revelation* 14:6: 'Then I saw another angel flying in midheaven with an eternal gospel to proclaim to those who dwell on earth.') No complete copy has survived, but Gerard seems to have collected together some of Joachim's writings, and attached an introduction putting his own construction on them. He said the Bible no longer had authority in itself, and that Joachim's inspired interpretation of it constituted a new scripture, with barefoot friars as its destined custodians. The Age of the Holy Spirit would begin soon. By the barefoot friars

Gerard meant Franciscans, or rather super-Franciscans, recruited from existing religious bodies and superseding them. His exorbitant claims caused great annoyance. A classic of French literature, the *Roman de la Rose*, calls his book 'diabolical'.

An ecclesiastical commission studied the *Eternal Evangel* and reported adversely. The Pope himself picked out Gerard's introduction for special condemnation, but did not mention Joachim, being well aware that the Franciscan had misrepresented him. The abbot had never given the slightest hint that the Bible was out of date, much less that anything could take its place. However, a provincial church council at Arles broadened the attack to Joachimism in general, including the theory of the three ages – probably because of its exploitation by extremists like Gerard and the Spiritual Franciscans. One result of the argument was that Gerard's book acquired a fame which lasted for centuries, while Joachim was apt to be misunderstood through being saddled with notions that were actually Gerard's. The atmosphere was not improved when Spiritual Franciscans put Francis on a level with Christ: as Christ had inaugurated the second age, so Francis, through his disciples, was inaugurating the third.

The over-publicised year 1260 came and went with no visible dawn. Believers (and belief continued, abundantly) coped with the disappointment as best they could. Obviously the date could be dropped as a miscalculation, or revised, without prejudice to the rest. Or something might have happened unobtrusively, something that would lead to visible events later. After all, the Age of the Son had started with a birth in Bethlehem that hardly anyone noticed.

But presently a few ceased to need such hypothetical comfort. They had found the initiator of the third age, living among them in a most unexpected guise. Guglielma Boema of Milan was revered in that city as the Holy Spirit incarnate.

Little is known about Guglielma, but she had begun to proclaim original teachings around 1260. By 1271 she was heading a recognisable group. Her disciples explained that as the Son had become a man to establish the second age, so the Spirit had become a woman to establish the third. Guglielma doesn't seem to have been a charlatan or a deranged fanatic, and some of her followers were well-educated and comfortably off, with a stake in society: they included members of the family of the Duke of Milan, the Visconti.

Guglielma proclaimed that the male papacy was finished. One of her women followers would take over as pope and appoint women cardinals. This was Manfreda, who was probably one of the Visconti relatives. As pope, she was going to heal religious divisions and even convert the Jews and Saracens. A male disciple, Andrea Saramita, would preside over the composition of new gospels and other scriptures. We owe the scanty accounts of Guglielma's teachings to Manfreda and Saramita. Guglielmism was not anathematised in the founder's lifetime. One modern Italian historian, F. Tocco, who has examined the records, has described the 'dream of Guglielma' as 'the most beautiful and seductive of all contemporary hallucinations'.

She died in 1282, and was buried in a monastery of Cistercians – Joachim's order – at Chiaravalli. Her group stayed together and held gatherings around her tomb, perhaps with a hope of resurrection. In 1300, when it was clear that the sect would not expire of its own accord, the Church clamped down. About thirty adherents were inculpated. Saramita, Manfreda, and one other woman were put to death as heretics. Inquisitors extracted Guglielma's bones from the tomb and burned them, presumably to destroy any notion that she would rise again.

*

Thus Joachimism's first phase came to a tragic end. It might have dwindled into a topic for academic study and throwaway comments by other authors, but the vision of the leap to a transformation was too alluring. Indeed, it was ineradicable. Joachimism survived by undergoing a revision that had begun before 1300, overlapping the Milanese phenomenon. It became ideological, even semi-political. The approach to the Age of the Holy Spirit grew more complicated, more sophisticated, and less liable to be derailed by events. In due course, Joachimism was linked with popular movements, and sent out ramifications extending to English would-be prophets in the seventeenth century and Offbeat Radicals in the nineteenth and twentieth.

Its new exponents, who can be labelled as 'Joachimites', developed the system. Instead of trusting in divine action alone for the great transition, they added two human characters.

They began to talk about an 'Angelic Pope'. This pontiff is an unexplained figure in medieval mythology. He is first mentioned in 1267 by the Franciscan Roger Bacon, famous as a pioneer of experimental science. Bacon says this pope has been foretold for some time (by whom, no one knows). He will cleanse the Church of corruption, end its internal disputes, and win over its enemies by his devotion to truth and justice. The schismatic Greeks will return to the fold, the Jews will acknowledge Christ, Tartars and Saracens will be converted. Wherever this prophecy came from – and it rather looks as if Guglielma heard and adapted it – Joachimites annexed the Angelic Pope to their programme. To judge from Joachim's teaching, he might well be a poor man, a friar or a monk or even a hermit, setting the tone for the Age of the Spirit as it unfolded.

The other new character, the Angelic Pope's imperial counterpart, was the Second Charlemagne. Early Christian fantasies had focused on the notion of a 'Last Emperor' who would win the Church's battles and prepare the way for Christ's return. But he was, specifically, a Last Emperor reigning towards the end of the world, and irrelevant to Joachim's system, though his imaginary career supplied hints for the Second Charlemagne's.

The real Charlemagne had united most of Europe and refounded the western Roman Empire in the year 800. His huge domain fell apart, but a reduced Empire survived as its chief inheritor through the Middle Ages, mainly in Germany and Italy. Still, the belief that the Empire ought, ideally, to comprise all Christendom was persistent. Dante maintained it eloquently. One of the Empire's thirteenth-century rulers was the brilliant and ambiguous Frederick II, nicknamed the 'wonder of the world'. Some saw him as a Messiah, others as Antichrist. His spectacular reign encouraged Joachimites to imagine an even greater one.

Crowned by the Angelic Pope, this Emperor would assist in the work of unification, master the anticipated wave of troubles, and usher in the third age. Talk of a more or less comprehensible 'good time coming' had a broad appeal that Joachim's basic prophecies seldom enjoyed. It encouraged outbreaks of protest and revolt. Other prophetic utterances became current. Even the outpourings of Merlin himself, as Geoffrey of Monmouth had published them with such sweeping results, were rediscovered and enlisted by an Italian author named Asdante.

There was one wild moment when it seemed as if the Angelic Pope had actually arrived. Pietro di Morrone was a venerable and saintly hermit, the informal head of a scattered cluster of communities. In 1294 the cardinals elected him pope, virtually by acclamation. He resisted, but finally consented, taking the name of Celestine V. On the way to his coronation he was cheered by enormous crowds – two hundred thousand people, reputedly. He rode humbly on a donkey, with the kings of Naples and Hungary in attendance, walking. This reception of a very old man who, on the face of it, was completely unsuitable, showed that the revised version of Joachimism was already more than the daydream of a theological clique.

The 'brief shining moment' passed: Celestine actually was completely unsuitable. Finding Rome uncongenial, he aroused antagonism by trying to govern the Church from Naples, but he lacked the knowledge and capability to govern it at all. After five chaotic months he gave up and resigned. The arrangements for this unprecedented action were pushed through by a cardinal who promptly stepped into the vacancy and became pope himself. As Boniface VIII, fearing trouble from sympathisers with Celestine, he despatched his predecessor to a prison where he soon died. (Dante called Celestine's abdication 'the great refusal' and consigned him to a dismal antechamber of Hell. Not everybody took such a censorious view, and he was canonised in 1313.)

Nonetheless, Joachimites made Celestine's reign and martyrdom into a sort of anticipatory myth. Boniface was now one of their villains, because of his conduct in office as well as his treatment of Celestine. Though they became more inclined to regard popes with suspicion or hostility, they did not reject the papal institution itself. Joachim had said it would go on; there were good popes as well as bad; and the Angelic one would put things right. Still, there was never another candidate with as much plausibility as Celestine. As for the Second Charlemagne, attempts to cast an existing ruler in the role were equally unsuccessful and futile arguments broke out over his probable nationality.

Yet both the expectations survived, and another crisis of prophetic excitement exploded in fifteenth-century Florence, under the aegis of the spellbinding preacher and reformer Savonarola. He was certainly aware of Joachimism, and claimed, rather erratically, to be inspired himself. Then in 1494 the French king Charles VIII led an army into Italy to take possession of Naples, and passed through Florence. French poets and propagandists urged him to assume the role of the Second Charlemagne. An Italian Friar, Luke of St Genignano, made a fresh attempt to link Joachim's prophecies with Merlin's.

The king was an uninspiring figure, and it did not help that he was understood to have six toes on each foot, but at least his name was Charles. One of the poets foretold that he would conquer all Italy, become king of Greece, and subjugate the Turks – quite a good start. However, he did none of these things. In any case, there was no Angelic Pope to crown him. As it happened, the pope at that time was the extremely un-angelic Borgia, Alexander VI. Charles went home.

George Eliot's historical novel *Romola* is set in Savonarola's Florence. She knows more about the prophetic aspect of events than most nineteenth-century historians. One character says: 'The warning is ringing in the ears of all men; and it's no new story; for the Abbot Joachim prophesied of the coming time three hundred years ago, and now Fra Girolamo [Savonarola] has got the message afresh. He has seen it in a vision, even as the prophets of old.'

Eliot describes Charles VIII entering Florence with his army and being greeted as the new Charlemagne. She also knows about the Angelic Pope. In the Proem at the beginning of the novel, she introduces a Florentine who 'heard simple folk talk of a Pope Angelico, who was to come by-and-by and bring in a new order of things, to purify the Church from simony, and the lives of the clergy from scandal'. At the end of the Proem she adds a few words of her own: 'The sunlight and shadows bring their old beauty... and men still yearn for the reign of peace and righteousness.... The Pope Angelico is not come yet.'

Joachimite flights of fancy never effaced the primary vision. Botticelli preserves it intact. His *Mystic Nativity*, painted in 1500 and hanging in London's National Gallery, has been praised as 'one of the greatest documents of Joachimist thought'.[†] The artist has attached a note to it, stating his belief that he is living in the tribulation predicted by Joachim, before the great change. It will give way to joy with the chaining of the Devil, 'trodden down as in

† Reeves, Marjorie. *The Influence of Prophecy in the Later Middle Ages*, pp. 436–7.

this picture'. The angels whom he paints in the sky are not appearing to shepherds – that has happened already – but dancing ecstatically and timelessly. The lower part of the picture is a strange landscape with no spatial relationship to Bethlehem, though a path leads to it. It ought to be fairly close to the stable, but is far off. A small, vanquished Devil slinks away – an image that, as the artist's note makes clear, places this landscape in the future. Here, angels are embracing humans in a union of heaven and earth that does not exist yet, but assuredly will.

Botticelli, of course, is too cheerful. Nevertheless, it is clear that, even in 1500, Joachim's vision of transformation had not exhausted its potency. It had entrenched itself in successive minds as a kind of archetype, which could express itself in different ways, could survive multiple disappointments, could fade out and be reactivated or reinvented.

'Archetype' is a risky word to use, and it invites the retort that there is nothing more profound in all this than sustained wishful thinking. If that were true, however, there ought to be many parallel cases, since wishful thinking is a fairly common trait of humanity. But the truth is that there are no parallels at all, or virtually none. In Christianity, nothing like Joachimism appeared in the centuries before Joachim. Jewish expectation of the Messiah is something else. Outside the Judaeo-Christian tradition, all the world's wishful thinking has seldom or never inspired a comparable hope. Greek philosophers invented a cosmic cycle that would some day bring back the mythical Golden Age, and Virgil flattered Augustus Caesar by pretending that it would come back under imperial auspices; but few later subjects of the Empire would have taken the poet seriously on this issue, or looked ahead to the Golden Age's return as an event in a foreseeable future. The quantum leap to a qualitatively better society is Joachim's idea alone. We confront a motif which he planted in European minds, so widely and deeply that the word 'archetype' is legitimate. Wishful thinking may have helped to keep it there; wishful thinking did not put it there in the first place.

After Botticelli, however, it could not maintain cohesion in the shattering conflicts of the Renaissance and Reformation. It persisted, but it fragmented. Guesswork, of course, could still happen. There were still enthusiasts willing to assure the public that some contemporary ruler would turn out to be the Second Charlemagne, or that some contemporary pontiff would turn out to be the Angelic Pope. Few were convinced, and speculation about the Angelic Pope sank shortly towards a *reductio ad absurdum*. In 1516, a friar named Bonaventura claimed to be the Angelic Pope himself, and excommunicated the real one. The claim was also made for Marcellus II in 1555, but he died so soon after his election that there was no time to tell whether he was angelic or not. Several re-interpreters of Joachim, including Columbus, detected the ascendancy of the Holy Spirit in the conversion of newly discovered nations. A few saluted the Jesuits, with their worldwide missions, as at least partly fulfilling the abbot's prophecy of new religious orders.

Then a renewal came where no one would have expected it. England had not previously been part of the story, though some scholars during the Reformation quoted Joachim's work. But in the seventeenth century, England – Protestant England! – suddenly revived his vision. Some of the writers and speakers in this extraordinary phase know Joachimism explicitly, with its main developments. Others know it through misleading versions like Gerard's *Eternal Evangel*, which Donne attacked in a sermon. Others seem to have absorbed bits of it through a kind of osmosis that can be inferred but not traced.

In 1615 James Maxwell† assembled a collection of prophecies from various sources. Like most Protestants at the time, Maxwell is strongly

† The names and particulars on this and the succeeding pages are cited from Reeves, Marjorie. *Joachim of Fiore and the Prophetic Future*, pp. 157–63.

anti-Roman, yet he invokes Catholic prophecies to foreshadow the Catholic Church's purification, and criticises extremists who think that 'no good thing can come from Rome'. He knows about the Second Charlemagne and the Angelic Pope, and is willing to believe that the latter will effect a total reform of Christianity. He suggests that this Pope or Pastor (he isn't quite sure what to call him) will come from England. 'It may well be that God will honour this same Island with the reformation of the Church of Rome and her daughters.'

As for the Second Charlemagne, who is to bring universal peace, subdue Islam and so on, Maxwell invokes legendary pedigrees derived from Geoffrey of Monmouth to prove that Britain's monarchs are descended from the emperor Constantine who liberated the Church – a British monarch may be the right person, by descent, to fulfil the Second Charlemagne prophecy. Maxwell toys with the remarkable notion that the small, stammering heir-apparent Prince Charles, the future Charles I, will qualify. Over thirty years later, another author ridicules the idea of a Stuart apotheosis, but it is still well enough known to be worth refuting.

Maxwell's conjecture, however, would hardly have fitted in with the main English neo-Joachimist trend, which rose to an apogee in the 1640s. A study of 112 ministers who produced books and pamphlets during the Civil War and its aftermath showed that nearly seventy percent believed in a new spiritual kingdom of glory, about to appear on earth. Most of them were Protestant radicals, in rebellion against the compromise that had established the Church of England. They imagined the change in religious terms, but it was going to bring social change with it.

Milton himself echoes their hopes in *Aeropagitica*, his plea for freedom of the press, written in 1644.

> By all concurrence of signs, and by the generall instinct of holy and devout men, as they daily and solemnly expresse their thoughts, God is decreeing to begin some new and

> great period in his Church, ev'n to the reforming of Reformation it self; what does he then but reveal Himself to his servants, and as his manner is, first to his English-men.

Even with the Civil War going on, and despite his own strongly partisan stance, Milton does not picture the change as a violent revolution. Winning the war is a prerequisite, but it will not bring the quantum leap. That will come in some other way, and all Milton professes to be sure of is that it will be an English thing, led by his divinely-favoured compatriots. Like the extremist pamphleteers, he thinks of it in religious terms, but he expects it to bring social change as well; that can be inferred from his other activities and writings, before and after.

Joachim's third age is a theme for others around this time. William Dell, a preacher, refers to it in 1646. William Saltmarsh speaks of the three dispensations of 'Law, Gospel and Spirit', with a step-by-step ascent, though he does not actually name Joachim. Another William, Erbery, speaks of the third dispensation 'which we are now entering upon', with more stress on human agency in its advent, and on social as well as religious transformation.

After the execution of Charles I, the astounding spectacle of England as a republic could excuse a belief that something entirely new was dawning. It was not. Cromwell died without having won over a majority of the people, or anything like it, and the last of Milton's published tracts is a desperate protest against the Restoration. But the archetype of transformation was now embedded in England. It could lie dormant for generations and then revive, and it eventually did in various forms, some religious, some mythic, some secular. This revival constituted Offbeat Radicalism.

*

On the Continent, Joachimism's rediscovery came later, with a different bias. One outstanding figure in the eighteenth-century

Enlightenment, the German critic and dramatist Gotthold Lessing, knew of it – or, to be precise, knew of the notions of publicists such as Gerard, who more or less preserved the essential pattern, but distorted it by proclaiming (for example) that the Bible would be superseded. Lessing wrote an essay *On the Education of the Human Race*, published in 1780, predicting that humanity would some day arrive at 'the highest step of illumination'. His tone in speaking of the Joachimists is a shade patronising, but favourable:

> Perhaps even some of the enthusiasts of the thirteenth and fourteenth centuries had caught a glimpse of a beam of this new eternal Gospel, and only erred in that they predicted its outburst as so near their own time. Perhaps their 'Three Ages of the World' were not so empty a speculation after all, and assuredly they had no contemptible views when they taught that the New Covenant must become as antiquated as the Old had been.... Only they were premature. Only they believed that they could make their contemporaries, who had scarcely outgrown their childhood, without enlightenment, without preparation, men worthy of their Third Age. And it was just this which made them enthusiasts.

Joachimism was in the air again, not obtrusively, but quietly present; and it did not go away. For a while the cataclysm of the French Revolution overshadowed any forms it might take, but these forms retained a capacity to survive and evolve. As Norman Cohn points out in *The Pursuit of the Millennium*, the idea of history moving through three stages became part of the intellectual baggage of western Europe.† Even Hegel took it up, though he gave the series a different meaning; and it made its way into the

† Cohn, *op. cit.*, p. 109.

pioneer French socialism of Saint-Simon, and the positivism of Auguste Comte.

Its oddest occurrence, however, was in the German philosophy of F. W. Schelling. In a lecture, he spoke of the three ages with a fervour which gave hearers the impression that they were witnessing the birth of a new religion. Like Joachim, he related the Persons of the Trinity to the series, with the Age of the Spirit as the culmination. Like Joachim, he drew parallels between characters in different parts of scripture, and discussed them as expressing different aspects of the process. The strange thing was that he had worked it all out himself. He was surprised when he found that the Calabrian abbot had done it first. Possibly, though, he had read about Joachim and forgotten.

In France and Germany, the main emphasis was laid on the forward-moving historical stages, rather than on the climactic third and the transition to it, though its climactic character was accepted. For this reason and others, Offbeat Radicalism, which kept the seventeenth-century emphasis, remained a principally British phenomenon. But the abbot was a presence on both sides of the Channel, whether recognised or not. Professor Roger Garaudy of the University of Poitiers remarked in 1972 that the 'first great revolutionary movements in Europe' are 'all more or less imbued with the ideas of Joachim of Fiore'. An exaggeration, perhaps, but defensible.

A QUESTION POSED

2

Wordsworth, Coleridge, Godwin

The French Revolution was hailed as a transformation of society by vast numbers who had never heard of Joachim, or the antecedents of the way they were thinking. Causes were at work, of course, which were not theological or even ideological. France was being upheaved by the incompetence and bankruptcy of its monarchy; by the nobles' outrageous privileges; by the peasants' poverty and anger; by the ambitions of entrepreneurs whom an outworn system restricted. Yet the Revolution was not solely reducible to factors like these. Something tremendous was happening.

For informed onlookers in Britain, the event that brought it all into focus was the fall of the Bastille, on 14 July 1789. It made no difference that the old prison had ceased, for practical purposes, to be a stronghold of tyranny. Few in France and none in England could have named any of its handful of inmates. (The last notable one, until ten days before, had been – of all people – the Marquis de Sade. He had made himself a nuisance by improvising a megaphone and urging the crowd outside to attack. The governor got him transferred to a lunatic asylum.) When the attack actually came and the Bastille fell, it held only seven prisoners, and they were not there for political reasons. Nevertheless the building was symbolic, quite rightly, and its fall was apocalyptic.

British assessments of the new France, as the upheavals across the Channel went on, varied considerably. Aspects of the Revolution that were positive and powerful on its own soil were not necessarily endearing to Britain. The explosion of sceptical rethinking associated with the name of Voltaire had no real insular counterpart. King George's more conventionally-minded subjects disliked and distrusted the ancient enemy in whatever guise. A respectable body of opinion looked on the Revolution with a certain benevolence, in the belief that France was struggling towards the liberty which Britain already enjoyed. Some of the intelligentsia, on what may (with a slight anachronism) be called the Left, were ecstatic about this nemesis of authority, and expected France to lead Europe to undreamed-of heights. A small minority – large enough, all the same, to disturb the Government – went further in admiration, plotting and pamphleteering to start a revolution at home.

These were obvious responses. There was another, less obvious, that gradually created a different attitude. The best way to anatomise this process is to trace it in the minds of poets, for it is in a literary setting that the earliest stirrings of Offbeat Radicalism can be detected.

The first of the poets to call for consideration is William Wordsworth. Born in 1770, he was inspired by the Revolution and spent some time in France, talking with people and watching developments at first hand. He tells the story, or some of it, in his long autobiographical poem *The Prelude*, which includes a famous retrospect of his feelings as the national transformation unfolded:

> France standing on the top of golden hours,
> And human nature seeming born again . . .

Bliss was it in that dawn to be alive,
But to be young was very Heaven! O times,
In which the meagre, stale, forbidding ways
Of custom, law, and statute, took at once
The attraction of a country in romance!

Wordsworth had a French love-affair, not mentioned in *The Prelude*, which resulted in an illegitimate daughter. But his recollections of joy must not be psychologised away; and Bertrand Russell's allegation that he wrote good poetry when he was 'immoral', and poor poetry after he reformed, is quite untrue. His early poems are poor, the good ones come much later. The inspiration that he recalls was genuinely public.

He certainly knew nothing of Joachimism, but he felt, for a year or two, that he was witnessing a quantum leap. Another poet, Samuel Taylor Coleridge, who would later be Wordsworth's friend and collaborator, experienced the same excitement without the first-hand contact. He too looked back later and recalled these days, romantically invoking the powers of Nature:

When France in wrath her giant-limbs upreared,
    And with that oath, which smote air, earth, and sea,
    Stamped her strong foot and said she would be free,
Bear witness for me, how I hoped and feared!

The poem passes on to a double disillusionment, and Wordsworth shared it. Why?

Britain continued for several years to have plenty of sympathisers with the Revolution, and a sprinkling of activists wanting to imitate the French. France still seemed, perhaps, to be heading for constitutional freedom, and Louis XVI was still nominally enthroned and, under protest, co-operative. But the constitution-making was constantly frustrated. Popular demonstrations and royalist opposition led to a crisis. Pro-revolutionaries in Britain were still willing to applaud in 1792, when a mob stormed the palace in August, and a republic was proclaimed in September. The execution of Louis the following January was another matter. True, Charles I had also been executed; but what made the sympathisers' position more and more difficult was that the French king's death marked not an end but the beginning of a new and alarming phase. Other sovereigns undertook armed intervention against the French Republic, and Britain joined them. At first Wordsworth and Coleridge could deplore the involvement, and even, quietly, welcome defeats. But as the war dragged on, anything like support for France acquired an air of disloyalty. Taken a little further and called treason, disloyalty provided a pretext for official suppression.

Then something worse happened, something that threatened to discredit the Revolution itself. In April 1793 the Reign of Terror began. The Jacobin party, now in power throughout most of France, justified their killing of thousands of people by invoking the national emergency. Mercy could not be shown to royalist conspirators or to collaborators with the enemy. Yet many of the victims hardly qualified under either heading. An ideology was at work. Only a little while before, it had inspired the uprising for liberty which Wordsworth and Coleridge saluted. Now it was being exploited by fanatics who turned it to homicidal ends.

The inventor of this revolutionary mystique was Jean-Jacques Rousseau, who died in 1778 – long before he could witness its consequences. Rousseau had devised a myth that could be pushed to extremes and legitimise almost any atrocity perpetrated by those in power. Humanity, he asserted, had once been free and equal, living according to Nature in noble savagery. This primordial Eden had succumbed to the march of civilisation, propelled largely by base motives. Civilisation had produced gross inequalities, and set up kings, nobles, priests, plutocrats, and other tyrants. Such elements must be curbed or eliminated, so as to restore natural equality; age-old corruptions must be swept away. Rousseau's ideas were popular because so many people wanted so many things swept away.

Rousseau maintained that a new, equal society could be constructed on the basis of what he called the Social Contract, and could be ruled by what he called the General Will. His General Will is a somewhat metaphysical concept, a sort of consensus that is invariably right. Though democratic after a fashion, it isn't the will of the majority as an election might reveal this. In practice, it has to be inferred from the situation by an elite that understands Rousseau.

In 1793 the Jacobins were headed by Maximilien Robespierre, who was one of Rousseau's most thoroughgoing disciples. For a while he had virtually dictatorial powers. During that time, Rousseau's theories justified guillotining numerous aristocrats and many other more or less privileged persons, as well as anyone else who dissented, or was accused of dissenting, from Robespierre's interpretation of the General Will. The Reign of Terror lasted for more than a year and projected a horrifying image across the Channel, responsible, in due course, for *A Tale of Two Cities* and the *Scarlet Pimpernel* saga. Even in 1939, George Orwell could write: 'To this day, to the average Englishman, the French Revolution means no more than a pyramid of severed heads.'

A major reason for French acquiescence in this regime was the foreign threat. It was patriotic to rally round the Jacobins, and they did wonders organising resistance. In France, the year 1793 would always be looked back upon as a year of heroism. The Marseillaise was popularised during this crisis. As France's national anthem, it still exhorts her citizens to resist the 'ferocious soldiers' who violate her territory.

In Britain, at war with France, patriotism worked in the opposite direction. A pro-French stance was difficult to maintain, and became more so when France was no longer fighting for survival but going over to the offensive, 'compelling the nations to be free' by military occupation. The Terror ceased with Robespierre's fall in July 1794, but the damage was done. While the gains of the Revolution were real and visible, France was no longer a beacon of inspiration outside.

Wordsworth shed his pro-revolutionary ardour, and moved – not headlong, but steadily – towards a healing moderation. Coleridge did the same, not with quite the same steadiness.

*

A crucial question was beginning to frame itself, though few – so far – were audibly asking it. Britain's home-grown evils had encouraged the early enthusiasms, and those evils had not gone away. The nation still carried a burden of injustice, poverty, and oppression, with no prospect of improvement. There were still many challengers of the existing order, who had given up on France but had not given up completely. What position could they take now? It was becoming normal to react against the Revolution, and forget any notion of imitating it; but could this be done without merely reacting into conservatism? To put the question more positively, was there any way to repudiate the Revolution as a political model, yet still be, in some sense, a revolutionary?

Wordsworth never really examined that question. It didn't concern him. Coleridge responded to it by launching an experiment. With the poet and literary scholar Robert Southey, he proposed to turn away from the miseries of Europe, and found an egalitarian settlement in Pennsylvania, on the banks of the Susquehanna. By coining an ideological term, pantisocracy, 'all-equal-rule', he implied a hope that the settlement would become a prototype for a new sort of society. The project collapsed for lack of funds, leaving him coupled with a none too congenial wife, whom he had married as part of it; but it deserves an honourable mention, as the forerunner of numerous nineteenth-century attempts to create mini-Utopias in America.

Presently Coleridge joined Wordsworth in a different challenge – a challenge to literary conventions. They wrote innovative poetry and published it in a small but influential book, *Lyrical Ballads*. As for the Revolution, a French invasion of Switzerland was the last straw for them.

Was it, then, possible to remain revolutionary while renouncing the Revolution? Affirmative answers to the question were to be given by two other poets and, surprisingly, by a captain of industry. From these, as we shall see, an outline of Offbeat Radicalism would emerge; but it would take some time doing so.

*

At this point it is worth remarking on a curious contrast.

French thinking is supposed to be logical, to be dominated by clear ideas. Yet Rousseau's mystique was, on the whole, emotional. It relied on feelings rather than facts. Its prophet admitted that the ideal 'state of nature' from which he deduced his system was a necessary fiction: it was a state which 'exists no longer, perhaps never existed, probably never will exist, and of which none the less it is necessary to have just ideas, in order to judge well of our present state.' In his general thinking, he relied on intuition and the alleged dictates of the heart.

The irrational English, on the other hand, produced their own subversive doctrine, which delighted the pro-French intelligentsia so long as they persisted in being pro-French; and it was relentlessly rational. It turned out to be a dead end, at least from any constructive point of view; but a careful reader of its inventor's book (most of its readers were anything but) could use it to arrive at an end that was full of potential.

William Godwin is claimed by some modern anarchists as their founding father. He began his adult career in the nonconformist ministry, but abandoned it, and religion in general. After several years among sceptics and progressives in London, he wrote a two-volume work entitled *Enquiry Concerning Political Justice*. Published in February 1793, it was an instant success. Pitt, the Prime Minister, who suppressed other dangerous books, is said to have spared this one because it was too expensive for the seditious to buy. If so, it seems not to have occurred to him that several seditious readers could pool their resources, and some probably did. In any case, plenty of dangerous characters could afford the book unaided, and it became, briefly, their bible.

Political Justice has been described as 'calmly subversive of everything'. Hence, it was a welcome endorsement of the subversion of many things in France. Godwin is a rationalist who takes rationality, or what he thinks is rationality, so far that it verges on caricature. He insists that human beings are 'really' dominated by reason when it is given a fair chance. Reason is 'really' stronger than passion. In one of several illustrations that enliven the argument, Godwin claims that a man in the full tide of sexual activity – he doesn't put it in quite those words – will lose interest at once if you give him a factual message: for example, that he has won or lost a large sum of money. (It might be objected that anyone would be put off if Godwin rushed in with an interruption, of whatever kind; it wouldn't have to be informative; and even the message about money, if the victim took it in at all, would appeal to self-interest rather than reason.) Godwin also thinks 'intellectual resolution' can prevail over pain. He echoes a Greek philosopher of the Stoic school who argued that a truly good man would be happy on the rack. As Benjamin Jowett, sometime Master of Balliol and a great classical scholar, is said to have observed: 'Perhaps, if it was a very good man, or a very bad rack.'

If reason is so utterly paramount – or rather, if it is given the primacy that rightly belongs to it – what moral guidance does it offer? Virtuous conduct means doing things that are beneficial, not just to friends or relatives or even a wider circle, but to the world at large. In defiance of religion and most traditional morality,

Godwin opts for a situational ethic, a moral calculus. Given a choice, you must take the course that will be of most benefit to humanity, if you can decide what it is.

He proposes an example, picking, for some reason, on Archbishop Fénelon, a celebrated author in the time of Louis XIV. Imagine the Archbishop trapped in a burning house with his valet. You can rescue one of them, but only one. You must save Fénelon, Godwin argues, because he will probably go on writing books that are beneficial, and the valet won't. Godwin presses his point. He doesn't consider, for instance, that the valet might have dependants. What he does say is that the valet ought to die willingly, recognising his comparative unimportance. The same applies even where personal loyalties come into play: if you had to choose between the Archbishop and your own father, say. What then? The answer is the same. You must save the Archbishop and let your father burn.†

Godwin believes in 'necessity', or, as we might say, determinism. All behaviour is cut-and-dried with a machine-like motivation. There is no room for hesitations, exceptions, nuances. This raises a question about truth. Complete truthfulness is best, but is that an absolute, universal rule? Godwin's situational ethic might suggest otherwise, but it doesn't. He takes up several pages discussing a situation in which a householder who has a servant is expecting an unwelcome visitor. Can he instruct his servant to go to the door and tell the conventional fib 'not at home'? No: this would coerce and degrade the servant. The householder should talk to the visitor and explain coolly why he isn't wanted, giving him a chance to mend his ways. Well, we may feel – maybe.

Why was Godwin so popular with the left-wing intelligentsia? The answer is that, by applying his notion of what constituted

† This is how Godwin states the dilemma in the revised edition which his modern editor takes as the standard. In the original, the other occupant of the house is a maid, who could be 'my wife or my mother'. Leaving your mother in the flames may be an intolerable notion, but it is not clear that changing the maid to a valet gets rid of the difficulty.

virtue, he undermined almost all authority. A king and his ministers don't ask how to benefit humanity – in their position, they can't – nor do they invariably, or even habitually, tell the truth. They are harming and corrupting millions of people, their subjects. They are not even serving their own interests; not really. They may think they are, but they are actually unhappy, including the king himself, who may well be the most miserable of the lot. And so forth, essentially, down the line to all forms of authority. Godwin calls government 'the brute engine which has been the only perennial cause of the vices of mankind'. It must go. The iniquities of wealth and rank, denounced and deconstructed in much the same way, must go likewise.

Political Justice had its hour of triumph, but it declined towards neglect as pro-revolutionary sentiment waned. Even Wordsworth had tried (like Coleridge) to apply ultra-rationalism, and given up on it.

> So I fared,
> Dragging all precepts, judgments, maxims, creeds,
> Like culprits to the bar; calling the mind,
> Suspiciously, to establish in plain day
> Her titles and her honours; now believing,
> Now disbelieving; endlessly perplexed
> With impulse, motive, right and wrong, the ground
> Of obligation, what the rule and whence
> The sanction; till, demanding formal *proof,*
> And seeking it in everything, I lost
> All feeling of conviction, and, in fine,
> Sick, wearied out with contrarieties,
> Yielded up moral questions in despair.

Wordsworth expressed his disillusionment in an unactable and almost unreadable play, *The Borderers*.

No glorious transformation was going to come through the French Revolution, or through a home-grown imitation. Yet seeds had been planted, in the confusion of the British response to it. When Offbeat Radicalism did begin to emerge in the work of a younger poet, it was, in part, a delayed consequence of Godwin's writing, but an indirect and backhanded one. It could happen as it did because Godwin had *not* offered anything constructive himself.

To examine what he did offer is to see why *Political Justice* was a dead end, and why even a disciple, seeking a way forward, might feel a need for something more. It is discouraging in itself that his attempts to picture a future are crammed together in the last part of his massive book; a reader has to be persevering to get to them.

Looking ahead, *Political Justice* holds out only the prospect of a slow 'social amelioration' with no programme, no goal, and no timescale. The improvement will be kept in motion solely by the increase of enlightenment, through wise and public-spirited individuals. Violence in any form can only retard the process. There will be no point in forming associations or movements or other agencies of change, to help it along. In Godwin's opinion, all such things will generate faction and falsification, and, like violence, retard the process. His dislike of co-operation is so intense that he views even plays and concerts with disfavour, because the actors and musicians have to co-operate, and in doing so, they surrender their individuality.

He insists, all the same, that humanity's progress is certain. It has been secured by the invention of printing, which guarantees an ever-widening spread of information. He never considers that it may also spread misinformation, and worse. He expects that in some vague future, probably so far off as to be hardly worth speculating about, 'amelioration' will make everybody equal. Each person will be dedicated to the good of all. Property will be evenly divided. A simple but sufficient economy, without luxuries, will be maintained by every man doing half an hour's work each day – individually, of course, not in groups; technology will eliminate teamwork.

There will be no war, no crime, no judiciary, no government above the parish-council level. There will be no marrying and no propagation. All will be adults, and, thanks to the conquest of disease, will live much longer. It is not clear how, unless they are actually immortal, the inevitable wastage will be made up. Nor is it clear what these long-livers (to adopt Bernard Shaw's term from *Back to Methuselah*) will do with their time. Some of the negations, such as the absence of war, are entirely desirable, but there are vast silences on the positive side. Work will not only be minimal, it will be uninteresting. Godwin's dislike of combined activities must be adverse to many – sport, for instance. He won't allow his future people the chief forms of entertainment. Presumably they can still read, but one notes with misgiving that while he approves of *Gulliver's Travels* as instruction, he regrets that Swift makes it so enjoyable.

Some might yet find this future attractive, but any zeal for action is knocked on the head by Godwin's insistence that nothing can be done about it. Apparently it will all just happen, and it won't happen manifestly or measurably. The quantum leap is totally foreign to his mind.

As the negations pile up, a reader may be reminded of a conversation in *The Tempest*:

Gonzalo Had I plantation of this isle, my lord,
I' the commonwealth I would by contraries
Execute all things; for no kind of traffic
Would I admit; no name of magistrate;
Letters should not be known; riches, poverty,
And use of service, none; contract, succession,
Bourne, bound of land, tilth, vineyard, none;
No use of metal, corn, or wine, or oil;

No occupation, all men idle, all;
And women too – but innocent and pure;
No sovereignty...

Sebastian No marrying 'mong his subjects?

Antonio None, man; all idle; whores and knaves.

(II.i.140–153, 161–2)

The last lines are apt, in an oblique way. It was in this part of his book alone, while ruminating about an enlightened society, that Godwin attacked the institution of marriage. Critics abused him as if this was a major theme of *Political Justice*. It was nothing of the kind, and he didn't even get there until quite near the end of the book. Admittedly, when he did, he was emphatic. Marriage was an evil bond, and voluntary companionship would be better.

Godwin followed his own precept. He entered into a partnership with the pioneer feminist Mary Wollstonecraft, whose *Vindication of the Rights of Woman* had made her famous, or notorious, according to one's point of view. She refused to give up her independence, and he did not want her to. They lived apart for a good deal of the time, only marrying for her sake in 1797 when she was pregnant. On 30 August she gave birth to a daughter, the future author of *Frankenstein*. Ten days later she died.

Her husband never fully recovered. In his professional life, such as it was, nothing eased the burden. As a follow-up to *Political Justice* he had written a fairly successful novel-with-a-message, *Caleb Williams*, but he never repeated even that success, and had to struggle along with hack writing and bookselling, seldom making enough money for his household. He had brought out a second, revised edition of *Political Justice*, and after Mary's death he brought out a third, but few of the public seemed interested. A second marriage gave little comfort.

Then, in 1812, something happened. Out of the blue he received a letter: the sort of communication that begins, more or less, 'You won't know me, but. . . . ' The writer was another poet, of a post-Wordsworth generation, who knew *Political Justice* and thought it wonderful.

Percy Bysshe Shelley, born during the French Revolution, had acquiesced in his family's attitude to it, but was quite incapable of passivity. Estrangements beginning in 1810 had led him to buy Godwin's book, and he revelled in the iconoclasm, the denunciation of injustice, the demolition of conventional values. Godwin, reading the fan letter, rejoiced to find that he had not laboured entirely in vain. His reputation was still alive. He had a young and intelligent disciple, who, as he learned, belonged to the landed gentry, was heir to a baronetcy, and had financial expectations. They corresponded, and met. In spite of the difference in age, they became friends, but less harmonious relations were in the making, as would appear.

At this time Shelley was confronting the issue that others had confronted and backed away from. The British reaction against the Revolution had become deeply entrenched, first by the adventurism of the Republic, then by the Napoleonic wars following on from it, which had carried enmity much further. War-related hunger and general suffering had caused riots, but not so much as a tremor of insurrection. There was almost no pro-Revolution sentiment left. Wordsworth had written patriotic sonnets. Coleridge had turned to journalism, so effectively that he annoyed Bonaparte himself.

While all this was beyond dispute, Shelley had become an ardent rebel, because of trouble with the authorities at Oxford, and then, as a result, trouble with his father, who was Member of Parliament for New Shoreham in Sussex. The question arose again: how to be subversive, even revolutionary in spirit, while acknowledging that Gallic violence was not the way.

To a careful and thoughtful reader, as Shelley was, *Political Justice* could supply the beginnings of an answer. At the height of its popularity, when most of its readers in England were in favour of the Revolution, the two enthusiasms – for Godwin and the Revolution – had tended to go together. They composed, so to speak, a package deal. But after nearly twenty years, the dust had settled, and it was possible to look at Godwin again and see that the package deal was illusory. The delight of the intelligentsia at his iconoclasm had diverted attention from his real attitude to the Revolution. Whether or not his vision of human progress was attractive, it was absolutely non-violent. There was no place in it for revolutions of any kind. More particularly, he condemned violent revolt in principle, including, by implication, the French; only, he did it in scattered passages that were easy to overlook. A revolution, he said, may be an excusable response to the tyranny of the rich and powerful. It may be an assertion of liberty. But it will not produce liberty. The passion and strife will inhibit rational conduct, and hold back progress; the revolt against tyranny will set up a tyranny of its own.

So the dilemma disappeared. The anti-revolutionary passages in *Political Justice* – with their warning against a new tyranny, which the rise of Napoleon had borne out – were in harmony with the rest. Shelley could distance himself from the Gallic bloodbath and still keep Godwin's subversiveness, and his demolition of monarchs, governments, and institutions generally. It all held together.

On this insight Shelley was able to build. The result, as it turned out, would not be Godwinism but an inspired development from it, reaching imaginative heights beyond Godwin's ken. Non-violent revolution was not yet a clear conception, but it was a self-consistent one. As a poet, Shelley would expand it and make it the theme of an extraordinary appeal to the oppressed, which had an impact a century later and far away.

Thus he moved towards Offbeat Radicalism. But he was not the only person who did. Still another poet was moving in the same direction, though very differently: William Blake.

3

Blake

And did those feet in ancient time
Walk upon England's mountains green?...

One of the best-known English poems, in its inseparable musical setting, has been called a second National Anthem. It may be too familiar for its own good. The phrase at the end, about England's 'green and pleasant land', has become so perfect a cliché that it is constantly quoted out of context, and with no apparent awareness of its being a quotation at all. Of the thousands who sing the famous words, most know very little about the author or what he meant. The poem in its setting conveys a general uplift which suffices. Its power is real, almost incantatory, and the precise meaning hardly seems to matter. And yet that meaning, for many of those who sing, might prove surprising.

Here it is in full: the poem which William Blake did *not* entitle 'Jerusalem'. Originally, it was arranged in four verses. Hubert Parry's music combines them like this:

And did those feet in ancient time
    Walk upon England's mountains green?
And was the holy Lamb of God
    On England's pleasant pastures seen?
And did the Countenance Divine

Shine forth upon our clouded hills?
And was Jerusalem builded here
Among these[†] dark Satanic Mills?

Bring me my bow of burning gold!
Bring me my arrows of desire!
Bring me my spear! O clouds, unfold!
Bring me my chariot of fire!
I will not cease from mental fight,
Nor shall my sword sleep in my hand,
Till we have built Jerusalem
In England's green and pleasant land.

Much of Blake's mature radicalism is compressed into this poem. He wrote it around 1804, giving it no title, and embedded it in the preface to one of the 'prophetic books' in which his poetry and art go together. It acquired its unique distinction during the First World War, thanks to Sir Francis Younghusband, an explorer and empire-builder with wide interests. In 1916 he founded a patriotic society, 'The Fight for Right'. It promoted writing and lecturing about the conflict, by authors and others in the cultural milieu.

Sir Francis and his associates thought the society should have a song of its own, a signature tune, so to speak. Robert Bridges, the Poet Laureate, picked out Blake's verses as expressive of hope and aspiration – it is doubtful whether he or anyone else inquired into the meaning more deeply – and invited Parry to set them. The result was one of Parry's last compositions, and, as it turned out, the most successful. Women's Institutes have kept it vigorously alive. It has been sung, times without number, at school assemblies, church

† Some versions have 'those' instead of 'these' in the eighth line, but this is not what Blake actually wrote.

gatherings, sporting events; I have heard of its being requested for a wedding.

*

William Blake was born in 1757, the third son of a manufacturer of stockings. He was baptised at St James's Church, Piccadilly, which is still there. His father apprenticed him as a boy to James Basire, the head of a notable family of engravers. He developed his rare artistic talent by making copies of statues in Westminster Abbey for the Society of Antiquaries, and went on to a career of engraving, printing, and book illustration; he made improvements in technique. This was a living, but it never paid well, in spite of the genius often manifested. Much of it was hack work, and there were lean times between assignments.

In 1782 he married Catherine Boucher, the daughter of a Battersea market gardener. Catherine was attractive and a good household manager (she needed to be), and she co-operated with her husband's requirements; when he printed pictures that had to be coloured, she sometimes did the colouring herself. The marriage was childless, generally untroubled, and affectionate. Blake could be pugnacious, especially in artistic matters, but the pugnacity seems not to have disrupted the home. One or two anecdotes mention conduct irregular by the standards of the time. The Blakes are said to have received a visitor in a summerhouse, both naked. There is a story of William upsetting Catherine by suggesting a *ménage à trois*, but if so, he quickly dropped the idea.

During the early 1790s his work brought him into contact with several well-known pro-revolutionaries, among them the chemist Joseph Priestley, who discovered oxygen, and Thomas Paine, author of *The Rights of Man*. He illustrated a book by Mary Wollstonecraft; not, however, her *Rights of Woman*. Sharing their outlook, and experimenting with writing himself, he produced a long, rhetorical narrative poem entitled *The French Revolution*.

How long it was meant to be, we don't know, for the surviving text breaks off abruptly – probably because Blake underwent the recurrent anti-French reaction, and either destroyed the rest or never wrote it. He certainly underwent the reaction, judging, like many more, that while revolution could overthrow a tyranny, it would end by setting up a new one. He faced the same issue that others faced – how to react against the Revolution without reacting into conservatism. Remaining radical in his outlook, he solved the problem, eventually, in his own way.

Two small books of lyrical poems, *Songs of Innocence* and *Songs of Experience*, reflected contrasting moods. These contain most of what is universally familiar in Blake's poetry, including nearly all the anthology pieces. The Songs of Innocence are simple, melodious, even childlike in their language ('The Lamb', 'On Another's Sorrow'). The Songs of Experience are also simple in form, but their themes and imagery are darker and more powerful ('The Tiger', 'London').

Apart from a spell at Felpham near Bognor, under the auspices of a rather trying patron, the Blakes always lived in the capital – in Lambeth from 1790, at 17 South Molton Street later. Professional work proceeded as ever, with ups and downs. Blake exhibited sixteen original paintings of his own in 1809. *A Descriptive Catalogue* supplies important insights into his views. The exhibition, however, was a failure. Hardly anyone came to see it and no pictures were sold.

Few contemporaries thought of Blake as a poet. If they thought of him at all, it was as an artist, and mainly a commercial artist at that. The immense labours of his later years, when he was creating a whole mythology like no other, attracted hardly any interest until long afterwards. His work was too audacious and too difficult to gain a readership. It supplied excuses for an accusation that he was mad, though no unprejudiced person ever said so.

*

In that unparalleled myth-making, his lack of formal education was an advantage. It tended to isolate him from the better-off who had received such an education, and his avoidance of their influence was all for the good. T. S. Eliot regretted that there was no definite tradition in his work, but that was part of his strength. He made up a tradition, or its equivalent, as he went along. He studied as he wished, reading his way through English literature and teaching himself languages. A side effect was that he was more open-minded than the approved curriculum allowed. He was at least aware of people whom others dismissed as cranks or eccentrics. However crankish or eccentric they were, it was sometimes possible to pick up hints from them.

One was Richard Brothers (1757–1824), a former naval officer who called himself 'the nephew of the Almighty', and was jailed for demanding the abolition of the monarchy. He declared that the English were the true heirs of ancient Israel, an idea with sweeping religious implications. There is no evidence for direct contact with Blake, but, significantly or not, Brothers was the first person to talk about rebuilding Jerusalem. The layout had been divinely revealed to him.

Among Brothers' disciples was William Sharp (1749–1824), an engraver like Blake. He transferred his allegiance to Joanna Southcott, the farmer's daughter from Devon who said she was the apocalyptic Woman in Revelation 12, and enrolled a considerable body of fee-paying believers. Sharp knew Blake professionally and tried to convert him, without success. Blake's only observation on Joanna was a short, amused poem, *On the Virginity of the Virgin Mary and Joanna Southcott*. A fellow-Southcottian was William Owen Pughe, who translated *Paradise Lost* into Welsh verse. When Joanna proclaimed (erroneously) that she would be giving birth to a messianic child, Pughe and Sharp designed an outfit for him to wear. Pughe made Blake's acquaintance; Coleridge's friend Robert Southey records their meeting, though he misdates it. No conversion resulted in this case either. However, Pughe introduced Blake to a mass of ancient Welsh lore, some authentic, some not, but all of value to him.

Understandably, Blake took an interest in what is now sometimes called alternative history. To some extent this aspect of him has always been recognised. Readers and singers of the first quatrain of the wrongly-named 'Jerusalem' often take it for granted that it refers to a legend which historians do not accept, and seldom mention.

A friend once asked me, 'Whose feet?' As he later became a clergyman, it is strange that he missed the point of the phrase the 'Lamb of God'. This is a metaphorical expression for Christ, occurring first in the Gospel of John (1:29, 36). When John the Baptist sees Jesus, he exclaims, 'Behold the Lamb of God!' The idea which Blake is putting forward is that Christ was in England in 'ancient time'.

It is frequently assumed that Blake means this literally, and is recalling a legend of Glastonbury in Somerset, which the tourist can read on the wall of its Abbey's visitor centre: that Jesus made the long voyage to Britain in his youth with Joseph of Arimathea, who afterwards, as a disciple, provided his tomb. The story of Joseph's coming to Britain is on record in the Middle Ages: Blake knew of it. In one of his pictures he portrays 'Joseph of Arimathea among the rocks of Albion'. But the version that brings Jesus to Britain in Joseph's company is comparatively modern.

This more recent legend asserts that Jesus spent some time on the site of the future Glastonbury Abbey. It may be due to a misunderstanding of a medieval story about a vision. It also claims that he visited Priddy, a place on the nearby Mendip hills. (The objection that Blake couldn't have meant the Mendips because, though green, they are not mountainous, is inconclusive. Henry Fielding, who was born within sight of them, calls the Somerset hills 'mountains' in *Tom Jones*.) However, the Priddy tale may have been started unintentionally by a village schoolmistress. Blake's use of these stories – even the possibility of his knowing them – is problematical.

What matters is that, with or without specific Somerset hints, Blake's drift is clear. Jesus was present in this country, not perhaps as a crude historical fact, but in some profounder sense, a long time ago. Since Blake accepts his divinity, though very much in his own way, he is telling us that England has a special place in the divine scheme of things. He puts it in question form, but the tone is of wonderment, not interrogation. Browning has a short poem about meeting a person who was uninteresting to him, and then being startled to learn that this person once met someone else whom Browning ardently admired.

> Ah, did you once see Shelley plain,
>   And did he stop and speak to you,
> And did you speak to him again?
>   How strange it seems and new!

Browning isn't asking. Nor is Blake.

This British presence of Christ is only one feature of Blake's myth-making. Antiquarian speculation during the eighteenth century had been spreading novel ideas about Britain's past, ideas that gave it new dimensions. This was the time when Druids became fashionable, and were credited with building Stonehenge. Several imaginative historians ranged far beyond that. Over the years, Blake made use of their theories in his invented mythology, which, under scrutiny, explains the rest of the 'Jerusalem' poem. It also reveals his highly original radicalism.

The version of the past which he favoured can be traced back to Milton, for whom he had a warm if critical admiration. Milton saw Britain as a fountain-head of Ancient Wisdom:

> Writers of good antiquity and ablest judgement have been perswaded that ev'n the school of Pythagoras, and the Persian wisdom took their beginning from the old Philosophy of this Iland.

In a book entitled *Celtic Researches* (1804), Edward Davies carried this notion much further. He claimed that the Druids, in their British headquarters, were custodians of a pre-Deluge wisdom belonging to a primordial golden age. After the Deluge, they taught writing and other arts to Noah's descendants, and tried to hold them together in a non-violent society. With the advent of violence and division, humanity declined, and so did the Druids. But their teachings created the lore of the Celtic peoples and also the philosophies of Greece and India.[†] Some of Davies' bolder followers dared to add the Hebrews, saying that the doctrines of Scripture and the Druid religion were the same thing if you went back far enough.

Blake seems to have believed this; at any rate, he wrote as if he believed it. In the absence of any real knowledge of prehistory it was entirely legitimate to make use of such theories. In his mythology he adapted and expanded them, and he went back well before the Flood and the biblical narrative, making Adam himself quite a late comer on the scene: 'All Things Begin & End in Albion's Ancient Druid Rocky Shore.' In that pronouncement, Blake is using Britain's oldest name in its geographical sense. That is not the only sense in which he uses it.

*

Jerusalem is brought to our attention by the famous poem, before Albion demands it in any sense. What does Blake mean by Jerusalem, and how does any kind of radical thinking emerge from these mysteries?

† Todd, Ruthven. *Tracks in the Snow*, pp. 29–60.

Queries multiply. How was Jerusalem built long ago, in the country destined to be polluted by the Industrial Revolution, if we take the Satanic Mills at face value? If it was, why does it have to be built again, and what does 'building Jerusalem' mean?

In the second part of the poem, where Parry's music rises to a crescendo, some have detected a sexual subtext in the metaphorical armament. If present at all, this is definitely 'sub'. Not because Blake shied away from the subject: he could be more specific and positive, in this respect, than any of his literary contemporaries. Another poem, which may owe something to Mary Wollstonecraft, laments the frustrations of English women under a regime of respectability, and includes fairly explicit lines about masturbation. But it would be futile, and offensive to Blake, to trivialise the whole 'Jerusalem' poem with a psychoanalytic farrago.

The basic problem in understanding it is that it cannot be lined up with anthology pieces like 'The Tiger' and construed in their light. It is different in kind, and opens up the whole formidable topic of Blake's prophetic or symbolic books. Composed in the intervals of his work as an engraver, these were created on plates combining text and pictures in an amalgam that builds up his mythology. The pictures are often difficult to relate to the text. No one knows where his images came from. Many seem to have flashed upon him spontaneously, charged with meaning; it has been suggested that some were hypnagogic, visiting him in the borderland between sleep and waking.

Blake saw himself as resembling the biblical prophets, who were not primarily 'foretellers' but 'forthtellers'. Some of his own forthtelling is less than lucid. The meaning of large tracts of the prophetic books is not so much 'what they say' as 'what you arrive at for yourself by a sustained effort to understand them', with the aid, naturally, of interpretive scholarship. When an author whose book Blake was illustrating complained that the illustrations didn't speak for themselves, he replied: 'The wisest of the Ancients consider'd what is not too Explicit as the fittest for Instruction, because it rowzes the faculties to act.' The faculties of a reader of the prophetic books have to act very persistently indeed. But meanings do appear, sometimes with a power and vividness that reward the effort.

They are in unrhymed verse. The lines in the larger ones are very long, and tend to take leave of scansion as well as rhyme. A few shorter poems that do rhyme and scan are woven into accompanying essays; 'And did those feet' is one of them. Blake deploys an array of invented characters. The most important symbolise human nature in various aspects.

The principal prophetic book is a work in several thousand lines which Blake does call *Jerusalem*. He composed it slowly during the years 1804 to 1820, with the other books in mind. Complicated, and almost out of touch with regular metre, it has a bewildering medley of themes and characters. It does not yield to a single reading, or to any definite number. I think it is best approached with that knowledge. A reader can skim through it and discern its main outlines, without getting held up by attempts to understand the details. Further rapid readings will bring out more, and so on indefinitely according to taste. The particular theme that explains 'And did those feet' is the principal one, and can be deciphered meandering through it.

*

This theme can be summarised, with the aid of sidelights from the other prophetic books. It takes up the notion of the primordial golden age, as conceived by Blake on the basis of the theories of Edward Davies and others. Humanity, centred on Britain, was once united, wise and creative. Jerusalem in this context is not the earthly city, which supplies only the motif of holiness. It stands for the glory of humanity as it was meant to be, and as it was when the divine presence dwelt in it. More specifically, Jerusalem stands for Liberty in the highest sense, the prerequisite of everything else. The divine presence was most fully manifested in Britain, from which all wisdom flowed. Then came a fall (not the biblical one). Humanity was divided outwardly and inwardly, declining into error, spiritual and mental impoverishment, violence. But all was not lost for ever.

Blake sums up his overall theme as humanity's 'fall into Division and Resurrection to Unity'. In the long poem *Jerusalem*, this finds its focus in a character he calls Albion. The geographical meaning of 'Albion' as Britain is not forgotten, but here Albion is a symbolic Titan who represents all humanity. This is possible, even logical, because of the 'fringe' theory of prehistory that Blake adopts. Everything significant ultimately derives from Britain, so it follows that the figure representing Britain, Albion, can comprehend everything. The other main characters, who represent aspects of human nature, are projected (so to speak) as separated from Albion by the 'fall into Division'.

When Albion flourished in his pristine integrity, Jerusalem (who 'is called Liberty among the Sons of Albion') was an 'emanation' of him. In *Jerusalem* he becomes self-alienated from the divine vision, and self-divided from the eternal realities, pursuing false aims and rejecting Jerusalem, who is personified as female. He becomes sick, and sinks into a deathlike sleep, lying on a rock. His sleep symbolises humanity's fall. Chaotic and terrible results follow.

Now comes a mythification of real history, and it is not totally unhistorical. It can be disentangled from several of the prophetic books, not *Jerusalem* only, without violating them as poetry, and once disentangled it is a seriously interesting social analysis. It leads through the millennia to a quantum leap as radical as Joachim's.

In much of humanity's suffering, Blake detects a sort of perversion of the intellect, due to priesthoods and other elites. Human beings are cut down to fit systems. He symbolises this process in another of his invented beings, Urizen. The name may have been suggested by a Greek word meaning 'to limit'. Urizen, like the other main characters, is originally an aspect of Albion, but the Fall has given him a sinister autonomy of his own.

He is for ever trying to control and consolidate, to force life into a spurious order, at the expense of those who live it. Masquerading as God, he is responsible for legalistic religions, for impossible codes of morality, for ideologies that justify wars and persecutions. They never work out as he intends, and they have bitter consequences. Behind the French Revolution is Rousseau's artificial philosophy of nature, which led to the Terror and Robespierre's dictatorship. We might expect Blake to approve of science as liberating, but no. He sees science as in practice reductionist, condemning human beings to 'single vision'. It has produced technology and the new slavery of the factory.

A passage in *Jerusalem* pulls much of this together. It denounces the destruction of traditional crafts by the technicians and calculators, and their replacement by mechanised industry, with mass-production looming in the middle distance.

> Then left the Sons of Urizen the plow & harrow, the
>   loom,
> The hammer & the chisel & the rule & compasses;
>   from London fleeing,
> They forg'd the sword on Cheviot, the chariot of war
>   and the battle-ax,
> The trumpet fitted to mortal battle, & the Flute of
>   summer in Annandale;
> And all the Arts of Life they chang'd into the Arts of
>   Death in Albion.
> The hour-glass contemn'd because its simple
>   workmanship

Was like the workmanship of the plowman, & the
water wheel
That raises water into cisterns, broken & burn'd with
fire
Because its workmanship was like the workmanship of
the shepherd;
And in their stead, intricate wheels invented, wheel
without wheel,
To perplex youth in their outgoings & to bind to
labours in Albion
Of day & night the myriads of eternity: that they may
grind
And polish brass & iron hour after hour, laborious
task,
Kept ignorant of its use: that they may spend the days
of wisdom
In sorrowful drudgery to obtain a scanty pittance of
bread,
In ignorance to view a small portion & think that All.

Blake turns to the warfare which Britain's industrial power sustains. In this lament to Vala – a personification of Nature – we hear the voices of men dragged away to fight by the pressgangs.

Now, now the battle rages round thy tender limbs, O Vala!
Now smile among thy bitter tears, now put on all thy
beauty.
Is not the wound of the sword sweet & the broken bone
delightful?
Wilt thou now smile among the scythes when the wounded
groan in the field?
We were carried away in thousands from London & in
tens

Of thousands from Westminster & Marybone, in ships
clos'd up,
Chain'd hand & foot, compell'd to fight under the iron
whips
Of our captains, fearing our officers more than the enemy.

This is hardly what admirers of Blake, familiar only with his lyrical anthology pieces, might expect. It is not obscure mysticism or antiquarian daydreaming. It is informed, specific, contemporary condemnation, hard to match in any other poet of the period.

Everything has followed from the sleep of Albion and the primal disorganisation of human psychology. The story is not one-sided. *Jerusalem* assigns an important role to another symbolic character. Los, who is a prophetic figure standing for the imagination and all that opposes the Urizenic trends. He 'keeps the Divine Vision in time of trouble'.

Jerusalem's complication of mythic themes has no chronology, and there is no point in trying to construct a story. However, it ends in a future when 'Time is finished'. Personified England repents misdeeds which she sees as responsible for Albion lying dead. But he is alive.

Her voice pierc'd Albion's clay cold ear; he moved upon
the Rock.
The Breath Divine went forth upon the morning hills.
Albion mov'd
Upon the Rock, he open'd his eyelids in pain, in pain he
mov'd
His stony members, he saw England. Ah! shall the Dead
live again?
The Breath Divine went forth over the morning hills.
Albion rose

In anger, the wrath of God breaking, bright flaming on
all sides around
His awful limbs; into the Heavens he walked.

An apocalypse ensues, in which all that was lost is restored. Human nature recovers its integrity. Delusions and systems are no more. True science replaces the reductionist kind. Jerusalem, Albion's lovely 'emanation' who is called Liberty, 'overspreads all Nations as in Ancient Time'.

*

Albion's awakening is Blake's quantum leap. It is, of course, a poetic myth rooted in an incredible prehistory, even though some of his views on later events, when demythologised, are so perceptive. Nevertheless, he has prose notes and exhortations which show that he thinks of it as standing, however bizarre its imagery, for a future fact, something conceived as actually happening. The world's multiple wrongness will become so glaring that it will precipitate a revulsion. Enlightened human beings will free themselves from the systems that cut them down and shut them in – authoritarian religion, 'thou-shalt-not' morality, reductionist science, and so forth – essentially by seeing through them. They will overcome everything that divides, and grow into freedom and fulfilment, into a higher sanity.

There is nothing political in this. After shedding his early enthusiasms, Blake rejected politics utterly. When criticising society he could be as extreme as anyone, but it is an error to claim him for the Left. His radicalism meant (to sum it up in a phrase) *living differently*. A century later, H. G. Wells brought something resembling Blake's quantum leap into one of his less-known novels, *In the Days of the Comet*. Being H. G. Wells, he invented a sci-fi phenomenon to cause it. For Blake, the great clarification that will bring the change is to come chiefly by way of creative vision, as with the Hebrew prophets. He equates the prophetic inspiration with the artistic, and imagines poets, painters, sculptors and architects guiding humanity towards transformation.

Such a vanguard may not inspire much confidence. But Blake urges his readers to take action themselves. 'To labour in Knowledge,' he says, 'is to build up Jerusalem' – as in his famous poem. When the corner is turned, 'the New Age' will dawn; he uses that phrase far ahead of its latter-day popularisers.

In the notes in his *Descriptive Catalogue* to a picture called 'The Ancient Britons' (since lost) he says: 'The British Antiquities are now in the Artist's hands; all his visionary contemplations, relating to his own country and its ancient glory, when it was, as it again shall be, the source of learning and inspiration.' He expects Britain, the literal Albion with its ancient primacy, to lead the way. Here too, he employs mythical imagery; here too, he means it.

While disavowing conventional patriotism, Blake is very much a patriot in his own style. *Jerusalem* teems with allusions to British places, even whole lists. There is an underlying sense of regenerative power in the landscape, which has never been extinguished by the evils that have surged over it. This lingers in the cathedral cities, and in the satellite villages around London, since engulfed by the metropolis.

> The fields from Islington to Marybone,
> To Primrose Hill and Saint John's Wood,
> Were builded over with pillars of gold,
> And there Jerusalem's pillars stood....
>
> Pancras & Kentish-town repose
> Among her golden pillars high,
> Among her golden arches which
> Shine upon the starry sky.

Blake was a trail-blazer in virtual isolation. Some of his themes in the prophetic books became known to a few in a fragmentary way, partly through his pictures and the notes accompanying them. Hardly anyone read the books themselves, or knew what they were about, or even realised that they existed. Their discovery and decipherment was to be very gradual.

Robert Southey, now an outstanding instance of the revolutionary-turned-Tory, described Blake as 'a painter of great but insane genius'. Allowed a glimpse of *Jerusalem* as work in progress, he called it a 'perfectly mad poem' and, as evidence, picked out an alleged assertion that 'Oxford Street is in Jerusalem'. He was wrong twice over: first, in assuming that Blake's Jerusalem was the geographical city; second, in saying that he located Oxford Street there – he mentions it once, and puts it, correctly, near Hyde Park.

Towards the end of his life he was wrapped in his studies and meditations, and generally tranquil. A group of young artists who called themselves 'The Ancients' – Samuel Palmer was their leader, so far as they had one – gathered around him and treated him as their sage and mentor. Their admiration cheered him after so many years of inadequate recognition by other artists.

He died in 1827, singing. His grave is in Bunhill Fields, a small nonconformist cemetery now surrounded by London. Catherine survived for a while as a friend's housekeeper, often conscious of William's spiritual presence. She died in 1831 and was buried in the same cemetery.

*

Blake says less than we might expect about King Arthur, whose saga, after all, is the pre-eminent British myth. He seems only slightly interested in it. The reason is that he sees it against the background of his own larger myth. In the *Descriptive Catalogue* he says: 'The stories of Arthur are the acts of Albion, applied to a

Prince of the fifth century.' Albion's history of sleeping and waking, with all its consequences, is reflected in the traditional theme of Arthur's passing and prophesied return. A limited golden age existed in Britain while he reigned. He was betrayed and passed away, and his kingdom fell. But perhaps he is sleeping like Albion – in a cave, according to popular belief – and perhaps he will wake like Albion and return. His golden age will return with him.

What is noteworthy is that in Blake's scheme of things, the new society that will dawn with Albion's waking is, in substance, a lost ancient society resurrected – like Arthur's kingdom. We still have a quantum leap like Joachim's, and it still carries humanity into an equivalent of his third age. But the leap is not into a previously unparalleled state.

With some other cases of Offbeat Radicalism, the same is true. We find the quantum leap, and the new society, but the leap reinstates a long-lost glory or promise, with intervening corruption swept away. As we shall see, a return-of-Arthur motif may be said to have attached itself, in these cases, to Joachimism.

4

The Shelleys

In the early nineteenth century, Blake was the only English author who created a mythology, but he was not the only one who created a myth. While he was busy with *Jerusalem*, two new myths entered the public consciousness. The first gave a word to the language, and was re-invented long afterwards as a cinematic theme. The second shaped an Offbeat Radical call for action, and was re-invented as a factor in imperial politics. The creators of these myths were a couple living together, both, ironically, linked with the ultra-rational Godwin, one as his daughter, the other as a former disciple.

*

On 3 January 1812, when Percy Bysshe Shelley sent Godwin his momentous letter, he was nineteen years old. His family home was Field Place near Horsham in Sussex, where his father, Timothy Shelley MP, presided. The family was well off, mainly because Timothy's own father, Bysshe Shelley, had made two lucrative marriages. Bysshe received a baronetcy, becoming Sir Bysshe. Timothy was heir to the title, with Percy next in line.

Percy had spent his childhood at Field Place in the company of sisters. His father sent him to school at Eton, where his studious habits and lack of interest in games exposed him to bullying. He was already writing verses and Gothic stories. In October 1810 he went up to Oxford. The University was at a low ebb, but a spell of residence was acceptable as part of a gentleman's education. At Oxford, Shelley made one friend, Thomas Jefferson Hogg, who was struck by his volatility, his ability to read fast and retain what he read, his fascination with science – as a private pursuit, not an academic subject – and his curious shrill voice. Hogg would later give the world a good deal of information about him, plus a good deal of misinformation.

Family tensions were building up to a crisis, which came in December 1810 on religious grounds. Timothy Shelley was not pious. His religion was simply the routine Anglican conformism of his class, and meant very little, but it did stand for respectability. Percy had discovered *Political Justice*, and was stung by resentment over personal wrongs, real or supposed. He blamed Christianity and yearned for its abolition. In collaboration with Hogg, he put together an anonymous tract entitled *The Necessity of Atheism*, applying what he regarded as strict reason to arguments for God's existence, and finding them wanting. An Oxford bookseller put copies on display, but withdrew them in the face of complaints. Shelley, however, had compiled a mailing list and sent the tract to all the bishops and heads of colleges.

Its authorship became known, and the authorities asked him questions which he refused to answer. On 25 March 1811, he and Hogg were expelled from the University. His father was horrified, more by the disgrace than by the atheism. Painful correspondence and interviews followed, pushing Timothy's son towards exclusion from Field Place as well as Oxford.

Further turbulence was not long in coming. Shelley was friendly with a London family named Westbrook. The younger of the daughters, Harriet, was under his influence and evidently had designs on him. Claiming that she was being persecuted, she 'threw herself on his protection'. The appeal achieved its object. He took her to Edinburgh, and they were married in August, stretching the truth a little to make out that they were older than they were, and that they had fulfilled the residential requirements. Hogg joined the honeymooners remarkably soon, and an odd threesome developed. Before long he was making sexual advances to Harriet. Apparently her husband would have been willing to share her with him, but she was not willing to be shared.

Shelley wrote to other notable strangers besides Godwin, and might have made the principal contact sooner, only he was under the impression that Godwin was dead – a telling comment on the once-famous author's status, or lack of it, with the reading public. Towards the end of 1811 Shelley discovered his error. In that first approach on 3 January, he began, none too tactfully, on a note of pleased surprise at having found that his mentor was still living. A friendly reply came back to him. He wrote again with some personal details.

> I am the son of a man of fortune in Sussex. – The habits of thinking of my Father and myself never coincided.... I saw your inestimable book on 'Political Justice,' it opened to my mind fresh & more extensive views.... I am heir by entail to an estate of £6,000 per an.... My Plan is that of resolving to lose no opportunity to disseminate truth and happiness.

Godwin, who lived in a perpetual financial crisis, saw the potentialities. Not only did his young devotee have expectations, which he could presumably borrow on; he sounded ready to spend money in an unbusinesslike manner. While Godwin was against primogeniture, circumstances alter cases. He quickly advised Shelley not to fall out irrevocably with his father.

Shelley's realisation that he could disavow the French Revolution in the form it had taken, yet still be subversive and even revolutionary, went only so far. In February he tried an exploratory step beyond, towards a positive programme. He crossed over to Ireland and supported a campaign for repeal of the Union with Britain, addressing a public meeting in Dublin about its pernicious effects, and standing with Harriet on a balcony scattering pamphlets of his own authorship over the passers-by (many of whom could not read). He also spoke in favour of Catholic emancipation. In another pamphlet he went back to fundamentals about the French Revolution, saying it had succumbed to tyranny because the gap between rich and poor was so wide: the poor had no idea how to act constructively when they were given the chance. The object of his diagnosis was to lead up to a proposal for a chain of study-circles that would maintain libraries, draw in the workers, and help them to educate each other.

He sent the pamphlet to Godwin and was shocked by his reaction. Godwin was absolutely opposed. It was, of course, difficult to grasp that he was really and truly against associations for any purpose at all. Shelley had assumed that he meant only the political kind that could stir up trouble. Not so: after all, it was hardly to be supposed that Godwin, who objected even to orchestras, would approve of an educational network that could only function by becoming much bigger than an orchestra.

Shelley attempted a defence. With another slight lapse of tact, he remarked that *Political Justice* had been in existence for nearly twenty years and didn't seem to have had much effect. The Irish poor, he went on, were hardly superior in intellect to oysters, and lived huddled together in animated filth. Something had to be done. Godwin retorted that if these oyster-humans were encouraged to take action for 'redress of grievances', the result would be terrible. 'Shelley,' he wrote, 'you are preparing a bath of blood!'

The rebuff was not fatal to their connection. They met in London that October, and several times during the following weeks. For the moment, however, Shelley called a halt, apart from antics like launching model boats and balloons with seditious literature attached to them. One biographer has argued that by deflecting him from activism, Godwin made him a poet. That is going much too far. Nothing could have prevented Shelley from being a poet, and the incident in itself was not very significant. Godwin was a has-been, and out of touch; Charles Lamb said he read more books that were not worth reading than any other man in England. Shelley was young, naïve, and totally unqualified to organise adult education – in Ireland, at that, and especially if he put its people on a level with oysters. But the check did prove that this project for spreading neo-Godwinian enlightenment had no future. He would work his way through his own creative processes to his own Offbeat Radicalism.

*

Adopting a phrase from another author, Shelley once acknowledged that he had 'a passion for reforming the world'. It was showing already when he made his Irish foray, and now it was to show further, in a form better suited to him. He had been gradually composing a long ideological poem, *Queen Mab*, dedicated to Harriet. In the spring of 1813 he had it printed with notes for distribution to a select circle. He sent it to Byron among others; however, they did not meet until three years later.

Queen Mab is written in a modified blank verse echoing *Thalaba,* an epic by Southey. It tells the story of an imagined out-of-the-body experience. The soul of a girl, Ianthe, is taken aboard the Fairy Queen's magic chariot and conveyed through the sky to her celestial palace, commanding a panoramic view of the universe. The choice of the name 'Mab' is puzzling. Shakespeare mentions Queen Mab as an inspirer of dreams, but she is very small, and the image of a chariot with room for a human passenger – even a disembodied one – is hard to accommodate. Later, Shelley rewrote parts of the poem dropping the incongruous fairy.

As Mab's revelation proceeds, vistas of the past and present show the horrors of war, exploitation, and tyranny. Her general theme as she comments is that nature is good but humanity is corrupted. The evil is blamed especially on 'kings, priests and statesmen' who 'blast the human flower'. Above them is the supreme evil of religion; its God is an 'Almighty Fiend'. Much of *Queen Mab* is an extension of Shelley's Oxford outpourings, in more passionate language. God is a monster created by illusion and imposed on the world by priests, to keep it in subjection. The poem's hatred is so intense and vivid that God, even as his existence is denied, seems to acquire a sort of reality. Shelley offers a further cause of corruption: eating meat: he was one of the first in England to advocate vegetarianism on the ground that humanity has been spoilt by an unnatural diet.

The Fairy Queen shows Ianthe the future as well. Nature, an almost personified Nature governed by Necessity, will gradually improve things. Reason will prevail. Meat-eating will cease. The illusions and tyrannies will fade away in a happy Utopia. What is most significant here is that Shelley fails to suggest any concerted action by which humanity can better itself. It does not appear that we can do anything but spread enlightenment to help Necessity along. This is still Godwinism, if with a livelier picture of the future. Shelley's superimposed anti-God frenzy would one day inspire, indirectly, a more constructive passion – but not yet. As an enlightener, the author of *Queen Mab* might be doing his share to reform the world. Eventually, however, he disowned the poem himself as an 'intemperate juvenile effusion', and complained when publishers issued unauthorised reprints.

After *Queen Mab* Shelley almost dried up. He wandered about with Harriet in Wales and Devonshire, while their marriage showed signs of unravelling and she even talked of suicide. During this unproductive time he became more closely acquainted with Godwin's peculiar family. It comprised the author himself, his second wife Mrs Jane Clairmont, and the offspring of several marriages and liaisons. The principal members of the younger generation were Godwin's daughter by his first marriage, named Mary Wollstonecraft after her famous mother, and a daughter of Mrs Clairmont by her own first marriage, who was named Jane but came to be known as Claire.

Godwin never had an income that would support the whole household, and Shelley felt an obligation to help. In the early phase of their relationship, he was in financial trouble himself, yet a great deal of the cash he raised from moneylenders found its way to Godwin, and Godwin was a persistent cadger. This entanglement lasted for years; he extracted a total of £4,700. Such was the second consequence of Shelley's discovery of *Political Justice*.

The third was climactic. He fell ardently in love with Godwin's daughter Mary, and the ardour was mutual. In July 1814 they eloped to France, taking Claire Clairmont with them. Shelley was still married to Harriet. Godwin's anti-matrimonial theories had no effect on his attitude in this actual crisis: he was furious. However, he could not afford to break with the man who so generously subsidised him.

The illicit connection was a partnership of genius, whatever the ethics of the process that had led to it. But tragedy followed when, after some miserable correspondence, Harriet drowned herself in the Serpentine. She was pregnant by someone else. Her husband exaggerated her moral turpitude and married Mary. A court denied him custody of his children by Harriet on the grounds that an atheist was not a suitable guardian for them.

As Mary's companion, he began to compose poetry again, and better poetry. Yet the partnership's first masterpiece was hers, not his – produced at a time when few women wrote, and no other woman wrote with such an impact, so young. It was the first of the two myths which the couple created. The first was to supply hints for the second.

The story of the initial inspiration has been told often, but seldom with enough stress on the unlikeness of the result to its Hollywood and post-Hollywood versions. It begins during another spell on the Continent, when Percy and Mary spent some time beside Lake Geneva. Byron, self-exiled by the scandals surrounding him, was staying nearby, accompanied by his doctor, John Polidori. One evening in June 1816, the four agreed that each should make up a ghost story. None of them actually did. Shelley lost interest. Byron and Polidori conferred, and the doctor began a story of vampirism, a more original theme then than now. He finished it and it was published. Readers attributed it to Byron himself, who was most annoyed.

Mary at first had no ideas at all. Then, after she listened to flights of fancy by the two poets, an image came to her in a waking semi-nightmare, and she wrote. In a sentence that she set down, we can identify a point where something new enters literature:

> I saw the dull yellow eye of the creature open; it breathed hard, and a convulsive motion agitated its frame.

Around that image a paragraph grew, and around the paragraph a novel: *Frankenstein.*

Mary's story reflects a contemporary interest in the nature of life and the possibility of creating it. Victor Frankenstein of Geneva is an experimenter (the word 'scientist' had not yet been coined) who succeeds. Recoiling in horror from the resulting ugly hominid, he rushes out of his laboratory and is afraid to go back. The deserted creature – only occasionally called 'the monster' – drifts about the country. He has no in-built morality and is potentially good, but by the time he meets Frankenstein again he has become embittered by the hostility of frightened humans, and resentment at having been created at all.

He asks his maker to fabricate a female companion for him, so that they can migrate to some distant retreat and live alone. Victor consents, and begins work, but has second thoughts and dismantles the incipient spouse. In revenge, the creature murders Victor's best friend and his bride. Victor sets off in pursuit, and is lured on and on into an arctic wilderness, where he is taken aboard by an exploring ship, tells his story, and dies of exhaustion and exposure. Presently the creature arrives and boards the ship. After an anguished dialogue with the captain, he goes away promising to end his own life, and vanishes in the distance.

Frankenstein's creature is not what he becomes in films, an inarticulate, violent artificial human. Frankenstein even confesses that he had hopes of launching a new species. His creation is bigger than a man – eight feet tall – and could not have been made by merely assembling parts of normal-sized corpses; the implied technique is more mysterious. Moreover, far from being inarticulate, the creature is eloquent. He is in fact mentally superhuman. He teaches himself to talk by eavesdropping on a family, and teaches himself to read by surreptitiously borrowing books. His reading matter includes *Paradise Lost*. He identifies with Satan because he regards Satan as a victim, and reverts to this parallel in his parting speech to the captain.

Frankenstein has created a life-form with no place in the natural order, and cannot come to terms with his own creation, or understand him. Mary never humanises the creature by giving him a name. Hence the erroneous notion that 'Frankenstein' means the creature himself, and hence, also, the use of the phrase 'a Frankenstein' for something that destroys or ruins the person responsible for it.

The novel implies possibilities beyond anything conceivable at the time, or today, for that matter. It expresses scepticism about scientific overreaching, which Mary felt even if Percy did not. But she dropped two hints that came to fruition in his work. The full title is *Frankenstein; or the Modern Prometheus* – Prometheus being the mythical character who stole fire from Heaven. Satan and Prometheus: Mary's book supplied both, one at significant points in the story, the other on the title page.

*

During 1817 the couple lived at Marlow, beside the Thames. Shelley's 'passion for reforming the world' had been in abeyance for a while. The friendship with Byron had not immediately revived it: Byron was a shrewd critic of current society, but not a constructive one. During the Marlow phase, however, Shelley wrote a *Proposal for Putting Reform to the Vote* showing more political acumen than hitherto, and sent copies to people who might be expected to take an interest. One was Robert Owen (see Chapter 5), the pioneer of enlightened industrial management, whose 'New View of Society' was attracting attention: the editor Leigh Hunt had mentioned him in a letter. Shelley also studied the French Revolution more thoughtfully than hitherto, and wrote a narrative poem about an unsuccessful struggle for liberty. But its title, *The Revolt of Islam*, showed at once that the setting was not France. It was an imaginary country, vaguely eastern and a long way from home.

He wrote this poem in a boat on the Thames at Bisham. Not far upstream was the imitation abbey of Medmenham, the former headquarters of Sir Francis Dashwood's parody of a religious order, commonly nicknamed the Hell-Fire Club. His pseudo-friars gathered there for orgiastic parties and ribald ceremonies ridiculing church services. When the Shelleys arrived, the fraternity had become a local legend, and a memoir by Nathaniel Wraxall had just added dubious rumours of black magic, which made it sound more wicked than it actually was.

The Abbey had a Rabelaisian motto over its door, *Fay ce que voudras* – 'do what you will'. Its rakish flouting of conventional morality was not quite in Shelley's style. Yet its motto did have a certain relevance for an author who dwelt on liberty, even if he meant something different; and John Wilkes, the only eighteenth-century politician who proclaimed liberty in Shelley's anti-authoritarian sense, had been a member of the Medmenham coterie. As for its notorious blasphemy, this was largely comic. Yet a tirade in *The Revolt of Islam* reveals that the anti-God fervour of *Queen Mab* was still smouldering. It would be piquant to fancy that Shelley picked up a hint or two from the ghostly revellers near his workplace. He certainly took visitors, including Godwin, on boating trips to look at the pseudo-Abbey.

The Revolt of Islam was poorly reviewed. Godwin, predictably, grumbled. But Shelley was now writing quite copiously and undeterred. One of his best-known sonnets, *Ozymandias*, was composed at Marlow. In the following year, 1818, partly for health reasons, he and Mary moved to Italy, a country they both loved, and stayed there.

It was during this agreed exile, after a faltering start, that Shelley attained his full stature. He did so in spite of recurrent family grief, for Mary had children who did not survive infancy. Many of his poems written in Italy, lyrical, reflective and otherwise, remain deservedly celebrated. It was here too that he arrived at his unique Offbeat Radicalism. While he took the main steps towards it in Italy, it came to be focused on England, and later inspired mass action in a third country remote from both.

Critics and biographers have tended to go astray because of a misinterpretation. They have assumed that Shelley is always, at heart, dreaming of a revolution in the accepted sense, however irrelevant to almost all English opinion at the time. They note his acknowledgement that France got the revolution wrong, but suppose that the goal of his political and social thinking is to get it right. They have even claimed that he wants it to be 'proletarian' – a revolution initiated and powered by the industrial workers, leading to their dominance. That is a Marxist idea which is not in his writings, and could not have been. Marx was still a child, and even in England, where industrialisation had gone farthest, the workers were neither numerous enough nor united enough to challenge the established order. Shelley never even shows the awareness of them which Blake does, in those vivid lines of *Jerusalem*. His denunciations of English oppression are general rather than class-oriented.

His mature radical thought found expression on two levels, in prose and in poetry. In occasional essays like his *Proposal for Putting Reform to the Vote* he sketched a possible transition towards democracy. In the England of his time, with its restricted franchise and its aristocratic assumptions, his ideas were bold, and, from the viewpoint of those in power, subversive; but they were restrained, constitutional, and ahead of their time.

Poetry was another matter. Shelley was always more a poet than a political theorist. Pursuing his vocation, he soared into a realm of apocalyptic and libertarian myth, and evoked a quantum leap such as no one had imagined before. During the creation of his great work, *Prometheus Unbound* – and it was a very great work indeed – he set his more mundane cogitations aside. It happened that Blake was awakening Albion at about the same time. On the face of it, there was a fundamental difference. The change that Albion's waking symbolised was to be expressed in human action, the rebuilding of the mystical Jerusalem. Shelley, in the ardour of composition, did not picture his quantum leap as involving similar action. The myth was a myth, not a manifesto.

One day, however, an unforeseen event connected it with the everyday world, the world of the newspapers that reached him in Italy. He suddenly saw its theme transposed into the social context. Paradoxically, he returned to politics – though not the politics of prosaic reform – by way of his myth. The unforeseen event, coming into contact with it, inspired one of the most tremendous exhortations in English poetry.

*

Shelley's myth had its origin, true to form, in reflections on tyranny and the struggle against it. Living in Italy, he was seeing some of the issues differently. The peninsula was still far from unification. It was divided among several regimes, all repressive, with no springboard for opposition. The Catholic Church, centred on Rome, imposed its authority everywhere. To someone as much concerned with protest as Shelley, it was clear that courses of action which might be feasible in some countries would not be effective in Italy, or even safe.

This closure of doors is the likeliest reason for a shift in his thinking which undoubtedly did happen, and set him on course towards his myth. He reconsidered his old enemy of *Queen Mab* days, the God of religion. He had glanced at God again in *The Revolt of Islam*. Now he could scrutinise his face at close quarters. Even in Protestant England God was dreadful enough, but in Catholic Italy he was the source not only of oppression but of downright evil. In a preface to his play *The Cenci*, telling the story of a famous Italian crime, Shelley wrote:

> Religion in Italy is not, as in Protestant countries, a cloak to be worn on particular days. . . . Religion coexists, as it were, in the mind of an Italian Catholic, with a faith in that of which all men have the most certain knowledge. It is interwoven with the whole fabric of life. It is adoration, faith, submission, penitence, blind admiration; not a rule for moral conduct. It has no necessary connection with any one virtue. The

> most atrocious villain may be rigidly devout, and without any shock to established faith, confess himself to be so.

In his late twenties, Shelley was no longer strictly an atheist himself. Echoing Platonic and neo-Platonic philosophy, he spoke sometimes of an inscrutable Creator who 'dawned on Chaos' in the 'great morning of the world'. But when he mentioned this true God, he was still utterly rejecting the God of Christian orthodoxy – in particular, Roman Catholic orthodoxy – as an atrocity and a blasphemy: the Almighty Fiend, source and symbol of evil, keeping a deluded humanity in servitude.

In the Italy of 1818, Shelley considered that God's tyranny had to be opposed, and his mind ran on ways in which, as an author, he was qualified to do this. He saw that it was futile trying to undermine him by argument as in the Oxford days. Also, it was poetically uninteresting. Instead of renewing the onslaught, he shifted the emphasis, with a stroke of genius that transformed mere polemic into something far more profound. He conceived the idea of a drama about a magnificent rebel, who would, so to speak, refute God by being superior to him. And in *Frankenstein*, Mary had drawn attention to two such rebels, Satan and Prometheus. The Shelleys had left England on the day *Frankenstein* appeared, and they must surely have taken a copy with them, burning a hole in their luggage.

When Shelley wrote the projected drama, he attached a preface discussing both the great figures whom Mary had introduced, and explaining why one of them had had to be ruled out. He would have been quite willing, in principle, to take Milton's conception further. In Shelley's eyes, Satan was the hero of *Paradise Lost*, and superior to God, as his own plan required. He praised the fallen angel's 'courage, and majesty, and firm and patient opposition to omnipotent force'. Many readers of the epic, not having got far enough into it to see how Milton strips Satan of his magnificence, would agree that God is reduced by the comparison. However, Shelley realised that Satan would not do for his purpose, because of his 'ambition, envy, revenge, and desire for personal aggrandisement'. The moral issue was clouded for any reader by an inevitable temptation to excuse Satan's faults because his wrongs 'exceed all measure'. This was a romantic view that would have horrified Milton. For Shelley, however, it eliminated Satan.

The other great defier of Heaven, the one named on Mary's title page, was acceptable as a hero because he had the grandeur without the flaws. Like Satan, Prometheus had already figured in a major work of literature, a trilogy by Aeschylus. Only one portion of this has been preserved. In Greek mythology Prometheus is one of the elder gods called Titans, offspring of Heaven and Earth, headed by Cronos. Cronos's son Zeus leads the junior Olympian deities in a revolt against the elders. Prometheus breaks ranks, helping Zeus to defeat and banish the Titans and become the supreme deity himself. Zeus has a low opinion of human beings and wants to abolish them. Prometheus, however, teaches them the arts that raise them above the animal level and enable them to survive: this is the crucial point in the story where he steals fire from Heaven for their use. He is a lover of humankind, the only one among the gods, and therefore pre-eminently fitted to be a Shelleyan hero. Zeus is enraged, not so much by the theft in itself as by Prometheus's championing of humanity, and has him chained to a rock in the icy Caucasus with a vulture periodically gnawing his vitals.

Aeschylus's surviving drama, *Prometheus Bound*, begins when the Titan is being chained. As soon as he is left alone, he bursts out in a soliloquy, proclaiming to all the universe that he has been wronged. Several mythical characters visit him, and he is urged to make his peace with Zeus, but he remains adamant. He foretells Zeus's overthrow by a stronger destiny or Necessity that is in the hands of the Fates. Moreover, he knows a secret. If Zeus proceeds with an intended marriage to the sea goddess Thetis, their son will be mightier than himself. Zeus is vaguely aware that such a threat overhangs him, but Prometheus refuses to tell his emissary the details, and Zeus intensifies his torments.

Here *Prometheus Bound* ends, leaving an unresolved conflict. To judge from fragments of the sequel, Aeschylus went on to imagine some accommodation allowing Prometheus to be released. He may have pictured both antagonists as mellowing. But the loss of this part of the trilogy left Shelley free to invent his own myth. He rejected the Greek's conclusion, or apparent conclusion, as feeble: he could not approve of a reconciliation between 'the Champion and the Oppressor of mankind'. Aeschylus had created the magnificent rebel who was superior to the Supreme Being, as then conceived; this was vital. The re-invented clash must end in the Almighty Fiend's nullification. Prometheus, embodying the good, had to win – but not in some absurd battle of gods. If Shelley's thoughts returned for a moment to Satan, he certainly realised that it would be wrong to imitate the Miltonic War in Heaven that occupies Book VI of *Paradise Lost*, even if he gave it a different outcome. But without the war, how could the victory happen? *Prometheus Unbound* was the answer.

W. B. Yeats made a magisterial comment linking Shelley and Blake.

> When I was in my early twenties, Shelley was much talked about.... When in middle life I looked back I found that he and not Blake, whom I had studied more and with more approval, had shaped my life.... I have re-read his *Prometheus Unbound* for the first time in many years...and it seems to me to have an even more certain place among the sacred books of the world.

Yeats's linking of the two poets is perceptive, yet there is no proof that either knew the other's work. Blake may mean Shelley when he refers to an 'immortal bard' of Oxford; the publicity over *The Necessity of Atheism* could have caught his attention; but this is only a guess. Certainly the atheism expounded in that juvenile tract is not the point here. C. S. Lewis, as a Christian critic, made a comment of his own:

> If any one who has read [*Prometheus Unbound*] still supposes that . . . Shelley is any other than a very great poet, I cannot help him.

*

Composed mainly in Rome, *Prometheus Unbound* is a lyrical drama intended to be read, not acted. It leaves Aeschylus far behind. Its wealth of characters and themes, and its spectacular imagery, are foreign to ancient Greek models. So is its metrical virtuosity. Shelley uses thirty-six different verse forms. It is debatable whether anyone rivals him for variety until the collaboration between Gilbert and Sullivan.

At the beginning, Prometheus is still chained to the rock after many years, and still obdurate. He has a consort, Asia, from whom he has long since been separated. The Supreme Being who condemned him – Shelley uses the more familiar name Jupiter, sometimes shortened to Jove – is conceived more subtly than he is in classical myth. He is a usurper. When he attained sovereignty with Prometheus's aid, it was on an understanding which was meant to safeguard humanity, but which he never honoured. Jupiter is now the source of all oppression, with numerous aspects, not only religious but secular. As the drama develops it becomes far more than a Mab-style diatribe.

Jupiter is still expanding his tyranny. Some of the characters have throwaway lines indicating that he would like to crush, not only humanity, but everything beautiful or outstanding. He even has notions of flattening the mountains. Humanity, by worshipping him, shares responsibility for its own subjection, and cannot see that this is so, because he has disguised reality with a 'painted veil' falsely called life. His marriage with Thetis is still under consideration. He still does not know that any child of theirs will be his nemesis, because, as in Aeschylus's play, he has failed to extract that information from Prometheus.

The *dramatis personae* include various gods, demigods, spirits good and bad, personifications, and Prometheus's mother Earth as a speaking character. Two nymphs, Ione and Panthea, move from place to place commenting on what they see, a skilful avoidance of the need for elaborate stage directions. The most important of the subsidiary figures – only, he turns out to be anything but subsidiary – is Demogorgon. He bears the name of an awesome being from classical mythology about whom hardly anything is known. Shelley probably took the idea of him from Aeschylus's line about 'Necessity' being stronger than Zeus. Demogorgon is Necessity, or, more exactly, the inexorable Nature of Things.

In Prometheus's opening speech, delivered at night on the verge of dawn, he addresses Jupiter.

> Monarch of Gods and Daemons, and all Spirits
> But One, who throng those bright and rolling worlds
> Which Thou and I alone of living things
> Behold with sleepless eyes! Regard this Earth
> Made multitudinous with thy slaves, whom thou
> Requitest for knee-worship, prayer, and praise,
> And toil, and hecatombs of broken hearts,
> With fear and self-contempt and barren hope.

The second line plants the idea that while Jupiter rules the universe, there is someone or something that sets a limit to his power. In the second act, the One is mentioned again and revealed to be Demogorgon.

Long ago, Prometheus uttered a curse on Jupiter, a prophecy of the tyrant's downfall carrying the force of his own senior divinity. This is quoted. It begins with the words 'Fiend, I defy thee', an echo of *Queen Mab*. But things have moved on. Prometheus confesses that the curse was an error, a surrender to passion and hatred, which he must withdraw.

> It doth repent me: words are quick and vain;
> Grief for awhile is blind, and so was mine.
> I wish no living thing to suffer pain.

He seems for a moment to have capitulated, but it is not so. He has achieved what is supremely difficult, the non-violence of the mind, rising above the passion and hatred, and all that perpetuates conflict. We know already that he is superior to Jupiter, and now he has taken a further step, on to a moral level where his strength will be decisive.

Jupiter's minions assail him with crueller tortures. They try to persuade him that everything he has done is futile. Attempts to help humanity, like his own, simply make things worse. A vision of Christ appears, mourning that he ever taught his fellow creatures and endured suffering for them, because his teachings have been perverted to justify wars and persecutions. Another vision confirms Shelley's attitude to the French Revolution, which is singled out as a supreme nightmare for the lover of humanity.

> See a disenchanted nation
> Springs like day from desolation;
> To Truth its state is dedicate,
> And Freedom leads it forth, her mate;

A legioned band of linkèd brothers
Whom Love calls children –
'Tis another's:
See how kindred murder kin:
'Tis the vintage-time for death and sin:
Blood, like new wine, bubbles within:
Till Despair smothers
The struggling world, which slaves and tyrants win.

Prometheus is filled with horror, which he communicates to others; but he endures. Though long since deprived of any power, he is a greater being than the god who torments him, and all the more so because of the spiritual progress he has made. This has caused a shift in the cosmic order. The hour appointed for Jupiter's fall has come. Jupiter does impregnate Thetis, believing that their child will help him in a final subjugation of humanity. But by doing so he incurs the doom Prometheus foresaw. The being whom his action has summoned to Olympus is Demogorgon, the eternal Nature of Things bringing irresistible change. Demogorgon dethrones the tyrant and consigns him to an abyss of nonentity.

The spell is broken. Prometheus is unbound, and his consort Asia rejoins him. The 'painted veil' of illusion vanishes, and humanity flowers into what it was always meant to be: united in love, liberty and wisdom. Jupiter's countless manifestations crumble away, and with them the evils of the world.

Prometheus Unbound was originally in three acts and ended here. Later, Shelley added a fourth act, an explosion of joy shared by all beings, including Earth and Moon, who hymn a universe reborn. Demogorgon speaks an epilogue in Prometheus's presence. He warns that evil may rise again, but if it does, it must be met with the response which Prometheus exemplifies.

To suffer woes which Hope thinks infinite;

To forgive wrongs darker than death or night;
    To defy Power, which seems omnipotent;
To love, and bear; to hope till Hope creates
From its own wreck the thing it contemplates;
    Neither to change, nor falter, nor repent;
This, like thy glory, Titan, is to be
Good, great and joyous, beautiful and free;
This is alone Life, Joy, Empire, and Victory.

*

In *Prometheus Unbound* Shelley created a new myth, or transformed an old one so thoroughly that the result was new; it hardly makes any difference. The drama branches out from a mere indictment of his old divine enemy into something more interesting and more profound. He imagines a quantum leap on a cosmic scale, with no real parallel in previous English literature.

Prometheus Unbound carried a general moral implication about abjuring violence of mind as well as body, and rising on to a spiritual level above hate and fear. But was there more to this than a generalisation? Did the myth point to anything that might actually happen, or might actually be done? Shelley kept up with the news from England, and fully understood that millions were living in poverty and squalor, appallingly overworked (children as well as adults) and subject to rulers whose only resource for handling criticism or protest was repression. Jupiter was enthroned in his principal English guises, the Established Church and the Monarchy.

Shelley does seem to have started wondering whether any real happening could be pictured that would correspond, on the mundane level, to his Promethean leap. In the preface to *Prometheus Unbound* itself, he hints at a development like Blake's cultural Jerusalem-building:

> The great writers of our own age are, we have reason to suppose, the companions and forerunners of some unimagined change in our social condition or the opinions which cement it.

There is no hint here as to what the change might be, or why anyone should expect it. But a sonnet, *England in 1819*, introduces the leap almost casually in its final couplet.

> An old, mad, blind, despised, and dying king, —
> Princes, the dregs of their dull race, who flow
> Through public scorn, — mud from a muddy spring, —
> Rulers who neither see, nor feel, nor know,
> But leech-like to their fainting country cling,
> Till they drop, blind in blood, without a blow, —
> A people starved and stabbed in the untilled field, —
> An army, which liberticide and prey
> Makes as a two-edged sword to all who wield, —
> Golden and sanguine laws which tempt and slay;
> Religion Christless, Godless — a book sealed;
> A Senate, — Time's worst statute unrepealed, —
> Are graves from which a glorious Phantom may
> Burst, to illumine our tempestuous day.

'Time's worse statute' means the Act of Union combining Ireland with Britain, against which Shelley had once campaigned.

Those who insist on finding violent revolution in Shelley's poetry try to make out that the Phantom symbolises just that. There is no reason to think so. The author of *Prometheus Unbound*, who exhibited the French Revolution as a tragedy when there was no obligation to bring it in at all, would hardly have nursed a longing for a similar English one. Mary, who edited her husband's poems with posthumous notes, confirms that he did not. The Phantom is unspecified. Its dawning is a glory to speculate about, like the dawning of Joachim's third age.

*

Then, abruptly, something happened that inspired Shelley's one outright exhortation, his one call to give reality to the quantum leap, in a true Offbeat Radicalism.

On 16 August 1819, a rally was held in St Peter's Fields near Manchester, protesting peacefully at hunger and unemployment, and demanding political reform. On the order of the magistrates, a troop of mounted dragoons charged the unarmed and largely working-class crowd, inflicting hundreds of casualties, including eleven dead. This was the atrocity that came to be called the Peterloo Massacre; the word is a bitter reminiscence of Waterloo, won by the tenacity of working-class soldiers. A report reached Shelley while he was writing *The Cenci*. He suspended work on the play, and poured out a long and extraordinary poem, *The Mask of Anarchy*.

'Mask' is 'Masque' in English spelling. 'Anarchy' has a special meaning given it by Rousseau. The assumption is that there are natural, traditional laws of human society, which despotic governments brush aside to rule in their own arbitrary way, so that despotic government is anarchy.

This is a vision-poem. It begins with sketches of several political figures of the day – Castlereagh, Eldon, Sidmouth – who are named, execrated, and paraded before the reader, with a host of sinister companions. Anarchy, personified, rides among them wearing a crown: he is 'God, and King, and Law'. His attendant mob pours through England trampling the people. Then a Being appears – in effect, the Phantom of the sonnet. Anarchy falls dead. A voice denounces the nation's afflictions and those who have caused them, and sounds a call for action.

Men of England, heirs of glory,
Heroes of unwritten story,
Nurslings of one mighty Mother,
Hopes of her, and one another;

Rise like Lions after slumber
In unvanquishable number,
Shake your chains to earth like dew
Which in sleep had fallen on you –
Ye are many – they are few.

Scathing contrasts between what *is* and what *should be*, with a condemnation of Peterloo, include a word of warning. Even after such an outrage, the people must not resort to force as they grow in strength:

Then it is to feel revenge
Fiercely thirsting to exchange
Blood for blood – and wrong for wrong –
Do not thus when ye are strong.

Their revolutionary act must be different.

Let a vast assembly be,
And with great solemnity
Declare with measured words that ye
Are, as God has made ye, free…

Let the tyrants pour around
With a quick and startling sound,
Like the loosening of a sea,
Troops of armed emblazonry…

Stand ye calm and resolute,
Like a forest close and mute,
With folded arms and looks which are
Weapons of unvanquished war,

And let Panic, who outspeeds
The career of armèd steeds
Pass, a disregarded shade
Through your phalanx undismayed.

Let the laws of your own land,
Good or ill, between ye stand
Hand to hand, and foot to foot,
Arbiters of the dispute.

The old laws of England – they
Whose reverend heads with age are grey,
Children of a wiser day;
And whose solemn voice must be
Thine own echo – Liberty! . . .

And if then the tyrants dare
Let them ride among you there,
Slash, and stab, and maim, and hew,—
What they like, that let them do.

With folded arms and steady eyes,
And little fear, and less surprise,
Look upon them as they slay
Till their rage has died away.

Then they will return with shame
To the place from which they came,

And the blood thus shed will speak
In hot blushes on their cheek . . .

And the bold, true warriors
Who have hugged Danger in the wars
Will turn to those who would be free,
Ashamed of such base company.

And that slaughter to the Nation
Shall steam up like inspiration,
Eloquent, oracular;
A volcano heard afar.

And those words shall then become
Like Oppression's thundered doom
Ringing through each heart and brain
Heard again – again – again –

Rise like Lions after slumber
In unvanquishable number –
Shake your chains to earth like dew
Which in sleep had fallen on you –
Ye are many – they are few.

This is no storming of the Bastille, but heroic non-violence and, if necessary, martyrdom. Something new is coming into the world. And the assembly will not talk about a hypothetical future, it will appeal to the 'old laws of England' and a 'wiser day'. Shelley implies, as Blake does, that a long-lost good can be reinstated, though Shelley's is much more recent. The 'old laws', nullified by modern oppression, can be resurrected to form a springboard for the great leap.

Shelley sent *The Mask of Anarchy* to the liberal-minded editor Leigh Hunt, who told him it could not be published. In the event, it appeared in print only after Shelley's death, when it could be dismissed as no longer relevant. However, it was taken up later by the Chartists, and its message resurfaced later still in Gandhi's non-violent campaigns against British rule in India. His programme of *Satyagraha* as he called it, Truth-Force, was entirely in keeping with Shelley's vision. *Satyagraha* incorporated particular features of *The Mask of Anarchy*, such as the moral force of suffering and martyrdom, and the conversion of opponents. Gandhi knew Shelley's writings and quoted them; he publicised an article by a student supporter who had discovered the epilogue of *Prometheus Unbound* and offered its last nine lines as a motto for *Satyagraha*. At his Centenary in 1969, Dame Sybil Thorndike gave a spirited reading from *The Mask of Anarchy*.†

Accepting Leigh Hunt's editorial verdict, Shelley wrote another essay on political reform, a perfectly sober one discussing the extension of the franchise (though he worked in a few lines paraphrasing part of *The Mask of Anarchy*). He also wrote *A Defence of Poetry*, taking a very broad view of what should count as poetry, and urging the claims of the imagination: poets, he concluded in a famous phrase, are the unacknowledged legislators of the world. He wrote many more poems himself, including the *Ode to the West Wind*, and *Adonais*, his lament for the early death of John Keats. He saluted uprisings in Spain and Greece. But *The Mask of Anarchy* stands alone.

Shelley died tragically in 1822, in a boating accident off the Italian coast. One – only one – of his and Mary's children survived, Percy Florence, named from his birthplace, as Florence Nightingale was. Mary took the boy back to England, where Sir Timothy contributed to his upbringing without much enthusiasm. Most of

† The copy she was handed had a misprint. I happened to be present, and gave her the correct reading. To have told this great actress what to say, even to such a slight extent, was a privilege that I still value.

her income, such as it was, came from literary work of her own. She wrote more novels, but none that were anywhere near to equalling *Frankenstein.* She edited her late husband's poems, faithfully and informatively, if with a tendency to make him sound less disturbing than he was. Percy Florence, who inherited the baronetcy, showed no signs of having inherited genius. He was a keen photographer, but not a pioneer in the art like Julia Margaret Cameron or Lewis Carroll.

Gradually, Shelley himself acquired a readership. Most of his Victorian admirers concentrated on his lyrical gifts and preferred not to take much notice of what he said; in their eyes he was admittedly a great poet, but wrong – a 'beautiful and ineffectual angel', in Matthew Arnold's phrase. Most of the readers who did take him seriously were on the Left, Chartists and early socialists, thanks to whom *Queen Mab*, the poem which Shelley himself disowned, went through fourteen pirated editions.

A NEW SOCIETY?

5

Owen

Blake and Shelley habitually said 'England' when 'Britain' would have been more correct. The first Offbeat Radical who actually did anything came from Wales, and began his major activities in Scotland. In the year of Peterloo he issued his own *Address to the Working Classes*. Like Shelley, he saw a change coming. Like Shelley, he was firm about non-violence, especially the non-violence of the mind. But unlike Shelley, he tried to initiate the change himself; and, very unlike Shelley indeed, he was a manufacturer.

Robert Owen was the first to sketch a constructive programme for building a new society in the shell of the old. He is counted as a founding father of socialism, but he was decidedly Offbeat himself. He was one of two famous contemporaries (Jane Austen was the other) who showed that a person of genius could achieve great things while taking no notice whatever of the French Revolution. The movement that he launched had no connection with what was left of the revolutionary tradition, even as a reaction against it, and very little with political radicalism in Britain. Politicisation came, but much later. Robert Owen was making converts to a 'new view of society' when Marx was not even on the horizon.

Owen was born in 1771, at Newtown in the then county of Montgomeryshire. His father was a saddler and ironmonger, and also the local postmaster. Robert was the sixth of seven children. In his schooldays he was a voracious reader, but not to the exclusion of other pursuits: he was good at football, and played the clarinet.

Thanks to the inventions of Arkwright and Crompton, the Industrial Revolution was unfolding, though it was still at an early stage. By what today might be called *chutzpah*, Owen bluffed his way, while still very young, into well-paid and responsible jobs outside Wales. He knew Coleridge slightly, but was never much interested in poetry; a more congenial friend was Robert Fulton, the inventor of steamboats, who was a fellow lodger in Manchester.

In 1799 he married Anne Caroline Dale, the eldest daughter of David Dale, who owned a cotton mill at New Lanark by the Clyde, south-east of Glasgow. She was a Scots Calvinist and they were uncongenial spouses, but his sons, in difficult times later, were loyal and supportive. Owen became resident managing director of the New Lanark mill, and subsequently a partner. Dale was a paternal employer, but his managing director soon realised that the mill presented problems which paternalism could hardly touch.

The population of the village was then about 1,300, but most of the workers had no roots in that part of Scotland. They were victims of what passed for progress – uprooted crofters and dispossessed highlanders, who had come to the hated cotton mills because they had nowhere else to go. Men, women and children worked long hours for minimal wages, and lived in squalid conditions. The labour force was supplemented with children dumped from orphanages. Generally these displaced persons were resentful, dirty, drunken and thievish. They diverted themselves, so far as any diversion was possible, with sectarian disputes. To add to the difficulties, some had such a distinctively northern pronunciation that non-northerners found them hard to understand, and wondered if they were talking Gaelic.

Owen grasped the need for drastic remedial action. Prejudice against him as an outsider was strong, but he acted step by step. He raised wages, reduced working hours, and spent money on decent housing, proper drainage and refuse disposal, and an honestly run company store. He stopped the intake of pauper apprentices and started a school for his employees' children. The school was one of his most successful innovations, and quite unlike most schools at the time. The curriculum included physical education, visual aids, dancing lessons and music lessons.

The workers gradually responded, becoming happier and more productive, and better behaved. Owen generated enough goodwill to allow a form of merit rating, assessing their conduct on a regular basis. This was done by means of 'silent monitors'. Beside each workplace was a small block with coloured sides – black, blue, yellow and white, corresponding to different levels of behaviour, from unsatisfactory to good. Departmental superintendents turned the blocks around periodically, so that in each place the side facing outwards gave a judgement of that worker's recent record. A procedure that might, in later times, have been furiously resisted, was accepted in the general climate of amelioration, partly because Owen, while by no means lax in his attitude, enforced factory discipline by suasion and consultation rather than punishment. Conduct did improve, and he actually managed to be popular.

In order to broaden the base of the project, and strengthen its foundations, he formed a new partnership, bringing in William Allen, a benevolent Quaker, and the Utilitarian theorist Jeremy Bentham. His policies paid, even in money terms: New Lanark had a stability that helped it through the violent fluctuations of early capitalism. It became a show place. Visitors made the journey to see it, an uncomfortable journey before railways. Many even came from abroad. Over a ten-year period, nearly twenty thousand names were written in the visitors' book.

*

Owen was beginning to see his experience as supplying the key to a change for the better in society. Under the *laissez-faire* economics that the factory owners favoured, industrialism was serving the interests of a few only, while impoverishing and degrading a much larger number. Owen did not reject technology like Blake. The new productive power was a fact; what was needed was to bring it under social control. As yet, no method of doing so existed. To suggest a way of harnessing it for the common welfare, Owen began to use a term that was not yet familiar: co-operation.

He proposed a government programme for setting up 'villages of co-operation', with a healthy balance between light industry and agriculture, planned housing, and education and cultural amenities. The villages would offer an alternative to industrial concentration, and check the blighting growth of slums. A prototype would not need to be large; it might have only a few hundred inhabitants. But its evident superiority, curbing industrial ruthlessness, alleviating rural poverty, and giving its people a visibly brighter life, would set off a chain reaction. There would be more and more like it, until the village of co-operation became the normal unit of society.

Owen's proven and publicised success at New Lanark made him an effective propagandist. By 1817 he was a celebrity, 'Mr Owen the Philanthropist'. (This was the year when Shelley, at Marlow, became aware of him and sent him the *Proposal for Putting Reform to the Vote*. Shelley, however, was not interested in anything so down-to-earth as New Lanark, and there is no evidence that the contact developed.) Owen went to a congress of European sovereigns at Aix-la-Chapelle, and met prominent people. Some of them listened, but he was too sanguine in supposing that they had any inclination to do more than listen. When he handed one potentate a booklet, the potentate simply handed it back, saying he hadn't a big enough pocket to put it in. Owen assumed naively that Europe's rulers genuinely wanted to improve their subjects' condition, and was shocked when a diplomat told him that they didn't. If the masses were better off, they would be harder to control.

He gave lectures on his proposals to a distinguished London audience, including several bishops and the Duke of Kent, whose daughter would presently ascend the throne as Queen Victoria. *The Times* reported favourably and the listeners were receptive, up to a point. But on 21 August 1817, at the City of London Tavern, he lost most of them, together with *The Times*. His fatal step was to condemn religion as a barrier to social progress. Many of his supporters deserted, and henceforth opponents could use the charge of atheism, in those days a damning one, against him.

Owen's rejection of religion went deeper than theoretical unbelief. It had begun as a reaction against the narrow Protestantism around him, including his wife's. One of his sons, long afterwards, recalled a childhood conversation when he had tried to reclaim his infidel father. The boy was under a vague impression that everyone who mattered, or almost everyone, accepted Christianity, so that it was a foolish eccentricity to reject it. Robert quietly set him thinking. He asked whether Roman Catholics were Christians. Oh no, said the son, the Pope was Antichrist. So the principal Christian body didn't count, his father replied. And then, Robert added, millions of people revered the teachings of Muhammad, not Christ, and had a sacred book of their own, the Koran. This time his son was really shaken. A rival Bible! The topic was not pursued.

More important than Owen's personal scepticism was his insistent denunciation of the 'great lie of religion', which would have to be got rid of if society was to solve its problems. He had touched on this in a pamphlet, *A New View of Society*, and in his lecture at the City of London Tavern he spelt it out. Religion, he said, teaches that human beings are individually responsible for what they are and what they do. His success in improving human material had convinced him otherwise. People are products of their environment, but not only that. In a broad sense their characters are formed *for* them, not *by* them. Godwin had argued on the same lines, and Owen met him occasionally, but he had worked it out for himself on the basis of practical experience.

Religion, by obscuring this truth, allowed all kinds of evil to flourish. An employer who was a heartless profiteer, as so many were, could rationalise his refusal to treat his workers better, because the Church assured him that their shortcomings and degradation were their own fault. The boss, as their superior, had every right to exploit them, forcing them to work and live in wretched conditions; and many of them, as good Christians, would make no protest. Owen was quite willing to admit that most of the workers, at present, might well be ignorant, dishonest, incapable of anything better; but they had been made so, and the wretched conditions kept them so.

At the upper end of the scale, moreover, the boss could believe he was superior – and entitled to behave as such – because the Church put no serious obstacle in the way of his thinking he was. It encouraged respect for a 'self-made man'. Yet his superiority, so far as it existed, was itself a deep-rooted product of his own lifelong conditioning. Even if the vicar tactfully urged him to reconsider his ways, the urging was unlikely to have much effect.

Owen had changed his workforce by changing the environment. In particular, New Lanark's schoolchildren were growing up to be promising citizens, and he was extending the educational process to others, in an Institute for the Formation of Character. His achievement could surely be extrapolated without limit. But human beings must break free from thousands of years of priestcraft, and turn their moral universe upside down, or rather right side up. All who embraced the truth should set to work creating different factories, different schools, different communities; new environments where humanity could be reconstituted – starting as early in life as possible – and could learn to take control of its destiny. The villages of co-operation would help to supply the kind of milieu where these tasks could be undertaken.

*

Owen dabbled briefly in politics. He supported a campaign to prevent the worst exploitation of child labour. Coleridge also supported it, and the first Factory Act was passed in 1819. It made very little difference in practice, because there was no provision in it for government inspection. However, it established a principle, preparing the way for effective Factory Acts later. Owen took no further interest, and resumed his own propaganda.

In the same year he tried, for the first time, to reach out directly to the workers. His *Address to the Working Classes* is mainly about his own theories. He recognises class conflict, but explains that it is all due to the context and nobody's fault.

> An endless multiplicity of circumstances, over which you had not the smallest control, placed you where you are, and as you are. In the same manner, others of your fellow-men have been forced by circumstances, equally uncontrollable by them, to become your enemies and grievous oppressors. In strict justice they are no more to be blamed for these results than you are; nor you than they.

If the workers show any desire to fight against the rich, or to dispossess them, the 'contention' will never have an end. They should see all their fellow creatures as being formed solely by the circumstances of their birth and environment; if they can't grasp this, the time is not yet come for their deliverance from mental darkness and physical misery. Furthermore, they should realise that the rich aren't necessarily so bad.

> It must be satisfactory to you to learn that I have the most evident proofs from many individuals, high in those classes, that they have a real desire to improve your condition.

Soon afterwards, in ironic contrast, came the Peterloo massacre and a very different address to the working classes, *The Mask of Anarchy*.

Owen's hopes of remoulding society from above were fading, but, as his exhortation shows, not quite extinct. While the bishops had dropped him, the Duke of Kent was still well-disposed and arranged a new continental tour, supplying useful introductions. For the first time Owen made contact with other educational innovators, visiting schools founded by Pestalozzi and Oberlin.† He preferred Oberlin's, but neither visit affected his own programme. Meanwhile the Duke headed a committee that tried to set up a pilot village of co-operation, but failed to raise sufficient funds.

Owen was having problems at New Lanark itself. His own school was attracting criticism from his partners. The Quaker objected to physical education as quasi-military: drill was drill whatever its purpose. Others disliked the dancing lessons, and condemned kilts as indecent. Owen weathered the quarrels and disappointments, but he was looking elsewhere for fresh possibilities. To an increasing extent he was guided by an illusion: a creditable one, but an illusion nevertheless. He never accepted that

† Johann Pestalozzi (1746–1827), from Alsace, and the Swiss Johann Oberlin (1740–1826) were well-known for their experiments in education.

his achievement at New Lanark was due mainly to his own exceptional personal abilities. Imitators were much less successful, but never mind! He put his faith in his theories. In 1821 he presented a proposal for an alternative social order in a *Report to the County of Lanark*. He argued that while labour created wealth, existing society could not distribute it so as to recompense the masses who did the creating. Again he called for a fundamentally new system based on his model villages, with appropriate education, and co-operative living that would prevent the uncontrolled growth of private fortunes.

The County of Lanark was unimpressed. William Cobbett, the most conspicuous radical of the day, had no use for any of this. He denounced the intended 'parallelograms of paupers'. Owen did not care much: he was moving towards a resolution to test his ideas in a free environment. In 1825 he withdrew from New Lanark. With his departure, public interest in it waned. Today, however, thanks to the sustained efforts of well-wishers, New Lanark is a World Heritage Site, open to the public. The principal buildings have been restored or reconstructed. There is a Visitor Centre supplying information and visual material. Guided tours introduce Owen's house and school, and replicas of the workers' dwellings illustrate their lives. It is even possible to buy and assemble your own silent monitor.

*

For a proving ground, Owen looked to America, like Coleridge and Southey thirty years earlier. They had never planted Pantisocracy on the banks of the Susquehanna, because they did not have the money. Owen, fortunately – or perhaps unfortunately – did. He was rich enough to finance experimentation. The Midwest still had plenty of elbow room where he could build an environment from the ground up.

The United States already harboured communities founded by

religious sects. One, the Rappites, owned 30,000 acres in Indiana. Their settlement was called Harmony. In 1825 they moved out and sold the land and buildings to Owen for £30,000. Here he inaugurated 'New Harmony' and issued a proclamation inviting 'the industrious and well-disposed of all nations' to assemble there and found a new kind of society.

New Harmony had a loose constitution based on division into six departments, occupationally defined. Within this framework Owen trusted the inhabitants to sort themselves out. His son William, who had the day-to-day running of the place, urged him to concentrate on getting the right kind of settlers. But he was too deeply committed to the notion that a co-operatively designed environment would make the settlers co-operative.

Eight hundred arrived in the first few weeks with hardly any selection procedure, and did not co-operate – at least, not adequately. They had incompatible aims. Some were simply drifters, and some were close to being criminals. One, a Captain Macdonald, rejected the constitution and broke away to form a community of his own. Another, named Taylor, negotiated an agreement with Owen allowing him to secede; he took farm equipment and cattle with him, in violation of the deal, and set up a whiskey distillery, which was also not envisaged.

New Harmony lasted three years. It was remarkable that it lasted as long as that. Owen admitted that people's ingrained individuality was too strong: a successful community would require 'precedent moral training'. He sold off most of the land. Ownership of the residue was vested in his sons, who stayed on and became American citizens. The remnant of New Harmony played a notable part in the cultural development of the Midwest. It was the early headquarters of the U.S. Geological Survey, and provided geological and natural science collections for what became the Smithsonian Institution. Today, the place is preserved as a historic site, like New Lanark. Some of the old buildings are still there. Guides conduct visitors on a tour, and a film tells the story for them, though the radicalism of Owen's experiment is soft-pedalled.

Owen continued to spend time in America after New Harmony's dissolution. With unfailing optimism, he went to Mexico and tried to interest President Santa Anna, best remembered – at least outside Mexico – for the dictatorial policies that led to the Alamo siege and the loss of Texas. After this doomed attempt, Owen returned to the United States and attracted some attention as a lecturer. He debated religion in Cincinnati with a well-known Christian minister. Among the audience was Frances Trollope, the mother of the novelist, who was gathering material for her book *Domestic Manners of the Americans*. She thought Owen a good speaker, and, by all accounts, he was. But he was not a good debater. He stated his own position clearly and persuasively, but he took no notice of anyone else's – even the position of the person he was supposed to be debating with. In the absence of any interplay, he became extremely repetitive: a man of one idea, as Hazlitt put it. Habitually calm himself, he could be infuriating to others.

When he went to Indiana in 1825, he had about £50,000. When he returned finally to England in 1829, he was down to £10,000. That was what his experiment cost him. He was still quite well off by the standards of the time, but much less so. His lack of money sense in his later life, contrasting with his earlier practicality as an organiser and manager, was due to a growing apocalypticism. He believed in a quantum leap as total as Blake's or Shelley's. Society could be changed almost overnight, at least in the sense of turning the corner, and it would happen when his message sank in. It just needed a push in the right direction, and the proper use of his money was to give that push, irrespective of normal prudence.

*

Coming home, Owen found his public position had altered, both negatively and positively. Hardly anyone was left who favoured his earlier notions of reform from above. The Duke of Kent was dead, and the demise of Owen's appeal to the gentry was marked, unobtrusively, by an episode that was not publicised and of which he probably never heard. It involved a *reductio ad absurdum* of his philosophy; yet it forced one of the ablest advocates of religion to confront Owenism as an alternative to his own beliefs, and to form a judgement on it.

John Henry Newman, Oxford scholar, Christian controversialist, and future Roman convert and cardinal, had a brother named Charles. Charles was intelligent but erratic, the black sheep of the family. One day he told John that 'for practical motives to action', Owen 'beat St Paul hollow'. As the only atheist Newman, Charles deeply disturbed the others. If he had been a good advertisement for Owenism, the result might have been public and interesting. He wasn't. He raved about being persecuted; John found a job for him as a bank clerk, but he lost it because of his noisy ideology. He got his inheritance from his mother in advance, and ran through it. He became a schoolmaster and was soon in trouble for biting one of the boys. He lived with a woman not his wife, who locked him up, pawned his clothes, and spent the proceeds on drink. At last he became entirely dependent on relatives. But as a convinced Owenite, he insisted that none of it was his own fault, he was simply what his environment had made him.

John's Christian commitment was unshakable, but the case of Charles forced him to think a little harder about others' lack of faith. Unfortunately, his brother's vagaries reinforced a suspicion that atheism did not deserve respect as a doctrine, and was merely a symptom of personal shortcomings in the atheist. So Owen's last gentleman disciple was a disaster. He carried the influence no further, and was unconsciously symbolic of the end of a phase.

If one door had closed, however, another was now wide open. In the course of Owen's American involvements, the British workers he had addressed so condescendingly were discovering his ideas and looking his way. Trade unionism at home was not a complete novelty: he did not invent it. In 1818 John Gast, the London shipwrights' leader, had formed an association called, picturesquely, 'The Philanthropic Hercules'. Gast was right about labour's potential strength, but his Hercules was premature. A few years later the situation was different. Union activists were pressing, not only for better pay and conditions, but for political measures as well.

Parliamentary reform was by this time a major issue. The House of Commons was grossly unrepresentative, not only because of the restricted franchise, but because the population map was fast changing. Some areas had many MPs who were nominated by a handful of electors, while far more populous areas, such as the new industrial regions, had very few. Middle-class radicals and the new rich campaigned for a Reform Bill that would get rid of such anomalies. Trade-union militants had no votes themselves, but supported the campaign in the belief that the benefits of a reformed parliament would trickle down to their membership. After a frantic moment when even revolution seemed possible, the Reform Bill became law in 1832.

Meanwhile, Owenite ideas had been taking hold among the workers. Some of the more thoughtful were even using a newly invented word, socialism, though not with the meaning it was to have later. Forward-looking groups were talking of forming co-operative communities in villages. The Reform Bill had not been on the statute book for long when it became apparent that it would not, after all, do much for the workers. Direct action became the watchword, and labour organisation developed on a much larger scale. Now Owen was in demand as never before. He spoke to working-class audiences everywhere. By the middle of 1833, at the age of sixty-two, he was the leader of the union movement so far as anyone was. The great change which he had failed to inspire from above was suddenly boiling up from below. He was neither a visionary like Blake nor a poet like Shelley, yet he proclaimed a quantum leap as tremendous as theirs. Society would be visibly altering within a year.

In 1834, with his blessing, several working-class groups combined to form the Grand National Consolidated Trades Union. It grew spectacularly; at its height, it may have had a full million members. Owen's advice to the workers was not to attack capitalism head-on but to bypass it, and create an alternative economic system based on association instead of private ownership. The superior power of co-operation would squeeze the capitalists out. Owenite optimists launched a co-operative store in London, and a builders' guild that actually did some building.

But destructive factors were at work within and without. The Consolidated Union had to be ready with industrial action if necessary. And it lacked the resources for major strikes. While Owen gave his support to minor ones, an old trouble surfaced again: most of the membership declined his package deal because it involved rejection of religion. The Government saw the labour movement's real weakness, and clamped down with legislation – this was the time of the Tolpuddle Martyrs, agricultural labourers in Dorset who were transported to Australia for trying to form a union. Owen protested without success. His apogee was past, and the Consolidated Union disintegrated.

In any case, Owen was drifting back towards the judgement he had formed after New Harmony: the great change required a profound reconditioning. Even at the height of his enthusiasm for trade unionism he was speaking of it as the agency that would usher in a 'New Moral World', and his emphasis was shifting further in that direction. He expressed his views through his weekly periodical, *The Crisis*, to which he appointed an eccentric preacher, J. E. Smith, as editor. Smith did the job well, but again the religious conflict was a stumbling block. Smith broke with Owen, invented a religion of his own, and eventually became editor of the *Family Herald*, that apparently immortal journal which would one day be the first to print stories by Annie Besant, and, improbable as it sounds, H. G. Wells.

In 1835 Owen tried again with another publication, *The New Moral World*, devoted to 'Truth, Industry and Knowledge'. He was now coming down definitely on the side of moral regeneration, and was firmly of the view that the workers' activities, as such, could never produce it. The year 1844 saw the beginning, in Rochdale, of the consumer co-operative movement that would presently cover the land with 'Co-op' stores paying dividends to customers instead of shareholders. Owen had ceased to take much interest in such practical initiatives. In the later nineteenth century, a typical northern manufacturing town would have three foci of working-class life: the Chapel, the Union, and the Co-op. Two parts of that triad were in some degree a legacy of Owen's thought. The Chapel, of course, was not.

The working-class militants left Owen behind and returned to political action in the shape of Chartism, demanding new reforms of the system to give the masses real political leverage. It was the Chartists rather than the Owenites who discovered *The Mask of Anarchy*; and in Disraeli's contemporary novel *Sybil* we are introduced to working-class characters who are radicals with political aims. An Owenite diehard, still believing in a different kind of radicalism, is a lonely figure in the story, to whom no one listens. Six Owenite groups that were still struggling on in 1850 had a tiny total income of two pounds, five shillings and threepence between them.

Owen himself was growing old, and his money had run out. There would be no more experimentation. But he wrote a volume of autobiography, and he continued to talk. One of his audiences included Friedrich Engels, Marx's collaborator, who was impressed by the story of New Lanark. Owen tried to interest

Victoria, the crowned daughter of his late ducal ally. He stuck to his belief in the quantum leap. The transformation would come, and its beginning at least would come soon. His reason for thinking so was the same as Blake's. Society's wrongness would be realised so widely that the turn towards rightness would be rapid.

The leap was a mirage, but he could still break new ground, both in person and through his reputation. At eighty-two he became a pioneer of spiritualism. While God might be out of the picture, post-mortem survival was acceptable. Owen was not merely following a trend. He embraced the doctrine before the medium Daniel Home, Browning's Mr Sludge, made it fashionable.

Forced to admit that religious delusions were still hampering the living, and delaying their adoption of his own philosophy, he entered into communication with the dead who might be expected to know better. His last years were fortified by contacts with several of the illustrious deceased, among them Thomas Jefferson, and his own supporter the Duke of Kent. Owen had more success with the Duke than with his daughter, and praised his punctual attendance at séances, while tactfully not reminding him of his non-repayment of a loan. Another visitor from the Other Side was, as he put it, 'my old friend Shelley'. It would be interesting to know in what sense the poet was an old friend. Shelley might have attended his London lectures in 1817, and met him briefly, but there is no evidence that he did so. The phrase may have been no more than an approving reminiscence of congenial reading: for instance, of the pamphlet which Shelley sent him, or even of *Queen Mab* when it was reissued and circulated.

Nevertheless, the 'old friend' would have been a kindred spirit, in more senses than one. Owen's own opposition to Christianity gave him eventual status as a pioneer of secularism, the anti-religious movement led by Charles Bradlaugh and – for a time – Annie Besant. Through this he continued to be an influence in a way he had not foreseen. Encouraged by the spirits, he lived until

1858, talking and writing to the last. His final collapse engulfed him at his birthplace, Newtown, while he was giving a lecture.

*

It is worth taking a step backwards in time and, briefly, across the Channel, to meet another inventor of ideal communities. Owen claimed to have inspired him, and perhaps he did, but, if so, the result was definitely un-Owenite.

France never produced a real counterpart to Offbeat Radicalism. The causes operative in Britain did not apply. The French were well aware that their Revolution had brought solid gains, in spite of the horrors that alienated foreign sympathy, and in spite of the long war that followed. They were dazzled by Napoleon rather than antagonised by Boney, and the Napoleonic spell lingered even after Waterloo. Only a minority recoiled into thoroughgoing reaction, and most of those who did became reactionaries truly so called, favouring restored monarchy rather than further experimentation.

Yet the Revolution's tally of victims had been real enough, and one of them – a survivor – did dream of charting a new course for society. His eccentric version of Offbeat Radicalism appeared during the heyday of New Lanark and New Harmony. If he did look to Owen for inspiration (he denied it), they were too unlike to collaborate. The Frenchman was a solitary theorist with none of the Welshman's industrial flair and experience. The system that he concocted in isolation was hard to take seriously. And yet people did, not only in France; they felt that he had given them a glimpse of something worth considering, even worth trying to put into practice.

Charles Fourier (1772–1837) was born in Besançon near the Italian frontier, the birthplace of another social theorist, Pierre Proudhon, and also of Victor Hugo. He was the son of a well-off linen-draper. Incidents in his early life gave him unpleasant insights into capitalistic ethics, which he never forgot. On his father's death, he moved to Lyons and started a business of his own. In 1793 the city revolted against the revolutionary regime, and was bombarded. Fourier barely escaped being executed himself, lost most of his money, and henceforth, understandably, had little use for the Revolution.

Employed sporadically as a commercial traveller, he saw a good deal of western Europe, but never had a real career and would not have wanted one. During the later part of his life, unmarried, he drifted through a succession of private hotels and furnished apartments, writing large, strange, repetitive books. He was commendably sensitive to the sufferings of others; he was fond of cats and flowers; he had an obsession with minute detail. As he evolved a programme for social regeneration, without attempting to learn from any predecessors, he became, odd as the description sounds, a furtive Messiah. He lived obscurely and his contacts were few, yet, somehow, he was going to enlighten humanity after millennia of darkness. 'To me alone,' he boasted, 'present and future generations will owe the origin of their immense happiness.'

Fourier diverges from Owen at once by basing his ideas on belief in God: not, however, the Christian God. His Deity has been experimenting with creation in many other worlds before ours, so that he knows what he is doing. We can trust in his goodness. But Fourier carries this trust beyond what it means in Christianity. Since God is entirely good – and, through long practice, competently good – nothing in his universe can be bad. So all our passions and desires come from him, and have his blessing. He implants in us a yearning for happiness. Therefore, we have a right to expect that happiness will be made available.

As matters stand, however, it usually isn't. Like Rousseau, Fourier regards civilisation as all wrong. It misdirects and corrupts our God-given longings, often through false morality. If we could drop morality and live by our natural impulses, we could move towards a happier state which Fourier calls 'Harmony'. Obviously, this can't just happen. A mere free-for-all would lead to chaos. What is required is a social organisation through which the change can be effected. This is a possibility, and not a remote or fanciful one. Fourier believes in a quantum leap as strongly as Owen, or, for that matter, Blake and Shelley. He thinks a first step, from which all others will follow, can be taken in two years.

Thus far, it all sounds fairly rational or at least fairly intelligible. However, the new social system which Fourier expounds is embedded in a mythology that is not derived, like Shelley's, from older sources, but very much his own. Some of those who discuss him prefer not to take much notice of it, because it makes him sound crazy and absurd. The trouble is that he actually *is* crazy and absurd, some of the time; and his system cannot be detached entirely from his mythology.

His universe teems with planets and stars which are living beings with personalities of their own – an interesting anticipation of Olaf Stapledon's sci-fi classic *Star Maker*. Human souls are immortal, and transmigrate. The fact that we all keep going away and coming back, and exchanging notes with others who are doing the same, is a good reason for taking an interest in humanity's long-term career.

Our planet has a predetermined lifetime of 80,000 years. For the human race, part of that time will be taken up 'ascending' – that is, progressing – in sixteen stages. Then another part will be taken up 'descending'. In the middle there will be a kind of plateau, and on this happy table-land we shall enjoy full Harmony, with an extended lifespan. After several thousand years the decline will set in. At the end of the descent on the downward side, also in sixteen stages, any surviving humans on earth will be transferred to another world.

Future phases of the process, above the level we have reached and before the subsequent decline, will bring surprising developments. Six moons will replace the present one. Seawater will turn into an agreeable fluid resembling lemonade. New animals will appear, replacing existing creatures with more human-friendly ones. There will be benign anti-bugs and docile anti-lions. Co-operative anti-whales will allow themselves to be harnessed to draw ships.

Most of this mythology is scattered through Fourier's writings, not presented in any one passage, and his motive for bringing it in at all is not very clear. The thoughts that surround it are of quite a different order, and far more substantial.

He leads up to his constructive proposals with a critique of society that gives him a lasting place in the literature of protest. As things stand, he says, civilisation makes Harmony unattainable. It prevents the completion of humanity's upward movement. It perverts the passions and thwarts the desires that should be leading us on. It warps human relations by deceit, intrigue, and antagonism. An entrepreneur has to make his way by falsehood – by adulterating food, for instance, or by selling defective goods. Success is liable to depend on others' misfortunes. Doctors have a vested interest in sickness; lawyers have a vested interest in litigation; soldiers have a vested interest in the death of other soldiers (because it leads to their own promotion); glaziers have a vested interest in windows getting broken; and so forth. Marriage is based on a false ideal of faithfulness, and breeds hypocrisy and mendacity. Civilisation doesn't even work well. It is a morass of waste and inefficiency, making vast numbers of people poor and vast numbers parasitic, especially women.

Fourier calls for a restructuring of society, enabling all people to do freely what they want to do, in unison instead of conflict. At present morality is on the wrong track, and especially because it tells us to love our work, whereas this is possible only for a fortunate few. What is required is 'to make work loveable'. It can be done, if people are arranged in a co-operative relationship.

His most famous proposal is for a social unit called the phalanx, to replace existing groupings. The phalanx is a body rather like an Owenite village of co-operation, self-supporting in essentials, but much more intricately planned. Fourier's love of detail prescribes an exact number of members – 1,680 – based on a classification of psychological types. (He allows some latitude – there could be another hundred or so.) Ideally, a phalanx should be in a pleasant situation, perhaps in a valley with a river, fertile land, and woods. All the members are to live in a great complex of buildings called the phalanstère. Fourier coined the word; which is anglicised as 'phalanstery'. The phalanstery is conceived as a very fine place to live, with dining-halls, dancing-halls, and a general opulence far beyond what most people know at present.

Left-wingers such as Bernard Shaw have tried to interpret the phalanx as an egalitarian commune. It is nothing of the kind. It has gradations. The members share in the ownership, but some own bigger shares than others, and draw bigger dividends. Everybody is comfortably provided for (Fourier dwells lovingly on the lavish meals), but while some mingle freely in the phalanstery's facilities, some are allowed to have service flats for themselves.

All, however, are active and productive in one way or another, doing what they like doing, with a great deal of consultation and programming. Fourier believes in a divine 'Law of Attraction' that will hold everything together if it is given free play. More is involved, of course, than purely individual choices. He recognises a 'passion cabaliste' that impels people to combine in groups and compete with other groups. This is to be encouraged. Some of his examples are rather trivial. He imagines a team of soft-pear growers competing against a team of hard-pear growers, and a team growing blue hyacinths competing against a team growing red hyacinths. Still, his point is made. He foreshadows the 'socialist competition' of Soviet Russia, when state owned factories were spurred to produce more by competing against other state owned factories.

Fourier is close to some other Utopia-builders when he

proposes to do away with marriage. Multiple and orchestrated eroticism is to be a feature of life in the phalanstery. As for the family, he wants to abolish it. One reason is that he doesn't like children, and objects to traditional ways of bringing them up. The majority of children, who are at least amenable, should be put through vocational training almost from infancy. And the less amenable? Fourier offers one of his most ingenious and notorious notions. Critics of ideal societies are apt to ask: 'What about the unpleasant jobs that no one will ever want to do – refuse disposal, scavenging and so on?' Fourier replies that one section of the population will be glad to do them. Plenty of little boys like dirt, so let there be gangs of little boys to attend to it.

These are the main features of Fourier's system. He never makes it clear how the phalanstery's population is to be kept stable – there will, after all, be births and deaths, and probably more births – but in planning it as a functioning unit, he shows a certain psychological insight. He has a peculiar trick of illustrating his points with little stories about the hypothetical membership, showing how much more fun they can have than the victims of civilisation, and how even ugly habits can be fitted in and made constructive. One of his characters has a fondness for eating spiders. This is recognised as a special taste, doubtless sexual in origin, and catered for.

On the whole, Fourier's fictional digressions are ill-advised. Yet the fact that he can be – so to speak – fiction-minded, and not purely prosaic in his thinking, raises an intriguing question. Explaining the phalanstery, he awakens echoes of a greater French author three centuries earlier. He is anticipated by François Rabelais. Owen would not have taken a hint from such a frivolous source, but a Frenchman might. In any case, the echoes are there.

In his exuberant fantasy about giants, *Gargantua and Pantagruel*, Rabelais introduces a highly un-clerical friar named John. Taking a liking to him, the all powerful Gargantua offers to make him an abbot. John replies that he would rather found a new abbey 'after his own devices' – meaning a libertarian abbey, the opposite of existing ones. The giant gives him an estate by the Loire, called Thélème. The name is a pun: *thélèma* is Greek for 'will'.

The anti-abbey which is built on this site is a huge hexagon containing living quarters, art galleries, libraries, a theatre, a swimming pool. The inmates, of both sexes, are nominally monks and nuns, but they have no regulations. They rise in the morning when they like, eat and drink when they like, sleep when they like, and, in fact, do things in general when they like. They have only one rule – Do what you will. This, it will be remembered, was adopted by Sir Francis Dashwood as the motto of his real mock-abbey at Medmenham.

The occupants of a Fourierist phalanstery are likewise doing what they will; that is the whole point of it. But Thélème is unstructured. Thélèmites can work if they want, and earn money, but they are free to do otherwise; the funds will provide for them. Many prefer to spend their time in unpaid cultural pursuits. They study, write, compose music, compete in games. Material needs are supplied by a subsidiary body of craftworkers, garment-makers, and so on, separately housed.

Even as a fantasist, Rabelais recognises that a random assemblage of human beings could never live together in peace if all were pleasing themselves, without restrictions of any kind. So he provides for a highly selective screening. He gives a whole list of people who are not eligible, such as lawyers, money-lenders, and pious hypocrites. Having imagined a community of people he does approve of – an impossibly large one, but he is prone to exaggeration – Rabelais thinks (or pretends to think) that 'Do what you will' is going to be a sufficient guide, because a benevolent Nature will keep them in accord: the whole elite company of 'generous and high-spirited' men, 'frank and fearless' women.

Thélème is a Renaissance daydream, not to be taken too

seriously. There is no suggestion of its being a prototype for a network of other communities. But Rabelais, accidentally, draws attention to a flaw in Fourier's system. The Thélèmites not only do what they enjoy without any schedule, they switch from one activity to another as the mood takes them; after all, boredom is not to be tolerated; and here Fourier himself has to confront a fact of life. Among the passions which he says God has implanted in us is one that he calls the 'papillonne', the butterfly passion. His people are doing work they enjoy, as the system provides for, but they won't want to do it all the time. They will feel the need for a change, like a butterfly flitting from flower to flower. The system must provide for that too.

Fourier accepts that the 'passion papillonne' is liable to strike with disconcerting rapidity. Restlessness may set in within an hour or two, and alternative jobs must be available. Could such jobs always be ready when required? Perhaps. But as critics have pointed out, the drawback with any large number of people, living together in mutual dependence, would be the lack of reliability. You would never be sure that a job you relied on someone to do would actually get done. The butterfly passion might create a diversion without notice. The passengers on a train would doubtless be pleased to know that the engine-driver liked driving, but they would be less pleased if he stopped the train to put in an hour basket-weaving.

Fourier never solved this problem, even theoretically. Yet he was confident that phalansteries could work, and that if their formation once got going, they would spread until they became universal. With his penchant for exactitude, he reckoned that there would eventually be 2,985,984, a worldwide federation of them, with each one capable of self-support in necessities, but linked by an interchange of goods and personnel. Meanwhile, a start could be made with a prototype. To set up even one phalanstery, with its complex human engineering and elaborate residential arrangements, would require a large initial outlay. But a single rich well-wisher could do it. Fourier announced that he would be at home in his meagre furnished room at a certain time each day, so that a sponsor would know when to call. No sponsor ever did; Fourier died alone.

With his odd fancies pruned away, Fourier is usually allotted a place in the history of socialism, like Owen. This is only marginally justified. Some of his social criticism entered the left-wing mainstream, but his system as a whole did not. Continental Marxists dismissed him. He was too blind to large-scale industry to work out how a phalanx, or even a combination of phalanxes, could organise it. His mode of thinking did reappear among anarchists, not however because the phalanx appealed to them, but because they liked to fantasise about a society where anybody could do anything.

Like Owen, Fourier attracted some notice in the United States, a country with space and scope for experimentation; and his admirers did more than the handful of community builders who were inspired by Owen. Thanks partly to publicity in the *New York Tribune*, under the historic editorship of Horace Greeley, about forty communities came into existence based on Fourier's theories to at least some extent. They subsisted on farming and light industry. Most of them soon expired. One at Red Bank, New Jersey, lasted until 1855. Visitors included William Ellery Channing, the head of the Unitarian Church. He was among the eminent persons who made posthumous visits to Robert Owen at séances. Descendants of Red Bank's original members remained on the site for several decades, quite happy, but free from ideology.

Such attempts were part of a wider phenomenon. Nineteenth-century America produced something like two hundred mini-Utopias. Coleridge's pantisocracy was the forerunner of all of them, though it is generally forgotten. Few of any kind survived after the first generation. Those that did usually managed it by becoming business organisations, like the Oneida Community in New York State, a Utopian project which transformed itself into a company manufacturing cutlery and silverware. It still does.

1. *Mystic Nativity* by Sandro Botticelli, 1500.

2. Etching of the 'Awakening of Albion' by William Blake, plate 95 of *Jerusalem*, 1810.

Chapter 7th

21 / 95

It was on a dreary night of November
that I beheld ~~the frame on whic~~ my man compleated; ~~and~~
with an anxiety that almost amount
ed to agony I collected instruments of life
around me ~~and endeavoured~~ that I might infuse a
spark of being into the lifeless thing
that lay at my feet. It was already
one in the morning, the rain pattered
dismally against the window panes, &
my candle was nearly burnt out, when
by the glimmer of the half extinguish
ed light I saw the dull yellow eye of
the creature open — It breathed hard,
and a convulsive motion agitated
its limbs.

~~But how~~ How can I describe my
emotion at this catastrophe, or how deli
neate the wretch whom with such
infinite pains and care I had endeavoured
to form. His limbs were in proportion
and I had selected his features ~~&~~ as
beautiful. ~~handsome~~ ~~handsome~~. ~~Handsome~~ Beautiful, Great God! His
yellow ~~skin~~ skin scarcely covered the work of
muscles and arteries beneath; his hair
was of a lustrous black & flowing and his teeth of a pearly white
ness but ~~these~~ luxuriances only ~~formed~~
formed a more horrid contrast with
his watry eyes that seemed almost of
the same colour as the dun white
sockets in which they were set,

3. Leaf from the first of two disbound draft notebooks, started by Mary Godwin at Geneva in the summer of 1816, with marginal corrections by Percy Bysshe Shelley.

4. Cruikshank etching of the Peterloo Massacre, as published by Thomas Tegg, 1819.

5. Tenement buildings from the settlement of New Lanark, provided by Robert Owen for his cotton-mill workers, 1820.

6. Annie Besant, English theosophist and Indian political leader, 'How to become a Mahatma'.

7. English author, artist and social reformer John Ruskin, 1859.

8. Portrait photograph of William Morris by Frederick Hollyer, 1884.

9. Conversation Piece: *Gilbert Keith Chesterton, Hilaire Belloc and Maurice Baring*, by Sir Herbert James Gunn, 1932.

NO COERCION!

VICTORIA PARK, SATURDAY MAY 21, 1887.

No. 10 Platform.

Chairman—H. A. BARKER.

SPECIAL RESOLUTION.

"That this meeting expresses its deep abhorrence of the Coercive Measures levelled against the Irish nation, and is of opinion that, the Land Question being at the root of the Irish troubles, no political change can have permanent value unless accompanied by, or be in the direction of the abolition of Landlordism in Ireland; and is further of opinion that the Irish nation should be left free to settle with the landlords without any restriction whatever from the English Parliament."

SPEAKERS.

ANNIE BESANT. WILLIAM MORRIS.
G. B. SHAW. H. H. SPARLING.
H. DAVIS. J. LANE. C. W. WADE.

The **Commonweal**, *Socialist Journal (1d. weekly), and pamphlets on Socialism, may be had from the Secretary of the* SOCIALIST LEAGUE, *13 Farringdon Road, London, E.C.*

10. The Socialist League pamphlet cover, advertising No. 10 Platform to be held in Victoria Park on Saturday 21 May, 1887.

6

Two Women

Owen's brand of socialism expired, but in many minds his irreligion survived. For him, those two things had constituted a package deal. He said – and sabotaged himself by saying – that the abolition of the 'great lie' of Christianity (in effect, the abolition of Christianity) was a prerequisite for the full realisation of his projects, because the people involved had to be liberated from Christian delusions that interfered. Finding the delusions more deeply implanted than he thought, he had fallen back on moral re-education, though he persisted in hoping for a sudden mass enlightenment – a quantum leap – that would put everything right.

For Blake and Shelley likewise, their visions had been linked with a nullification of Christian orthodoxy. But they did not consider this in Owen's way. The logic of a link between rejection of Christianity and thoroughgoing radicalism, Offbeat or otherwise, is not compelling. Plenty of Victorians grew doubtful and more than doubtful about the Church, yet remained good Conservatives or Liberals, not seeing the ecclesiastical loss of grip as leading to social or political change, or even seeing why it should. Irreligion began to take the offensive in the National

Secular Society, which was founded in 1866 and campaigned for particular reforms – but it was not subversive.

Two individuals, however, did continue to raise the issue of an Owenite type of package. Both were women. They do not enter the story as mere token characters. The older was one of the greatest authors of the time. The younger was one of its most conspicuous rebels.

*

Mary Ann Evans is always known by her pen name George Eliot. Having adopted this in the belief that a book with a male name on it would be more respected, she used it almost invariably.

She was born in 1819 on a farm in Astley, Warwickshire, where her father was an estate manager. Her mother died when she was seventeen, and she took charge of the household. She found time to read voraciously and employ visiting tutors to teach her languages and music. In 1841 Mr Evans moved to Coventry. Father and daughter opened their home to interesting guests. One was Robert Owen himself, now more or less disengaged from public activity. Another was Herbert Spencer, later to be famous as a philosophical writer, and to cross Mary Ann's path again. Also welcomed were Harriet Martineau, a writer of stories with a message, and Mr and Mrs Charles Bray. Bray was an expert on phrenology, which was then counted as a valid science.

Brought up in the Church of England, Mary Ann took Christianity seriously (as she took most things), and was soon launched on a phase of unease that carried her into strange company. Long after, in a middle-aged retrospect, she told a correspondent that the Church of England was the only religious body she had ever belonged to. Yet she regarded it as 'the least morally dignified' of all forms of Christianity since the Reformation, and only youthful associations had prevented her from joining a dissenting sect. This had hardly been a state of mind to encourage stability.

When still in her early twenties, she came under the influence of Bray's brother-in-law Charles Hennell, who was a Unitarian. He had written an *Inquiry Concerning the Origin of Christianity*, examining the Gospels in a critical spirit. His book attracted the notice of David Strauss, a German biblical scholar, who arranged for its publication in his own language. Strauss was well known as an extreme sceptic. His *Life of Jesus* dissected every episode in the Gospels and leaned heavily on speculative mythological theorising. Mary Ann was invited to translate it into English. She found it heavy going, but finished the job in 1844. By then she had decided that she no longer believed in the divine authority of scripture.

After a continental tour with Mr and Mrs Bray, she settled in London as a journalist. George Eliot, as she must be called from now on, lived in a large house on Fleet Street belonging to a certain John Chapman. Besides publishing books, Chapman had acquired a magazine, the *Westminster Review*, and she wrote for it, presently becoming assistant editor. His ménage was curious: besides the publishing, he took in paying guests, and rumours of sexual goings-on implicated his resident literary lady – probably unjustly. The books that he published were 'rationalistic', and George Eliot would have described herself as an agnostic, if the term had been invented then.

Christian orthodoxy was under attack from other quarters besides biblical criticism. Geologists such as Charles Lyell were showing reason to think that the world was millions of years old, and that species were not immutable descendants of pairs in the Ark. Tennyson's *In Memoriam* versifies some of the questions that were being raised.

In 1851 George Eliot's editorship brought Herbert Spencer into her life again. On her birthday they shared a theatre box with another journalist, George Henry Lewes, at a performance of *The Merry Wives of Windsor*. It was not a happy omen: during the next two years, she was neither a wife nor particularly merry.

The Shakespearean occasion opened up two potential partnerships. An immediately evident possibility was that she should marry Spencer. That step would have taken her on a different ideological course from the one she followed. Spencer was a pioneer of evolutionary theory, well ahead of *The Origin of Species*. He, not Darwin, coined the phrase 'The Survival of the Fittest'. George Eliot had ideas about marrying him in 1852, and wrote some fairly ardent letters, but he was less than ardent himself, and not inclined to reciprocate. He remained like that throughout a voluminously productive career.

The marital prospect faded. The pair remained on friendly terms, but the most important result of their acquaintance, if some biographers are right, was that Spencer started her on the idea of writing fiction. That certainly took hold. Before long a succession of books began to establish her as one of the supreme English novelists: *Adam Bede*, *The Mill on the Floss*, *Silas Marner*, *Romola*, *Felix Holt*, *Middlemarch* and *Daniel Deronda*. *Romola*, her single historical novel, has a Florentine setting. In this, as we saw earlier, she shows knowledge (rare in nineteenth-century England) of Joachim of Fiore and his three historical phases, leading up to the Age of the Holy Spirit. Although one of her characters, Felix Holt, is called a Radical, the word refers to conventional politics – Holt is simply an extreme Liberal – and it is useless to look in her opus for radicalism of an Offbeat kind. Politically, she was progressive, but moderate, much like her journalistic colleagues. Her deviation was non-political and unforeseeable.

It began during the 1850s, in what looks like a rebound from the Spencer episode. Her other companion on the visit to the theatre, George Henry Lewes, was Spencer's friend rather than hers, though she had met him at a shop in the Burlington Arcade. He was more congenial than the self-centred Spencer, and far broader in his outlook. To some extent he was simply a very good hack, contributing articles on all sorts of topics to a cheap encyclopedia and a medley of journals. But he also wrote well-researched histories and biographies, including lives of Robespierre and Goethe. George Eliot fell in love with him, and this time it was the real thing.

Marriage was impossible, because Lewes had an estranged wife who could not be divorced. In 1853 or 1854 the pair became lovers. They were widely known to be so, and they had to pay a price socially. Houses where they should have been welcome would not receive them. Some hosts would invite one of them but not the other. The gentleman was pardonable, the lady – the 'strong-minded woman', as Thomas Carlyle called her – was disgraced. Nevertheless, they strolled about in full view of passers-by who recognised them. They were not a beautiful couple: she was plain, he was less than handsome; but their love was quite evident.

In 1854 she produced her last work before the beginning of her experiments with fiction. This was another translation from the German. The book was *The Essence of Christianity*, by Ludwig Feuerbach. Exceptionally, she put her real name on the publication. Feuerbach was a minor philosopher who achieved a modest immortality in some notes on him by Karl Marx. The last of these is the famous dictum that 'philosophers have tried to explain the world, but the point is to change it'. Feuerbach himself was an explainer rather than a changer. As a materialist, he denied God and all things supernatural, yet he allowed them a shadowy reality as projections of human ideas and aspirations. So a kind of humanist religion took the place of the theological sort, as possible and desirable. For his English translator, *The Essence of Christianity* was an apt prelude to a new adventure of the mind.

*

In her mid-thirties George Eliot was following the path which Owen had indicated: she was passing from rejection of Christianity to a new radicalism which the rejection made possible. Like some others of the intelligentsia, she became interested in the French social theorist Auguste Comte. She had two reasons that were peculiarly her own. One was that Lewes gave her a book on Comte which he had written himself. The other was that Comte knew about Joachim, referring to him as 'the pious utopist whom Dante installed in his Paradise as endowed with the prophetic spirit', and constructing his own three-phase pattern of history, which was very different from the Calabrian abbot's, but had the same upward trend.

Comte invented sociology – in fact, he invented the actual word 'sociology' – and most would-be analysts of society are, if unconsciously, his heirs. He was born in Montpellier in 1798. His parents were Catholic and Royalist, but Auguste gave up on God at the age of fourteen. He received his higher education at the Polytechnic in Paris, where he had a reputation for turbulence. The capital was his home for the rest of his life. He attached himself to Claude Saint-Simon, a penurious aristocrat with an elitist programme for manipulating society, which has ranked him beside Owen and Fourier as a forerunner of socialism. Some of his disciples had smatterings of Joachimism, and there was talk in the movement of a New Christianity. Comte's early reflections on society were published in a Saint-Simonist journal, and he was the leader's secretary for a while.

He did not stay so for long. The break was fortunate, and perhaps perceptive. When Saint-Simon died in 1825, the movement was taken over by a pseudo-Messiah called Prosper Enfantin, and collapsed in scandal and ridicule. The Messiah, having searched for the right woman to be his co-Messiah and failed to find her, dropped it all and became a director of the Paris and Lyons Railway. Comte managed to detach himself from the later and wilder Saint-Simonists. Their antics confirmed him in a down-to-earth, non-mystical attitude which he showed for most of his life. The whole point of his 'Positive Philosophy' was to get rid of everything mystical.

His three historical stages are successive, but not rigidly so; they overlap. The first is the Theological. It began in the immemorial past. Human beings interpreted the world by imagining gods and myths and supernatural agencies that caused the phenomena around them. As long as this way of thinking persisted, rationality was confined to the immediately practical. Science was impossible, and so was any coherent rule of law.

Next came the Metaphysical stage, when theories and abstractions took hold. The universe was now supposed to function on principles that could be defined. But these were not deduced from real observation. An earth-centred astronomy charted celestial movements, but it postulated spirits or angels to account for them, and concocted astrology out of spurious notions of connection. Occult influences, supposedly at work in matter, produced alchemy. Philosophers talked of concepts like Plato's 'ideas'. Religion, thanks to its own philosophic mentors such as Augustine and Aquinas, gained in intellectual strength and inspired great achievements, in art, architecture, literature – but it was still religion.

Finally came the Positive age, which is now unfolding. This is the age of science, of precision and measurement, where objectivity reigns – or is supposed to reign. Real science has evolved from pre-science. Astronomy, for instance, has emerged from astrology, chemistry from alchemy, and so on. Comte's major claim is that 'social physics' or sociology, his own invention, will emerge likewise to replace the delusions that bedevil humanity. The right course for anyone devoted to human betterment is to campaign against superstition in every form and further the 'positive' trends. Authentic progress, effective altruism, must come through their prevalence and the realisation of the third age, the age of science in a broad and enlightened sense.

This vision of step-by-step advance is the central feature of positivism. The ramifications are enormous. Comte was extending his system from 1830 on, and he continued to do so for several decades. His books were not bestsellers, but they were read, and made his ideas known. As an individual he was elusive. Positivism – very properly – remained an ideology and never became a personality cult. Even when he had a public of sorts, a party of admirers wandered about in Paris for hours on a hot day, looking for the apartment where he lived; only the few who persevered actually found it.

The main reason for his withdrawn, non-celebrity existence was simply poverty. Positivism did not pay. His wife Caroline, who had a past, suggested that she should solve their problems by taking a rich lover. Auguste demurred and she walked out. Domestic strains temporarily unbalanced his mind, and he tried to drown himself in the Seine. Presently Caroline returned. Lecturing and tutoring brought in a small income, though never enough. One of Comte's pupils, a Scotsman named James Hamilton, happened to write a description of him. He was short and rather stout, clean-shaven when beards were common, and generally dressed in black. He was very punctual and attentive to detail; he kept conversation to a minimum, and was difficult to get to know; but Hamilton eventually liked him. In 1838 Caroline did take a lover, and the marriage came to an end. Auguste found another companion – not a mistress – with whom he was happier, but she died. He treasured her memory, and modified an anti-feminine tone which some readers complained of in his writings.

Positivism attracted George Eliot during the 1850s when she was approaching her richest phase of literary activity. Lewes's book on Comte effected a crucial transition for her. Personal abandonment of Christian orthodoxy could now be fitted into a majestic historical scheme. Comte's world began with naïve acceptance of gods and the supernatural, then took to thinking about them and asking questions, and then set them aside, but not in mere negativity. In a higher humanism, the sons and daughters of the dawning third age were transforming their inheritance. They would lead the way (like Joachim's new religious orders) into the daylight of the Positive era.

George Eliot was inspired by the Comtist panorama of humanity's enlighteners and benefactors. She wrote a poem, 'The Choir Invisible', saluting

> *Those immortal dead who live again*
> *In minds made better by their presence.*

Her highest aspiration would be to become like these, a humble member of the Choir Invisible. When she was preparing to write *Romola* she recalled Comte's affinity with Joachim, and reread him.

Positivism had other influential sympathisers in England. John Stuart Mill was one. He was never as close to discipleship as Comte liked to think, but he helped the impecunious Frenchman financially. So did George Grote, famous as a campaigner for voting by ballot, and as the author of a voluminous *History of Greece*. Comte's books were translated into English by George Eliot's old friend Harriet Martineau, now a well-known author in her own right. She too had discovered him through Lewes.

Comte welcomed his English supporters, and not only the ones who sent him money. He suggested that their government should renounce imperialism, and make a start by returning Gibraltar to Spain – a surprising way to begin, but he would have heard in his schooldays of France's recent assistance to Spain in an unsuccessful siege of the Rock.

*

Comte may have caused surprise with his Gibraltar proposal, but he had a bigger surprise in store, hardly calculated to please the intelligentsia. It began in a paradox. Positivism banished religion, yet its social objectivity forced the recognition of needs that required religious satisfaction; at least, there was no evident substitute. Comte squared the circle by inventing a religion himself. He invited the world to replace worship of God with worship of the *Grand Être*, the Great Being, Humanity itself.

Two objections are palpable. In the first place, there is no way of getting Humanity into focus as an object of worship, since positivist principles rule out abstraction or personification. With its billions of components, it is altogether too complicated. In the second place, Humanity as it actually is hardly seems to deserve worship.

A solution came from an existing religion. Comte never reverted to the faith of his upbringing, but he preferred Catholicism to Protestantism as a 'great system of spiritual organisation'. Its cult of the saints could be imitated. He drew up a list of 558 historical figures who could be focused upon, meditated upon, honoured, and, in some cases, held up as role models. Unlike the saints, they were presumably no longer living, in heaven or anywhere else; but they survived through their example and influence.

Comte followed the Church's lead by designing a positivist calendar. His calendar has thirteen months of twenty-eight days. Each month is devoted to a topic. The first is the month of 'Theocratic Civilisation', the second 'Ancient Poetry', the third 'Ancient Philosophy', and so through to 'Modern Industry' and other more recent themes. In each month, a number of individuals exemplify its topic. They are distributed among the days. Moses heads the list in the first month, Homer in the second, and so on. One day is left over, which is to be a Festival of All the Dead, and in a leap year the additional day is to be a Festival of Noble Women.

The lists reflect Comte's knowledge and interests. After the early months, he has very few non-Europeans, and he includes only a dozen or so named women throughout. Most of his selections are fairly obvious, even conventional. A few are bizarre.

In month twelve, 'Modern Statesmanship', he has the Paraguayan dictator José Francia, having happened, perhaps, to read a polite obituary; and in month thirteen, 'Modern Science', the names are headed by the almost forgotten Dr Bichat, a French anatomist. A reader naturally looks to see where Christ is listed, and fails to find him, because Comte accepts the Church's belief that he claimed to be divine, so he disqualified himself and must disappear together with God. But several figures from primitive Christianity are included, such as St Paul, and so are Dante and other outstanding Christians in later times.

The calendar would have had to be revised and updated every so often, but that could be arranged. Comte supplemented his lists with recommended reading and a Positivist Catechism in the form of thirteen dialogues. He also devised positivist rituals and ceremonies. He was proud of the Religion of Humanity, and hoped he would live to be a hundred, and witness its inauguration in Paris. Like Robert Owen, he tried to enlist influential sponsors. One was the Tsar. Another, far-fetched as it sounds, was the General of the Jesuits. Comte autographed a copy of the positivist catechism and gave it to a friend to pass on. No one knows whether it reached its intended recipient, but it turned up in a second-hand bookshop, its pages uncut.

Comte died in 1857. English positivism drifted on. Several of its supporters, including Lewes, backed away from the Religion of Humanity. One who held firm was Richard Congreve, who translated the Catechism. He gave lectures to assorted audiences. Another was Frederic Harrison, a respected authority on law, who was as near as anyone to being positivism's leader in England. In 1866 he wrote to George Eliot urging her to present Comte's ideas in a Utopian drama or poem. She replied that the notion was attractive, but positivism had become a system – almost a creed – which she could not accept whole-heartedly; and she could not write an original work with the form and content laid down for her.

In 1877 Harrison tried again, telling her that she ought to be positivism's laureate. He had in mind her poem 'The Choir Invisible', which Congreve had read aloud at one of his lectures as a relevant text. Harrison and Congreve were composing a Positivist liturgy. Eliot accepted that she could not prevent them from appropriating her work, but she declined to co-operate. That remained the position until her death in 1880, two years after Lewes had died.

John Stuart Mill retained enough interest to write a book on Comte, but Positivism, as such, faded out. It had glimmered for a while as another kind of Offbeat Radicalism, but it ceased to be so. Most of its themes were coming before the public in new forms that tended to eclipse it. In 1859 Darwin had published *The Origin of Species*, and the anti-religious case was beginning to be stated on Darwinian lines. Christianity's greatest advocate, John Henry Newman, had no difficulty with evolution (having in fact anticipated it in work of his own) and said he was prepared to 'go the whole hog with Darwin'[†]; but he stayed clear of the conflict, while lesser ecclesiastics and injudicious laypersons kept the pot boiling. As for Comte's humanised religion, T. H. Huxley, the most active propagandist for Darwin, derided it as 'Catholicism minus Christianity'.

The issues of social evolution were taken up by Herbert Spencer, who relegated Comte to the background with nine volumes of his own 'Synthetic Philosophy'. And any appeal that positivism had had for the Left was extinguished by socialism. Marx even had his own theory of historical stages, which was more exciting than Comte's, because it led up to a revolution.

Comte's only specific legacy, however seldom acknowledged, is the academic discipline he invented and named: sociology. None-

† Newman, John. *The Philosophical Notebook of John Henry Newman*. Two vols. Edited at the Birmingham Oratory by Edward Silliem, revised by A. J. Boekrad. Louvain, Nauwelaerts Publishing House, 1969–70. Entry for 9 December 1863, vol 2, p158.

theless, that was a considerable achievement.

*

George Eliot made the transition from negation to ideology without any fuss. She did not proselytise, or go out of her way to argue. Most of the time she was too busy with her novels, and she accomplished far more in that way than she could ever have done in any other.

There was another woman, however, younger than Eliot, and her case history is a different matter. Instead of a single transition from the rejection of Christianity, she made two, the second following the first after an interval of several years. From an Offbeat Radical point of view, the second was the remarkable one, building up to a quantum leap that was not Victorian but post-Victorian, and was meant to supersede Christianity altogether. Looking back from a distant vantage-point, this woman, when no longer young, saw most of her life's Victorian phase as a prelude; the sequel, stretching into the twentieth century, was the part that mattered. She may be taken at her word. It is the prelude that brackets her with George Eliot, and the rest comes much later.

Annie Besant, originally Annie Wood, was born in 1847. When she was still a child, her widowed mother entrusted her to the care of Ellen Marryat, who kept a kind of informal school. Ellen was a sister of the novelist Captain Marryat, author of popular tales such as *Mr. Midshipman Easy*. Annie, with several other girls and boys, spent her youth in a happy and cultured atmosphere. As she grew up she had a personal religion, a romantic Anglo-Catholic piety, supported by extensive reading in early Christian literature.

The first tremor came – unintentionally – from herself. She tried to compose a 'harmony' of the Gospels, arranging passages in four parallel columns, with the ones that told of the same incident side by side. She assumed that the result would be a comprehensive narrative bringing everything in. She found, however, that the harmony did not work. There were discrepancies. The passages she had lined up side by side as having the same subject matter sometimes disagreed. For the moment, she shelved this discovery as an unresolved problem, but it was not forgotten.

When she was nineteen, a clergyman, the Reverend Frank Besant, asked her to marry him, and she consented. As his wife, she acquired his surname. There was an ambiguity about the proper way to pronounce it. Frank had a brother Walter who wrote novels. Walter always put the stress on the second syllable, and people referring to Annie would often do the same, but she herself insisted that 'Besant' should rhyme with 'pleasant'.

She entered marriage like many young Victorian brides, ignorantly. The first sexual encounter horrified her, and subsequent familiarity did not help much. The couple produced two children, a boy and a girl. But Frank, who became the vicar of Sibsey in Lincolnshire, was never endearing. When Annie began to write, and had a story accepted by the *Family Herald*, he pocketed the payment himself.

In 1873 she had an inkling of her vocation. She locked herself in her husband's church, climbed into the pulpit, and poured out an impassioned denunciation of the Christian view of the Bible. The pews were empty, but she imagined a congregation. They would not have seen much more than her head, just visible above the pulpit. But her voice was deep and spellbinding. So it would remain.

Her Christian belief had been dissolving, in the absence of anything to encourage it. She read sceptical books, and even wrote sceptical pamphlets herself, furtively and anonymously. Her marriage was depressing enough; the further prospect of living a complete falsehood was beyond bearing. It really would not do for the vicar's wife to be an atheist or near-atheist, yet that was what the situation was coming to. A refusal to take communion forced the issue into the open.

Her health showed signs of giving way, and she went to stay with her mother. Frank arrived in a rage, and demanded that she return to Sibsey and conform, or not return at all. She elected not to return, and took the children to live with friends. Now, it was feasible to write more pamphlets and put her name on them, and the publisher paid her a little money. She extended her reading further, and sampled Auguste Comte himself, though with more interest in his criticism of ancient illusions than in his hopes for the future.

One day in the summer of 1874, she walked into a Holborn bookshop looking for Comtist literature, and picked up a periodical, the *National Reformer*. This was the magazine of the National Secular Society, which she perceived to be an umbrella organisation for rationalists, atheists, and 'freethinkers' generally. It announced a lecture by Charles Bradlaugh, the president. Annie sent in an application for membership and attended the lecture, which was an excursion into comparative religion. Bradlaugh argued that the story of Christ was a reflection of the Hindu myth of the god Krishna. When he stepped off the platform and handed out membership certificates, he spoke to Annie and they had a brief conversation. His new recruit made a good impression. After a longer meeting a few days later, he offered her a job on the staff of the *National Reformer*, writing reviews, articles, and topical comment.

This was the beginning of several years of working together. They were sharply contrasted. Annie at twenty-six was slight and elegant, five feet five inches tall, with piercing grey-blue eyes and brown hair. Bradlaugh, forty years old and the pre-eminent figure in English unbelief, was large in all directions. He was a fine speaker without the spell-weaving that Annie was capable of; he could hold any audience, and reply courteously to any questioner. On the negative side, he attacked religion, especially Christianity, as spreading lies and causing terrible evils. On the positive side, he campaigned as a political Radical, often in the field of civil liberties, or in support of repressed nationalities – the Irish, for instance. He showed an interest, uncommon at the time, in India. Bigots abused him as a blaspheming infidel. He was subjected to venomous attacks; some merely crude, some sophisticated. An apocalyptist encoded his name to make it add up to 666, the Number of the Beast.

A long-drawn dispute kept him in the public eye for years. It concerned his right to be a Member of Parliament. He was elected as one of the representatives of Northampton, a two-member constituency. A problem at once arose over his taking the parliamentary oath, which introduced God. If an unbeliever took the oath, would it count? Quakers, who objected to oaths in general, were allowed to 'affirm', and Bradlaugh asked for the same permission; but he was not a Quaker, and dozens of churchgoing MPs were resolutely opposed to having an atheist colleague. The wrangling went on and on. He was re-elected and excluded, re-elected again and excluded again, once being physically thrown out of the building. At last, he was allowed to take his seat, but the struggle had been tiring and time-wasting, and it left him burdened with heavy legal expenses.

Nevertheless, he had always kept his secular activities flourishing. Annie, increasingly a polymath, had proved to be an excellent choice as assistant. She was versatile, lecturing, handling correspondence, helping with the magazine. In her first *National Reformer* column she wrote:

> There is a strange interest in standing on a mountain-top, watching for the first faint signs of the coming day. Here and there a tiny white cloud warms into soft yellow, or flushes rosy red; here and there a gleam flashes across the sky.... But a deeper, keener interest swells the heart of those who are watching for the rising

> sun of Liberty; each ray... brings to the foremost soldiers of the army of Freedom a message of hope.

Anyone who cherished such visions was looking further afield and further ahead than most 'freethinkers'.

She might have married Bradlaugh, but both of them had spouses living, and they observed the proprieties. That failed to save him from scandal and persecution, and Annie suffered too. She could always stand up to heckling, but other persecutions were far worse. Her husband deprived her of the custody of her children, the plea being the same as it was with Shelley – that an atheist was not fit to be a parent. She was allowed only limited access, and when the children were old enough to decide for themselves they came back to her, but the blow was cruel. She tried to take a degree in science, and the examiners failed her, not because of a lack of scientific knowledge, but because of her atheism – a reason that was never given officially.

*

In 1877 Annie and Bradlaugh got into trouble with the law over a book they approved of, but which was condemned as obscene. Entitled *The Fruits of Philosophy*, this hitherto little-known volume was about birth control. Annie wrote eloquently of the miseries of poor families growing in numbers with no check, who had to live in overcrowded and squalid accommodation. Christians opposed measures of alleviation, in this respect and in others, and their Christianity had to be denounced, as ever. But was that enough? Could there be a way to do more for sufferers?

She was beginning a slow move to the political Left. It took years. Other factors were also entering her life – factors that were not purely secular. She had never quite shaken off a nostalgia for religion, and while a return to Christianity was unthinkable, she was picking up faint signals from the East. In 1879 Sir Edwin Arnold, the editor of the *Daily Telegraph*, formerly principal of a college in Poona, published a long narrative poem entitled *The Light of Asia*. It told the story of the life and teachings of Buddha. For a poem, it was popular. Annie read it with only a rather tepid enthusiasm, but she did read it. The seed of an interest in India was planted.

Also, reports were reaching her that secularists in India were unaccountably flirting with a new religion (if 'religion' was the right word) called Theosophy. It was being expounded by a mysterious Russian woman, Helena Petrovna Blavatsky. In June 1882 Annie wrote an unusually ill-informed article about it, expressing the hope that true freethinkers wouldn't be led astray. Madame Blavatsky read the article and replied soothingly, also shrewdly. She suspected the possibility of a major conversion.

More significantly, for the moment, Annie's drift to the Left was continuing. The socialism that she approached was still embryonic. Marx's ideology was known on the continent, but hardly at all in England, even though he and Engels lived there. In so far as socialism was claiming attention, it was through advocacy by someone else, Henry Hyndman, who founded the Democratic Federation – later, the *Social* Democratic Federation. Hyndman was no proletarian himself. He was a well-off former Tory of conventional appearance and conduct; he habitually wore a top hat, normal at the time, but, ironically, a type of headgear that would become the badge of the capitalist in cartoons (it still is in Orwell's *1984*). Hyndman, however, was a competent publicist, and he spread an impression that the movement he led was more widely supported than it was.

On 17 April 1884, he and Bradlaugh, who was decidedly not a socialist, came face to face in a public debate. The meeting was chaired by Professor E. S. Beesly, a positivist – yes, there were still positivists. Honours were about even. But Annie was now definitely on the move. In 1885 she became a socialist, and announced the fact to the public.

This was the first of her two transitions. She had never adequately discussed it with Bradlaugh, and while he accepted that she was still secular, he knew that they had drifted apart. She would never have taken such a step as a matter of theory alone. It implied action. She joined in protests and demonstrations, and wrote propaganda. In this new setting, she was frequently seeing Bernard Shaw, who was also beginning to be known as a socialist, and she collaborated with him on various projects. For a while an actual liaison seemed to be on the cards, but he was unwilling to go so far. Meanwhile, she did good work for her chosen cause. The further shift that was on the way would in due course shock Shaw as well as Bradlaugh, and profoundly.

7

Loss and Recovery

At this point, there is a break in continuity. After the middle of the nineteenth century, a new kind of thinking – or rather, a refurbishment of a very old one – begins to shape Offbeat Radicalism. It is important, partly, because of what it reveals about a particular way of looking at things; partly, also, because of its manifestations, and the groundbreaking figures who were involved in them.

Robert Owen, George Eliot, and Annie Besant were all forward-looking, whether they favoured co-operation, positivism or socialism. Yet they did not stand simplistically for progress. They dissented, in fact, from the progress in which most optimists believed, and that the Great Exhibition of 1851 saluted: industrial and commercial progress. However, they did accept the converse of that belief: the idea that the past was superseded, and in no sense a source of inspiration.

Charles Dickens, though critical of the society around him, was very clear indeed about this attitude to the past. He had a shelf in his study with a set of dummy books entitled *The Wisdom of Our Ancestors*. The covers showed that the imaginary topics were 'Ignorance', 'Superstition', 'Dirt', 'Disease', and other undesirable matters. Not everyone went to such extremes of dismissal, but, in general, the past – particularly the medieval past – was dismissed. It could be studied as history, or romanticised in novels and poems, but society had unequivocally left it behind. The three Offbeat Radicals were less than enthusiastic about the philistine 'progress' which the Great Exhibition epitomised, but they shared in the rejection of the past, and found very little in it that was better than the world they lived in, or worthy of reinstatement as part of the forward movement they hoped for.

William Blake, their visionary precursor, had thought otherwise, and expressed his thought in the theme of humanity's 'fall into division and resurrection to unity'. The relevant Prophetic Books mythified a conception of history which he believed to be literally true. Far back in time, the world experienced a real golden age when his symbolic Jerusalem 'overspread all nations'. Even the masterpieces of classical art came much later, as inferior imitations of lost golden-age originals. When Blake anticipated the future, he had his golden antiquity in mind and spoke of the new age as essentially the old one restored. Humanity would find fulfilment in rebuilding Jerusalem.

Blake was inventing his own mythology, but not in a void. This alternative scenario of loss and recovery, giving a vital role to the past, has a long history in human affairs. It is far older than the notion of progress, which is hardly heard of before the French Revolution, and it weaves a spell of its own, producing what can fairly be called a syndrome. In Britain, as Blake recognised, this took a medieval mythic form in the story of King Arthur's passing and prophesied return. Shelley's *The Mask of Anarchy* gives it a more literal guise, with its retrospective appeal to the 'old laws of England', which modern oppressors have thrust into the background, but which can advance again to defeat them.

Some of the forms which the loss-and-recovery syndrome has taken, not only in Britain, are illuminating. They are antecedents to the versions of Offbeat Radicalism that emerge during the later nineteenth century: antecedents with stubborn psychological roots, suggesting how it is that the syndrome can have a strange compulsiveness even where it hardly seems to belong at all.†

Loss-and-recovery might be interpreted as a mere reflection of Christianity's pattern of fall-and-redemption. However, it is not that, and the proof is that it occurs before Christianity: to be specific, in the teachings of Confucius.

China emerges into historical daylight in the second millennium BC. From about 1100 the Chou dynasty was dominant, and its early phase became fixed in legend as China's own golden age, guided by enlightened rulers and 'Divine Sages'. Confucius, who lived about 551–479 BC, seems to have complied with legend by regarding the early Chou era as a time of wise government and social harmony. Since then, a long decline had set in. Confucius summed up the lost rightness of ancient China as the Tao, the Way – that is, the 'way' of the former kings; and his teaching aimed at its restoration.

He meant nothing supernatural. The Chinese of olden time were supposedly governed by morality, not physical force; they observed the golden rule, if in a negative form – Don't do to others what you wouldn't want them to do to you; they were cultured and ceremonious. Confucius had no Messianic pretensions. He was not another Divine Sage himself. So far as he can be given a professional label, he was an administrative consultant. As such, he taught the reinstatement of the lost good. A new Divine Sage or saviour-king might arise, but in his absence, Confucius believed that his own knowledge of antiquity supplied enough for the education of an elite, whose presence at the top level could steer society back towards what it once was, and ought to be again.

† I considered the reasons for it in my book *Camelot and the Vision of Albion*. Here, I think it is enough just to define it and recognise its persistence.

Confucius, admittedly, lived a long time ago, and this outline of his philosophy is open to question, but it certainly expresses the views of the disciples closest to him, from which Confucianism developed as a doctrine. The syndrome of loss and recovery did root itself in China. Better-documented instances appear during the Christian era, in the history of Christianity itself.

Christianity has its own past golden age, the apostolic era down to about the end of the first century AD, when people who had known the Lord were still living and testifying. That period saw the writing of nearly all the books composing the New Testament; it saw a mainstream agreement on the principal articles of faith; and it saw primitive Christians leading exemplary lives, some of them dying heroically as martyrs. If we move forward to the sixteenth century, the time of the Reformation, we find the Church splitting apart, yet there is a significant common ground among the antagonists.

Many Christians agreed on the Church's accumulated corruption and the need for reform. There were Catholic reformers such as Erasmus and Thomas More, who stayed within the Roman communion and hoped for change. There were the founders of Protestantism such as Luther and Calvin, who dismissed it as an organised apostasy, and tried to reconstitute the true Church outside. But no notable reformer talked of an evolutionary or 'progressive' Christianity in the style of a later age. All who agreed on the corruption agreed on a remedial policy. What was needed was to recover the apostolic purity which had existed once, and gradually faded.

They appealed to Christianity's golden age when it was still close to its founder. The right object of reform was to bring this pristine condition back, not as an impossible carbon copy, but as the same thing renewed under the changed conditions. Moreover, there was wide agreement on the most important specific measure. The New Testament, giving the authentic message of Christ and his apostles, had to be disinterred from the Church's official Latin and restored to public access. Erasmus edited and published the original Greek. Luther translated the whole Bible into German. Tyndale, using the work of both, produced a New Testament in English.

A motive for action, and a deterrent from any sort of experimentation, was the belief that the world might end soon; it was vital to supply Christendom quickly with the means of salvation, and the means of salvation were to be found in the legacy of its golden age.

But this motive of supernatural urgency had no role in another major case of the syndrome. We noted Jean-Jacques Rousseau in the eighteenth century, and the mystique that he supplied for the revolutionaries. The French intelligentsia, including Voltaire, had discovered China and Confucius, and were delighted with what they saw as morality without dogma, in contrast to Christianity. Whether or not Rousseau knew anything of the Confucian message, or understood it if he did, his own was a more elaborate version. He asserted that society in civilised countries had slid downhill from a former happy state, but the essentials of its lost paradise could be reinstated for a fresh start. In this context, he is worth a closer look.

Rousseau was a native of Geneva, then an independent city. During various wanderings, he looked back with nostalgia at rustic idylls that seem to have been largely imaginary; he dreamed of returning to a rural tranquillity which he fancied he had once enjoyed. The social doctrine in his books can be described as self-sublimation. However, although he was a most unendearing person, and developed a persecution mania that caused quarrels in all directions, he happened to be able to self-sublimate in a way that appealed to the discontented.

In effect, he adopted the motif of Eden and changed its implications. Christianity portrayed unfallen humanity in the garden of God, and its exile through disobedience to him. Rousseau made the story of the Fall purely human, with an amendment that transformed it. The primal good condition was natural, and its loss was a social process, not divinely ordained – so it might be recovered. Potentially, paradise lay ahead as well as behind. Its essence was an untroubled 'state of nature' which human beings experienced once and ought to experience all the time. Rousseau supported his theory with travellers' tales about the unspoilt natives of the West Indies and other places; the myth of the Noble Savage originated from him. Natural humanity, long ago, was free and equal and instinctively virtuous.

If so, how did it go wrong? 'Everything is good when it leaves the Creator's hands,' says Rousseau, 'everything degenerates in the hands of Man.' Yes, but how? It transpires that equilibrium began to be unsettled because people are not, after all, equal in everything. In tribal activities such as singing and dancing, some of the noble savages sang and danced better than others. They attracted fan clubs and had an advantage in finding sexual partners. Once privilege had got a footing, even as innocuously as this, it got other footings. For example, the best workers became overseers, and used their position to gain power and goods for themselves.

And so it went on. Arts and sciences are rooted in the worse side of human nature. Geometry was invented because individuals who had grabbed property needed land-surveying. Astronomy began in the delusions of astrologers. As society grew more complicated, dynasties, aristocracies, priesthoods, and conspiracies of rich men built up civilisation embodying their privileges.

Rousseau passed on from his historical mythology to ask what might be done to reverse the trend. The kings, priests, and institutions in general should obviously be got rid of. A new model state should be established to restore the reign of natural law and the spirit of the lost innocence. His discussion of governments and constitutions, in his book *The Social Contract*, is more cautious and rational than might be expected. But while he believes, after a fashion, in democracy, he gives it a special character highly convenient for his more extreme followers. For him, the voice of Nature speaks through the General Will. This is not the will of the majority as an election might determine it, but a collective 'something' that is always right. It cannot fully emerge in present society because existing institutions and sectional interests prevent it. Once they are gone, Nature can resume her beneficent sway, the General Will can assert itself, and everybody will conform to it. In practice, when Robespierre and other disciples of Rousseau were in power, they interpreted the General Will as they saw fit, and anyone who dissented could be treated as rebellious.

There is no real evidence for the recoverable paradise that is axiomatic to all the rest. Indeed, it has one very significant feature: Rousseau is none too clear whether he believes in it himself. He speaks of the 'state of nature' as one that 'exists no longer, perhaps never existed, probably never will exist'. Yet it is necessary to have 'just ideas' of it, in order to 'judge well of our present state'. Here is a psychological compulsion almost confessed. He *has* to have his golden age in the beginning, because the syndrome takes charge; he cannot think of history, of the corruptions of civilisation, or of the possibility of a fresh start, except in terms of this mythic pattern of loss and recovery.

Other reformers and revolutionaries have thought along the same lines. Even apart from its Chinese version, the syndrome is not purely European: one of its most spectacular modern forms, as we shall see, was almost as far away as China is. However, Rousseau's myth draws attention to something like it in a professedly scientific setting, where myth-making should surely have no place. The most famous revolutionary doctrine of all yielded to the spell, and the results were widely visible, not least among Offbeat Radicals.

*

The *Communist Manifesto* of 1848 built up Marx's revolution by tracing history through a series of stages, each characterised by a different economic system with a class conflict reflecting it. The constant feature in every stage was the existence of a ruling minority exploiting a ruled majority, and setting up governments and religious establishments to maintain its power. First, we are told, came the world of patricians and slave owners oppressing a much larger population of plebeians and slaves. Next came feudalism, with lords and guild masters on top, serfs and journeymen and miscellaneous hirelings underneath. After that came the achievement of power by the 'bourgeoisie', and the modern society of capitalists exploiting wage-slaves or 'proletarians'.

This process, according to Marx and his devoted collaborator Engels, would be terminated by a revolution in which the workers would conquer the capitalists and take over the means of production themselves. Since the workers were a majority, the old norm of minority oppression would at last cease to exist, and society would progress towards classlessness. There would still be government for a while, but it would be transitional, concerned mainly with wiping out the remnants of capitalism. Apart from that, Marxism did not pursue its post-revolutionary society further: in the historical scenario, the workers' victory was a climax and a conclusion, creating a dictatorship of the proletariat.

All this was called scientific socialism, in contrast with the Utopian socialism of Owen and Fourier. But in the 1870s a re-thinking began, extending the scenario at both ends. It had never included a golden age – or, indeed, any sort of age – prior to its series of class antitheses. Now, suddenly, Marx and Engels discovered the golden age after all. They *tacked it on* at the beginning, and they made out that their future society, after the revolution, would reconstitute it in a new form. Syndrome had triumphed over science.

The enlarged Marxist history or pseudo-history was quite like

Rousseau's, but the inspiration did not come from him – at least not explicitly. It came instead from an American anthropologist, Lewis H. Morgan, whose book *Ancient Society* was published in 1877. Basing his ideas chiefly on the reputed customs of the seventeenth-century Iroquois, Morgan gave the Noble Savage a new lease of life. He maintained that the Iroquois, and most peoples at the same cultural level, had a free and equal society based on communal property, with no government because none was needed. Ancient humanity was organised in 'gentes'; the State came later.

Marx welcomed Morgan's book and took notes on it. After his death in 1883, Engels worked up the notes into a book of his own, *The Origin of the Family, Private Property and the State*. In this he proclaimed that the State 'has not existed from all eternity'. It arose when the division of society into classes, as described in the *Manifesto*, demanded a sovereign authority to keep the rulers on top of the ruled. But now, following Morgan's lead, Engels unveiled a prelude. Before government, before class conflict, before the whole scenario of the *Manifesto*, humanity lived in a semi-idyll of 'primitive communism'. This of course was Rousseau's state of nature, given anthropological dignity as Morgan's *gens* society. Engels extolled an age of 'simple moral grandeur'. The *gens* society was ruined by 'theft, violence, cunning, treason'. Economic progress was started and kept going by 'the meanest impulses – vulgar covetousness, brutal lust, sordid avarice, selfish robbery of the common wealth'. In view of the moral grandeur at the beginning, it is not clear where all these iniquities came from, but, for whatever reason, they came. Engels' Eden was subverted as Rousseau's was.

To an English edition of the *Manifesto*, published in 1888, Engels attached a note explaining that the history which it surveyed meant recorded history only. Prehistory was something else. The proletarian revolution, when it happened, would lead towards a classless society reconstituting the lost Eden on a higher level. Engels found this in Morgan himself:

> Democracy in government, brotherhood in society, equality in rights and privileges, and universal education, foreshadow the next higher plane of society to which experience, intelligence and knowledge are steadily tending. It will be a revival, in a higher form, of the liberty, equality and fraternity of the ancient gentes.

Morgan's treatment of ancient society was not in fact sound, but, once Engels had given it the slant that he did, Marxists found the whole notion too valuable to drop, and it persisted.

The Origin of the Family was closely related to two developments which Marx and Engels had foretold. They accepted that the new order created by their revolution would be transitional, and would at first have much in common with capitalism, though with a different bias. There would still be government; there would still be cash values, material incentives, wages and salaries corresponding to work done. But they did have ideas of something better beyond, and the vision of primitive communism reasserting itself made this easier to picture. With growing abundance and changed attitudes, the familiar getting-and-spending scramble would disappear. All would receive simply according to their need. The State would become superfluous and likewise disappear – as Engels said, it had not existed from all eternity – and humanity would enjoy total freedom. The phrase which Marxists adopted for its disappearance was that it would 'wither away'. And so, the golden age would return.

8

Two Prophets

Many Victorians linked two contemporaries together as prophets: not because of any predictions they made, but because they called to mind some of the biblical ones ('forthtellers' not 'foretellers', as a scriptural scholar put it), with relentless ethical assaults and eruptive denunciations. Both challenged assumptions about society and the march of progress. Both detected virtues in the neglected past, and one of them pointed towards a radicalism aimed at recovering those virtues.

Thomas Carlyle, the senior prophet of the two, is a major literary figure in several respects. He belongs here, not as an Offbeat Radical himself, but as a shaker and stirrer who moved others in that direction. He was born at Ecclefechan in Dumfriesshire in 1795, the son of a stonemason. In his early years he made a precarious living as a teacher, translator and miscellaneous writer. The teaching was unacceptable to him; he decided that he would rather do anything than that. Yet he never ceased to teach in his own way, or to regard himself as having a vocation to do so, often in a strident and subversive tone that would lead Matthew Arnold to call him a 'moral desperado'.

Like Auguste Comte, Carlyle flirted with the social paternalism and 'New Christianity' of Saint-Simon. Goethe, whom he adored and dared to approach personally, advised him not to get involved, and he drifted away not only from Saint-Simonism but from Christianity in general. However, he was too positive in his outlook, too deeply committed to the 'Everlasting Yea' as he put it, to drift into plain scepticism. Influenced by German romantic authors, who found a sort of religion-substitute in literature, he arrived at a conviction that any definite belief was better than none. In this he foreshadowed uprooted individuals of later times, especially after the First World War, who thought similarly and fell into totalitarian traps. Joseph Goebbels, who became Hitler's propaganda chief, was one. For Carlyle a hundred years earlier, that was not a hazard, but it has a bearing on his development, and some of the ideological choices he made.

There was one immediate effect in the spiritual realm. Despite his rejection of Christianity, he preferred the mystical notions of Edward Irving – a maverick preacher who expected the Second Coming of Christ – to any negation, however rational. This preference had an unexpected result. Irving had tutored Jane Welsh, a doctor's intelligent and vivacious daughter, and he introduced her to Carlyle. They married, and lived for some years on the bride's family property at Craigenputtock, later moving to London at 5 Cheyne Walk, Chelsea. The marriage was a failure from the beginning and continued downhill. Tennyson remarked, rather unkindly, that it was a good thing they did marry, because, if they had taken other partners, four people would have been miserable instead of two. A friend in whom Jane confided is the principal source for a suspicion, repeated by biographers, of Carlyle's sexual incapacity. Whether or not that was a reason, or *the* reason, Jane suffered. Her husband's ideas must be seen against a background of marital tension, and also ill-health, since he suffered from stomach troubles throughout his life.

As a resident of London, he remained Scottish in his accent and his spoken vocabulary, but there was nothing regional about his prose. His early writings, mostly literary essays, built up gradually and perhaps unexpectedly to an amazing masterpiece, *The French Revolution*, published in 1837. France's Revolution was not ancient history. It had happened well within living memory; the French king Charles X, deposed in 1830, was a brother of Louis XVI whom the Revolution guillotined; and Carlyle himself was born when the Reign of Terror had only just ended. He was able not only to use recently printed and unfamiliar material, but to consult surviving witnesses. He learned, and in due course put in his book, that the composer of the Marseillaise was still living.

In his hands the theme inspired a unique style, full of allusions and observations and exclamations and verbal explosions. He was not pretending to write a sober narrative. The story is an epic in the form of an immense running commentary, which closes the gap between the past and the present. Carlyle's reader – on whom he makes considerable demands – may extract meanings from the temporal fusion that would not be extracted otherwise. His approach foreshadows a dictum of Arthur Christiansen, a great twentieth-century newspaper editor: 'There is nothing in the world that cannot be told through people.' The Revolution comes to life through thousands of participants. Today it is natural to regret the book's shortage of social and economic data, but Carlyle has one supreme quality: he never lets you forget that something tremendous is happening.

The process of composition reflected that fact. His first volume took five months of exhausting toil, often in sickness, and the appropriate mood and passion had to be sustained throughout. He said it all came 'directly and flamingly from the heart'. He had finished that volume and made a start on the second, when he was pulled up short by one of the cruellest disasters in literary history. John Stuart Mill had been supplying him with books, and Carlyle lent him the manuscript for his opinion. Mill left it lying about, and a housemaid took it for scrap paper and burned it.[†]

Carlyle told the publisher he would have to wait, wound himself up again, and rewrote the volume. To read it today, with the knowledge of its being a product of rewinding and rewriting, is to be awestruck. The rest followed. When *The French Revolution* was finished, Jane celebrated by cooking a bread pudding, and her husband went out for a very long walk.

The book ended anti-climactically, even inconclusively, and it had to. Carlyle was well aware that the story had no closure. The revolutionaries had been right to overturn the old order, with its degenerate aristocracy that neglected its duties. But once they had unleashed the forces that overturned it, their attempts to constitutionalise and stabilise were doomed. Power had passed to others who were unprepared for it, and while they would go on to achieve great things, they would not carry the Revolution to any finality.

*

Would another historical outcome have been possible? Carlyle, reflecting, extrapolated his belief in individuals. He decided that society, in France or anywhere else, needed great men. He gave a series of lectures on this topic, picking out historical figures whom he regarded as outstanding in various fields, and published it under the title *Heroes, Hero Worship and the Heroic in History*. His chosen characters exemplified 'The Hero as Divinity', 'The Hero as Prophet', 'The Hero as Poet', 'The Hero as Priest', 'The Hero as Man of Letters,' 'The Hero as King'.

The Hero as King is the climax of the series. Etymologically, the

† The maid is usually condemned as the culprit, but she may not have been able to read, and before the typewriter, Carlyle's manuscript would not have looked like anything special. Mill, on the other hand, inexcusably left it in the maid's path without even drawing her attention to it.

king is explained as the 'able' man, the man who 'can'. The desirable ruler need not be literally royal. Carlyle approved of Francia, the Paraguayan autocrat whom Comte made one of his positivist saints. He wrote an entire book about Oliver Cromwell, putting the Lord Protector in a favourable light. There was an obvious question as to how the 'able' man whom a situation requires can be discovered and recognised. For some reason Carlyle saw Sir Robert Peel, who reorganised the police and abolished the corn laws, as a prospective new Cromwell; but Peel was killed in an accident, and Carlyle offered no further candidates.

For the unheroic multitude he did have a message, his 'gospel of work'. Produce, produce! Better anything than nothing. But in practice he soon had to concede that discrimination was needed. Britain, of course, was very productive indeed, with its railways, factories and so on. In the absence of the higher authority that Carlyle wanted, this was uncontrolled capitalism piling up material wealth. Enthusiasts who rationalised the process talked Utilitarian theory about generating 'the greatest happiness of the greatest number'.

Carlyle questioned this kind of production, and did so with growing asperity. It was here that his memorable shaking and stirring really began. He denied that the country's true wealth could consist in an aimless accumulation of goods. Did this make for greater wisdom, or beauty, or – to retort to Utilitarian with their own word – happiness? The legendary King Midas had the golden touch, but it didn't do him any good, and he ended up with ass's ears.

Moreover, Carlyle pointed out, the benefits of unfettered free enterprise were anything but universal. It condemned millions to work and live in dreadful conditions, often actually hungry, and it reduced the unemployed to virtual destitution. The manufacturing towns were hideous and appalling. A good society could not exist when human beings were treated as mere economic units, and human relations were confined to a 'cash-nexus'. Within the present constitutional frame, nothing really worked anyhow. Such democracy as existed was based on a restricted franchise, and there was no reason to think that a broader one would make it much better. Unless the national leader arose to lick the governing class into shape, it would go on being the governing class, with no conspicuous talent and less sense of responsibility than former aristocracies had.

These jeremiads laid the basis for a new radicalism, though it was to emerge only slowly, and through another prophet rather than Carlyle himself. When it did come, it was inevitably Offbeat, not left-wing or revolutionary. By then, quite coincidentally, extremism was in abeyance. There had been rumours of revolution during the 1840s because of the Chartists' campaign for political reform. Some of them orated provocatively about 'physical force'. In 1848, when a wave of attempted revolutions swept across Europe, the Chartists spoke of making a move themselves. The Government, alarmed, enrolled thousands of volunteer special constables. The Chartists planned two major actions in April. They would present a huge petition to Parliament, and they would hold a mass rally on Kennington Common. In the upshot, the programme was a double fiasco. Under scrutiny the petition turned out to be largely bogus: most of the signatures were forgeries, or even jokes; and at the rally there were more police than demonstrators – five times as many, according to one estimate.

Nearly all the Chartists' demands were eventually conceded, one by one and without disturbance. But after 1848, revolution was out of the picture, even as fantasy. The way was cleared for Carlyle-derived Offbeat Radicalism. There was no serious competition.

He had made a contribution himself that affected its character when it came: he had introduced the loss-and-recovery syndrome. In the course of reflection on the possibility of a changed society,

Carlyle's vivid imagination, which had given reality to the scenes of the French Revolution, happened to fasten on some others in England's own past. He discovered the twelfth-century chronicle of Jocelin de Brakelond, which gives an account of his abbey at Bury St Edmunds. The reader sees through Jocelin's eyes, and is informed about the things that Jocelin finds interesting, but these are glimpses of a real, tangible past. The Abbey's land is not a diagram on a map, but, as Carlyle puts it, 'a green solid place, that grew corn and several other things'. Abbot Samson is seen working with others in the community, and the chronicle tells us what they do. Samson is too busy to spend time talking about his religion, yet the chronicle makes us feel that it means more than the religion of the present day. Without saying much, Samson and the other monks testify to a higher reality. Carlyle cannot resist slipping in a little gibe at Methodism 'with its eyes forever turned on its own navel' – long before it became a cliché to say it of Buddhism.

In the medieval setting, Carlyle discovered not academic history of the Dryasdust school, as he nicknamed it, but human beings as real as those around him, and some of them more admirable. Bringing an account like this into a contemporary discussion was completely original. As Carlyle communicated his awareness, readers started to realise how the past could live for them, could be relevant and respected, could even be turned to for inspiration. They saw the narrowness of the normal ignorance about it. They could absorb it into their own philosophy, make acquaintance with virtues that had dropped out of sight, and perhaps revive them to oppose the evils of the present. In the new Offbeat Radicalism, loss-and-recovery could be central.

*

Carlyle never went far along that path himself. While he could admire elements of the Middle Ages, he had no notion of grafting anything medieval on to his own hopes for the future, such as they were. The hopes themselves grew slighter and slighter. In a long essay entitled *Past and Present*, which introduces Jocelin and shows the effect of reading him, he could still put forward ideas for reform. But a reader today learns with misgiving that his favoured instrument for effecting this is the army. Being already used to discipline, Carlyle argues, it should be directed to wage a national battle against hunger, muddle and stupidity. Parliament need not be by-passed. It can clean up the manufacturing towns, and provide public baths and parks.

England must learn from the failure of the French aristocracy, and create a new one, a 'working' aristocracy. None of this can get far through ballot-box voting; there will need to be a respected minority striving for something higher than money, and making something better than the 'cash-nexus' between human beings.

Carlyle's *Latter-Day Pamphlets* are more morose and scornful. They are full of tirades against 'shams'. In *Past and Present*, he assumed that his readers were at least capable of shedding illusions and discovering moral truth. Now he doubts it. England lives by consecrated falsehood, which he blames, weirdly, on the long-term influence of the Jesuits. Can something truer emerge? Well, they got rid of traditional 'imposture' in the French Revolution – and the result was anarchy. An election may show a supposedly constructive consensus, but the consensus may be mistaken. Popular suffrage can't determine what the 'Laws of the Universe' are. Giving the vote to the workers won't help. They live in a poison-swamp, a cesspool of poverty, unemployment, and degradation. Carlyle recoils from the 'ape-faces' of a monstrous and bestial working class.

In any case, he now argues that Parliament shouldn't govern at all. Its proper function is consultative. It should tell the monarch what the people are thinking. Again we are introduced to his elite, a wise minority empowered by a kind of upside-down revolution, devoting its energies to the nation's real and living interests. But even this working aristocracy wouldn't be enough to bring a decisive change. Everything would depend, in practice, on a sovereign authority at the top, forcing co-operation: a real king, or another Cromwell, only more so. There is no sign of such a person.

Carlyle's monarchical fixation led him into an undertaking that came perilously close, in the end, to self-refutation. He set out to write the history of a candidate for the honour, Frederick II of Prussia, Frederick the so-called Great, who reigned from 1740 to 1786 with bitter consequences for Europe. Frederick played the flute, posed as a champion of the Enlightenment, and invited Voltaire to live at his court, an arrangement that ended in recriminations. His autocratic rule was, arguably, beneficial to his subjects, but his real interest was in his magnificent army and its potentialities for Prussia's expansion. His aggressions led to the Seven Years' War, from 1756 to 1763, in which he held out against Austria, France and Russia in alliance, creating a myth of invincibility that was still bedevilling Germany more than a century later.

The strangest thing about Carlyle's work on Frederick was that he hated it. He had a room soundproofed at the top of the Chelsea house, and toiled on and on for seven years, studying 'dull and dreadful' books on the Prussian king. Jane suffered all the time; she died suddenly soon after his six-volume history was complete, and he only realised how great her sufferings had been when he read her diaries. The glorification of Frederick seems to have been an obsession, a nightmare duty. After all that trouble the book was unsuccessful in England, but it was popular in Germany – eventually, with Hitler: in 1945, when Germany was collapsing, Goebbels read out a passage from it to remind the Führer that Frederick had made a miraculous recovery from disaster.

*

Carlyle's authoritarian notions never made any large number of converts. The critical and subversive thinking that nourished them was, fortunately, stronger in its effect: once again, it laid the groundwork for an Offbeat Radicalism at which Carlyle never arrived himself. After *Frederick* he wrote very little, but continued to shake and stir when opportunity served. He lived until 1881, and almost witnessed the dawn of socialism in Britain. As expounded by Hyndman it was utterly foreign to him; yet without Carlyle's attacks on capitalism it might not have begun when it did. There is no way of telling how many minds his work influenced, but the Carlyle phenomenon, in one form and another, was extensive. George Eliot compared him to an oak tree scattering acorns, and declared that if all his writings were annihilated, his multiple effect would go on.

His most enduring and honourable legacy, sprung from a very noble acorn indeed, is the London Library in St James's Square. In 1840, between *The French Revolution* and the publication of *Heroes*, he was going to the British Museum regularly for research, and becoming frustrated by the difficulty of getting the books he needed and studying them in peace.[†] Driven finally to take action, he played a leading role in setting the London Library up, with himself as honorary secretary and a distinguished committee including Dickens. The Library is still there, an unparalleled resource for readers and research workers: an institution launched, not by philanthropy, but by Carlylean pique.

*

When Blake and Shelley introduce loss-and-recovery in their visions, they are not indulging in Tory nostalgia or proposing

† According to an anecdote – perhaps not precisely true, but well invented – he happened to arrive one day at the same time as Macaulay. Macaulay was given preferential treatment, and allowed to jump the queue ahead of him. He was so angry that he went off and founded a library of his own.

merely to bring the 'good old days' back. The revival of the lost good is seen as a springboard to the future. The change that the waking of Albion symbolises is to inaugurate the rebuilding of Jerusalem; the resurrection of the 'old laws of England' is to inaugurate a new reign of justice.

After Carlyle's medieval hint, loss-and-recovery gradually begins to take hold with others. At first, however, the emphasis is novel. The lost good itself is what a thoughtful few discern and examine, led by the second of the two prophets, John Ruskin. The idea that it can be resurrected to shape a future, at odds with current orthodoxies, follows on. But it does not follow on at once.

Carlyle's shaking of his contemporaries was unsettling, as it was meant to be. Ruskin began his public career as an authority on art; then the Carlylean shock diverted it into subversive channels. The two prophets between them spanned the whole century. Carlyle was born in 1795, Ruskin died in 1900. Ruskin's output was vast and varied, and more positive than the Scotsman's. The record of his life is a strange case-history. He is the only author of genius in Victorian England who never escaped from parental dominance. How far this moulded his achievement is a matter for psychological speculation, but speculation should not distract attention from the achievement.

He was born in the Bloomsbury district of London in 1819, the only offspring of two strong-willed spouses. His father, John James Ruskin, was a prosperous wine merchant. His mother Margaret was an Evangelical Christian. She intended her son to enter the Church, and subjected him from childhood to regular and relentless Bible readings.

The family moved to Herne Hill on the capital's southern outskirts. When John was fourteen, his father gave him an edition of a topographical poem, *Italy*, written by Samuel Rogers and illustrated by Joseph Turner. This glimpse of foreign scenes made a deep impression on the boy, which was soon reinforced by first-hand experience. Ruskin Senior made frequent business trips, both in Britain and abroad, collecting orders for sherry, and he took his wife and son with him. Travel opened John's eyes, but the constant presence of his parents was a curb on his growth in social skills. In 1833 they visited his father's overseas partner, Monsieur Domecq. Three years later Domecq returned the visit, bringing his daughters. John developed a crush on one of them, Adèle, but was hopelessly gauche. Quite aware that the guests were Catholics, he talked about Protestantism. In spite of this tactless failure to connect, he was still having fantasies about Adèle several years later. But they did not reflect any desire to be with her in France: after foreign excursions, he was always happy to return to the 'blessed sameness' of Herne Hill.

In 1837 he went up to Oxford. His college was Christ Church. The family expertise in matters of wine gave him a mild popularity, but the advantage was soon stifled by the parents to whom he owed it. His mother moved to Oxford. She took rooms just up the street, and kept him under surveillance. His father visited at weekends. A student's natural escape route was closed to him. He only managed a pass degree. While in residence, however, he entered poems for the Newdigate Prize, and after failing twice, won it with a poem called 'Salsette and Elephanta', an anticipation of other cryptic titles which he was to produce at intervals for the rest of his life. He met Wordsworth, in Oxford to receive an honorary degree. His father, who had a high opinion of his abilities, and had burdened him at the age of eight by solemnly telling him so, began to think of him as a poet in the making. Certainly he was losing interest in becoming a clergyman as his mother desired.

In 1840 the Ruskins made another overseas foray, partly because of anxiety about John's health. He observed, but he did not enjoy. The family settled finally at Denmark Hill south-east of London, in a very large house. John was polite to visitors, but withdrawn. However, two things happened about this time that were to have momentous consequences. His father presented him with some pictures, including several by Turner, who had not yet achieved general recognition. Up to this point, John had only known him as Samuel Rogers' illustrator. The other event was a visit from Euphemia Gray – Effie, as she was usually known – the thirteen-year-old daughter of a family friend. John wrote a fairy story for her, *The King of the Golden River*.

Fascinated by what he now knew of Turner, he took up the painter's cause against hostile critics. Turner was living in obscure lodgings, dirty and untidy and accompanied by several thin cats, but no such personal factors deflated the admiration which John felt for his work. The result was a book, the first volume of what became a series, *Modern Painters*. Ruskin Senior handled the negotiations with publishers. John had to modify his exclusive enthusiasm for Turner, and broaden the book's scope, but in 1843 it was published. It was the beginning of a campaign to prove the superiority of modern painters over their predecessors, as not merely portraying exteriors (landscapes, for instance) but compelling the spectator to think, and offering ideas for reflection. Ruskin could draw very well himself, and he was extraordinarily good at describing pictures by others. Also, he had an eloquent style. He guided readers away from art that was generalised and conventional, and introduced them to unnoticed beauty and significance in the world around them. Presently, he would champion the Pre-Raphaelites.

Realising that as a self-appointed art critic, he needed to know more about old painters as well as modern ones, he travelled abroad to see their work. This time he travelled alone. But he wrote to his parents almost every day, and when he got home, he was as maladroit as ever in social relationships. He was taking a mild interest in another young girl, Charlotte Lockhart; yet seated next to her at dinner, he was utterly unable to make conversation.

On the other side of her was William Ewart Gladstone, already a rising politician; and John talked to him across Charlotte, about prisons in Naples.

Then Effie Gray, now grown up, re-entered the scene.

*

Whatever we choose to make of it, the two Victorian prophets shared a misfortune. Carlyle's marriage was a failure and he was said to be impotent. The same applies to Ruskin.

He wrote and spoke of love to Effie, and sounded genuine. She appealed to him as good-looking and lively; he appealed to her as handsome, kind, gentle – though he could give the impression that he pictured her as a kind of secretary, rather than a full companion. Wedlock was agreed upon. His parents, for the moment, approved – without that, the engagement would not even have got started – and made her welcome at Denmark Hill. The wedding, however, took place at Bowerswell, her parents' home near Perth, in April 1848. While there was no doubt about Mr Ruskin's prospective munificence, he did not attend the ceremony. He gave several reasons for staying away; one was that there might be a Chartist uprising in London.

The couple left for Blair Atholl on the first stage of a honeymoon tour. They completed the tour, but the marriage was not consummated, then or afterwards. Contemporary reticence makes it difficult to be sure what was wrong. The first attempt at intercourse seems to have disintegrated in panic, and while there were developments later, nothing ever happened that counted. The problem was psychological, and it might have been resolved with a little sexual sophistication on both sides. However, not much of that could be looked for in the victim of Mrs Ruskin's smothering love, and as for Effie, women (ladies, at any rate) were expected to come to marriage knowing very little – as Annie Besant did.

Weeks, months, years went by. The couple kept up appearances. They moved about, they mingled in London society, they travelled. During part of the time they occupied rooms at Denmark Hill. At other times they lived in a house not far away, which Ruskin's father provided. Regarding the marriage, Ruskin muttered rationalisations and excuses. One – which he did not produce at first, but came out with later – was aesthetic. Undressed women were all very well in art, but a real one, with physical features about which artists were insufficiently explicit, had put him off. Sometimes he said he was only postponing the crucial step because Effie wasn't ready. But it looked increasingly unlikely that he would ever take it. He hardly seemed to care, and his attitude was neither conciliatory nor encouraging. The end of the marriage, however, was some distance away, and the emergence of a little more of the truth was further away still. Meanwhile his work proceeded.

*

In November 1849, when Effie's situation was more or less bearable, she accompanied her husband to Venice for a long stay. This was the beginning of Ruskin's growth into something more challenging than an expert on pictures. He had started taking an interest in architecture as well as art, and both interests drew him to Venice. In a book entitled *The Seven Lamps of Architecture* he had deployed his admirable prose to discuss the moral and spiritual qualities that architecture ought to express. In Venice he passed from abstraction to visible reality.

The city, once the centre of a rich and powerful republic, had sunk into a decline since Napoleon ended its independence. English poets such as Byron watched and lamented. Venice was politically oppressed under Austrian rule. In 1849 a popular uprising had been crushed, and a strong occupying force was in control. Venetians were resentful and sullen. The Austrian commander

Marshal Radetzky (to whom the elder Strauss's *Radetzky March* was dedicated) was rowed along the Grand Canal past deserted quays and shuttered windows. People of the two nationalities sat in cafés on opposite sides of St Mark's Square.

The Ruskins, being neither Austrian nor Venetian, could avoid taking sides. They managed a certain social life. Ruskin refused to blame the Venetians' depressed mood on nationalism; he said it was the fault of the Catholic Church. He was drifting away from Christianity in general, and because of his mother's Evangelical teaching, and ecclesiastical quarrels in England, his rejection of it had an anti-Catholic tone.

He was assiduous in his researches. He examined old records. He drew and painted and measured and photographed – Daguerreotype was a recent invention, and he used it to the full. He climbed ladders and explored corners. At the age of thirty, he was an arresting figure, tall and slim, with fair hair and blue eyes, conspicuous among the Mediterranean people around him. He made interesting observations. Venice, he claimed, existed as it did because the sea was not absolutely tideless, but had very small tides. If there had been none at all, the canals would have been 'noisome'. If the water level had changed daily even by a foot or two, the doorways of large buildings would have presented difficulties. The city's architecture, he rejoiced to see, was a unique mixture. Roman, Lombard and Arab styles converged and were blended, notably in the Ducal palace.

To the objection that his anti-Catholicism was an anomaly, since all the buildings he admired had been built by Catholics, he replied as best he could. Papal power had been limited here. The Venetian achievement was the work of pre-Reformation Catholics, not of Catholics whose Church had done nothing memorable since it lost the Protestants. But the logic was not very convincing, and his opposition slowly became less vehement.

After the first spell in Venice, he realised that his project necessitated a second visit. This time the elite of the city were more active socially, and took more notice of the Ruskins – or, at least, of Effie. Radetzky himself flirted with her mildly. John, however, ridiculed the people she was glad to meet.

The book that resulted from these expeditions, *The Stones of Venice*, was an unquestioned masterpiece. Its style, its perceptiveness, its presentation of ideas, its wealth of information, were unprecedented. It introduced the Italian city to a new public in England. Ironically, Ruskin did more than anyone else to popularise Venice as a place to spend a honeymoon.

Because of one astonishing section, as we shall see, this book marked the beginning of a new phase in his life. The end of an old one almost coincided with it. In 1854, on Effie's initiative, the Ruskins' marriage was annulled. By this time she had a horror of their relationship, and the elderly, ever-looming parents-in-law were too much for her. In reference to Ruskin himself, the legal decree employed the phrase 'incurable impotency', but it applied only to this particular case, it was not meant to assert total incapacity. An ambiguity remained. Effie, however, was free. After a decent interval she married a mutual friend, the Pre-Raphaelite artist John Millais, who had painted one of the best portraits of her ex-husband. Ruskin had never stood in the way of their getting together.

Such matters were not publicised then. The privacy of private lives was, on the whole, respected. Some inevitable gossip was mainly adverse to Ruskin, though Carlyle, predictably, blamed Effie and accused her of deserting him. As he became more famous, many readers and lecture-goers knew vaguely of a broken marriage, but there were no journalists trying to worm out secrets.

He was back, finally and completely, at Denmark Hill.

*

One chapter of *The Stones of Venice* is headed 'The Nature of Gothic'. Arguably, this is the most important thing Ruskin ever wrote, though it was insignificant in bulk beside the rest of his output. It triggered the new Offbeat Radicalism, which would extend far into the future. The principal figure in that trend, William Morris, referred to Ruskin's chapter as 'one of the very few necessary and inevitable utterances of the century'. A discussion of medieval architecture might seem an unlikely candidate for such singling-out – but not when we see how Ruskin went on to develop the argument and its consequences.

The background to the chapter was a nineteenth-century Gothic revival, or ostensible revival, that had been gathering force for several decades. It was one aspect of a fashionable romanticisation of the Middle Ages, due largely to Sir Walter Scott's historical novels. The apostle of the neo-Gothic in architecture was August Welby Pugin, a Catholic convert who designed several churches, and had a hand in the embellishment of the Palace of Westminster housing Parliament, which replaced a predecessor destroyed by fire (a disaster painted by Turner). He thought his adopted religion helped him to recapture the spirit of medieval builders.

Ruskin attacked the revival as fallacious. One man, however gifted, could not reproduce a Gothic cathedral. Such a cathedral embodied a kind of perfection-through-imperfection. It was a patient growth over a long period, with no fixed design dominant throughout. Artists, sculptors, craftsmen collaborated, each working zealously in his own way, with no overall dictatorship. The building could exhibit humour, violence, grotesquerie, and other qualities only slightly related to conventional devotion. It was many-voiced, many-faceted.

All this changed in the Renaissance. Henceforth, a major building was a comparatively short-term project, created by one master designer, and executed by workers doing what they were told to do. The workers might be skilful and the result might be beautiful, but its perfection was of another kind, proud and elitist.

The authentic Gothic could not continue, Ruskin said, and it certainly could not return to life in the nineteenth century. The multiplicity had departed. Pugin could imitate, contriving any number of pointed arches, but the end product was a pastiche. His religious conversion was irrelevant, and Ruskin, still anti-Catholic, could say so with relish. Anglican-derived piety could hardly supply a rapport with Catholic builders half a millennium dead.†

More important, more profound in its implications, was the fact that the original conditions of the Gothic no longer existed. When Pugin created a pseudo-Gothic church, the project was a short-term one, following the course that had been the norm since the Renaissance. He planned it himself, and a team carried out his orders. Artists and sculptors and craftsmen still existed, but far fewer in proportion to the whole working population, and they would never combine to express themselves in a great structure, as their medieval forerunners did. The Gothic was a lost glory.

To say so was not to decline into a futile cult of the past. The author of *Modern Painters* would never have become a mere reactionary. In theory, a transformation of attitudes and conditions, with a corresponding transformation of work itself, might produce, if not the Gothic over again, something comparable – perhaps even an architecture that re-ignited the spirit of what could not actually be resurrected. In practice, mid-century England was not capable of it. Ruskin took a step that went far beyond the Gothic issue. He asked: Why not?

He confronted existing society, its commerce and industry, its

† Pugin had limitations of his own. There is a story that he was once showing a friend round a church he had designed. He pointed out a particularly sanctified area, saying no women were allowed there. At that moment the bishop walked across it with two lady visitors.

utilitarian outlook, and the so-called Political Economy that gave it an ideological basis. After mature reflection, he wrote a series of essays giving the results. In 1860 they appeared in the *Cornhill Magazine*, a very prestigious publication indeed. Or rather, four appeared; then the editor, no less a person than William Makepeace Thackeray, surrendered to a barrage from hostile readers and said 'no more'. The blow to Ruskin was severe, but he persisted, and published his essays in book form under the title *Unto This Last* (in his later years he had an increasing fondness for enigmatic titles).

Unto This Last is a critique of *laissez-faire* capitalism. Carlyle was the principal inspiration† and approved strongly. Some of Ruskin's analysis is not fully developed in the published text, but it is all there in his mind, as other writings show. Given absolutely free enterprise, governed by profit and nothing else; given unorganised labour, much of it downgraded by machinery; given the axiom that economic motives are the real driving force in all behaviour, and that this is how it should be – what actually happens? How do these principles work in practice? Is it right that wages and prices should be left to the operation of a free market? Does the accumulation of money and goods constitute real wealth? The bearing of all this on the possibility – or impossibility – of anything like the Gothic occurring again, is obvious. But architecture is only the beginning. More is involved, immensely more.

If an industrial employer is motivated solely by profit, he aims at efficiency. He makes the best use of machinery and the systematic division of labour. In Ruskin's time, the Ford-style assembly line is still far off, but there are already many approaches to it – and its consequences. The worker is alienated from his work, which is too elementary and repetitive, and cannot engage him as

† Cf. Abse, Joan. *John Ruskin*, p. 172.

a person. It is just a job bringing in a wage to support him and his family, and probably a poor wage, if the Political Economists have anything to say about it. From his own side, the worker will make whatever bargain he can, since his labour is all he has to sell. If he finds a different job that pays better, he will feel free to go to it; no inherent interest or loyalty keeps him attached to the present one.

Ruskin perceives all this as a sinister and spreading reality. In *Unto This Last* and related texts he opposes it, and the thinking that supports it. Economists, he argues, in the name of their pseudo-science, consider only factors that can be defined and quantified, with the associated motives. They omit the moral and social imponderables which they cannot handle. But the imponderables matter, and they can influence a system in which they occur. Sometimes they matter even in a strictly economic sense. A wise employer who thinks of other things – human things – besides tangible profit may do better than his competitors. He may achieve more stability and calmer industrial relations, and resolve disputes more easily through co-operation. Owen showed the way at New Lanark.

On the professional level, Ruskin observes, Political Economy has only a very limited application. Doctors attract patients, lawyers attract clients, by reputation and not by charging low fees. In some areas it doesn't apply at all: the armed services, for instance. A man may take the Queen's shilling because he is poor, and have his meals supplied by the British army. But he is not a mercenary, despite the sneer that was famously rebutted by A. E. Housman in his epitaph on the British Expeditionary Force of 1914; and when loyalty and comradeship develop, pay is simply not the issue. Nor, for that matter, is the fact that the soldier may have to do his duty at the risk of his life.

The respect shown to a doctor, lawyer, or army officer, recognises service to the community. The same respect is denied to 'trade', and the reason is not pure snobbery. The money-making merchant, like Ruskin's father, doesn't have the same reputation for service. Ideally he should, Ruskin says, and if he were to operate by high professional standards he might, but this could only happen in a general change of atmosphere.

Prices raise another issue. A manufacturer seeking profit, who wants to undercut rivals, has an incentive to reduce prices by lowering quality, and the customer suffers. If prices are determined by a free market, they may be unsatisfactory for the customer and unfair to the producer. Ruskin reverts to the medieval conception of the 'just price', defined by what the worker ought to receive, not by what necessity forces him to accept. If a free-market economist claims that prices can't be regulated, Ruskin answers that they can, because the rigid economic factor is not the only determinant.

He ends with some remarks about wealth in general. Ruskin observes that there is no value in mere accumulation. Let us by all means have possessions, but possessions that can be used or aesthetically enjoyed, not pointless clutter. Ultimately, there is no true wealth but life: 'That country is richest which nourishes the greatest number of noble and happy human beings.' He concludes *Unto This Last* thus:

> We need examples of people who, leaving Heaven to decide whether they are to rise in the world, decide for themselves that they will be happy in it, and have resolved to seek – not greater wealth, but simpler pleasures; not higher fortunes, but deeper felicity; making the first of possessions, self-possession; and honouring themselves in the harmless pride and calm pursuits of peace.

A believer in orthodox *laissez-faire* might dismiss that paragraph with relief, as innocuous if misguided moralising. Ruskin, however, gave *Unto This Last* a preface outlining some concrete proposals he had in mind. He accepted that human beings are not equal in their abilities, but he called upon those who were equipped for constructive leadership to supply it. He wanted state factories and workshops – not to compete with private enterprise, but to produce quality goods as models for imitation. He wanted state schools, meaning not compulsory education, but education that would supply guidance – vocational training, for instance. He wanted job creation for the unemployed, and public care – not charity – for the old and destitute.

*

Ruskin was the first person of national standing to talk like this about the quality of life. To contemporaries, the ideas in his preface were even more shocking than the essays. 'Socialism' was not yet a familiar term, and his proposals were not really socialist in any case, but they were still alarming. As it happened, *Unto This Last* was about as far removed from current realities as it could be. In 1860, free enterprise was triumphant, and free trade was reaching its apogee.

The essays enraged believers in *laissez-faire* – those, at least, who took any notice of them – and Ruskin's eminence in the art world was no excuse. There was clearly something wrong with him. Opponents attacked him fiercely and publicly. The book's sales were poor. It began to move later, helped along by the advocacy of William Morris and others, but not for some time.

Ruskin denied that he was taking a political stand. He refused to be pinned down, and he did not even care much about consistency, so long as he conveyed his essential protest. Like Walt Whitman, he was quite willing to admit that he sometimes contradicted himself. He had the audacity to appeal to the Bible, where, according to commentators, incompatible texts taken together could uphold a central, intermediate meaning. Truth could be polygonal. He described himself at different times as a socialist, a tory, a communist, an imperialist – though one label that he always rejected was 'liberal'.

His father, as a successful businessman, believed unwaveringly in *laissez-faire*. John's vagaries distressed him exceedingly. The atmosphere at home was not made any more comfortable by Mrs Ruskin's sorrow at her son's abandonment of religion. He assured her that he had not given up Christian morals with Christianity; but it was no use. Ruskin Senior's health was declining, and in his downcast mood, he took an 'after-all-that-I've-done-for-you' attitude to his son. It was true that he had spent considerable sums on converting part of his house into a sort of private gallery, fit for the reception of distinguished visitors whom John invited. These included Kingsley, Tennyson and Browning. They came, they admired, and they went away wondering at the spectacle of such a famous person living under the parental roof when past forty.

While the ménage was odd, it looked peaceful to outsiders. But it was quietly becoming intolerable. In the wake of the abuse of *Unto This Last*, and the disappointing response of the public generally, John himself sank into embittered depression. At last the long-brewing crisis erupted. His parents were old now, but the conflicts remained; he told them they had ruined him, and actually moved out for a while. He wrote to a friend, Lady Trevelyan:

> I know my father is ill, but I cannot stay at home just now. . . . If he loved me less, and believed in me more, we should get on; but his whole life is bound up with me, and yet he thinks me a fool.

The clash cleared the air somewhat. As he stood up to his parents, though they disapproved of nearly everything that he said and did, he felt more at ease than he had when he was compliant. He was defining himself by dissent from them. Ruskin Senior died in March 1864, and was buried in a churchyard near Croydon. John wrote an epitaph calling him an 'entirely honest merchant'. Despite all estrangements his father left him £120,000, plus the pictures. He was independent at last.

Independent, but, as it turned out, not psychologically free. Nevertheless, he tried. It has been said that while Carlyle and Ruskin were both tormented, Ruskin sometimes achieved a certain light-heartedness, even a certain optimism about society's prospects. His growing interest in social problems led him to teach at the Working Men's College in Red Lion Square, London, founded by the Christian socialist, Frederick Denison Maurice. The college had begun with subversive political aims, but was moving into intellectual and cultural fields. Ruskin conducted drawing classes, illustrated with pictures and specimen objects, such as stones and leaves. The classes were popular and well attended. He also wrote a series of tracts addressed to 'workmen and labourers', ninety-six in all. The title of the series was *Fors Clavigera*, a choice hardly calculated to achieve a rapport. It confirmed a remark by Benjamin Jowett, the Master of Balliol, that Ruskin 'never rubbed his mind against others'. He could think, write and speak brilliantly, but in social relationships that involved listening to people and considering their point of view, he was less successful.

*

During this time his life was subjected to another cycle of sexual bafflement, one that is even more distressing to contemplate than the first. It started in Lewis Carroll style with an attachment to a child, but of a different kind that never produced an *Alice in Wonderland*. In 1858 he was giving drawing lessons to Rose La Touche, a pretty and intelligent nine-year-old. He liked Rose's mother, and he liked Rose. But as the friendship continued, it became obvious that his fondness for Rose went further.

He wrote verses to her. In the atmosphere of the time, they could be seen as innocently romantic, but his ardour became excessive and self-centred. As Rose grew up, unavoidable hints at marriage made the situation more awkward. She responded, but not warmly enough to suggest the possibility of a partnership with a man easily old enough to be her father. She visited Denmark Hill, and gained time by insisting that serious matrimonial talk must wait until she came of age.

Ruskin himself was torn between infatuation and hesitancy. The main reason for delay was his apprehension that a second marital failure would damage his reputation. Here, biographers face the queries again, but with a few more clues. The wording of the decree that ended his marriage did not imply that an attempt with someone else would be foredoomed to futility. He was not null in this respect, as Carlyle very likely was. There is in fact evidence for masturbation, as there is for occasional passion, only it had never found an appropriate outlet; he had never made the usual connection.

This time, Effie herself had something to say. When Rose was sufficiently adult, Mrs La Touche addressed a confidential inquiry to Ruskin's non-wife, now married to Millais, and received a very firm reply. Ruskin was incapable, said Effie, of making a woman happy. His conduct had been 'impure in the highest degree' and he was 'quite unnatural'. The impression is not so much that Effie recalled nothing happening as that she recalled things happening which she regarded as unpleasant. At any rate, Ruskin's love affair was over. Rose and her mother agreed to break it off. About this time, he stated in a letter to someone else that he had 'never possessed any woman'. One notes his use of the word 'possess'. Probably the long parental regime and the religious pressure had given him an inhibiting and incurable sense of guilt. If so, it was exacerbated when Rose died prematurely.

Whether any of his literary output was sublimation, it is no use trying to guess, but one of his artistic enthusiasms is worth recording. During another visit to Venice, he took a disproportionate interest in a series of nine pictures by the little-known artist Vittore Carpaccio. They illustrated the legend of St Ursula. He made a copy of one of them, and fancied that the saint was in contact with him. According to the legend, she was a British princess in the fourth or fifth century. She refused to marry, and led a mass pilgrimage to Rome, with a membership consisting entirely of virgins – thousands of them – whom Ursula and her attendants educated at stopping places. They were massacred by barbarians on the way back.

*

Ruskin attained a peak of professional success in 1869, when Oxford University appointed him to its new Slade Professorship of Fine Art. His inaugural lecture was open to the public, and so many members of the public arrived that the venue had to be changed from the Museum to the Sheldonian Theatre. He led an impromptu procession from one building to the other. In a situation like this, he was a fine speaker, with carefully timed effects and a spellbinding voice. Dressed in a blue frock coat with a long watch chain and high Gladstonian collar, he read from a prepared text, but extemporised vivaciously, with dramatic gestures.

His record of springing surprises had aroused a certain apprehension, and he did surprise, but with good effect. Instead of discussing art academically and historically, he talked about its foundations, and its relation to the society producing it. Also – and this was a real surprise – he digressed into the topic of surplus population, exhorting British people to leave home, colonise Africa, and enlarge the Empire. Cecil Rhodes was in the audience, and was encouraged to start thinking about imperial projects of his own.

Ruskin too had projects. Unmoved by technological progress and reformist legislation, he wanted to make a start, however tentatively, towards creating an alternative society. In those days, before the imperial scramble for Africa had begun, his talk of emigration and peaceable settlement did not sound inconsistent. In 1871 he founded an organisation, St George's Guild, that collected parcels of land from sympathetic donors, and experimented with small-scale agriculture, craft revival and colourful clothing. The Guild is interesting chiefly as a far-off anticipation of distributism, the Offbeat Radical movement that attempted, briefly, to challenge twentieth-century political orthodoxies. Unlike distributism, however, St George's Guild struck some people as too much of a personality cult. They suggested that if it expanded, it would be a pyramidal structure, with its founder at the apex as a benevolent dictator. It never did expand, not noticeably.†

Soon after launching the Guild, Ruskin bought a house in the Lake District overlooking Coniston Water. His mother had died, and he at last gave up Denmark Hill. The move did not prevent further experimentation, a long way from the Lake District. He opened an artistically designed shop in Praed Street, Paddington, for selling quality teas to working-class customers; and he announced a plan for building a road from the village of North Hinksey to Oxford, with undergraduates doing the work and exemplifying the dignity of labour. Some volunteered. One was Arnold Toynbee, and another was Oscar Wilde, who boasted afterwards of having pushed Mr. Ruskin's wheelbarrow.

Actually Ruskin was abroad most of the time; he was never good at participation. He left his gardener to supervise the road building. Walter Besant, Annie's novelist brother-in-law, brought the scheme into one of his stories. The road petered out. A final observation was made later by one of the villagers: 'I don't think the young gentlemen did much harm.' It was Ruskin's principal follower, William Morris, who would make a success of practical projects.

† Quennell, Peter. *John Ruskin*, pp. 263–4.

More important, through its indirect and unobtrusive results, was Ruskin's friendship with Cardinal Manning, the head of the Catholic Church in England. Manning was profoundly concerned about the social problems of the day; in 1889 his intervention in the great London Dock Strike was to bring him immense prestige with the labour movement. *Unto This Last* was a key text for him. The two men met: one of Ruskin's letters describes having lunch as Manning's guest, and praises the cuisine and the conversation. Ruskin firmly declined to be converted, but he rearranged his opposition to institutional Christianity. Previously, he had attacked Catholicism; now, he was more inclined to attack Protestantism. Some of his ideas, as mediated through Manning, very possibly found their way to Rome. Pope Leo XIII's encyclical *Rerum Novarum*, issued in 1891, certainly marked a new departure in the social teaching of the Church, and Manning may have had a hand in its authorship.

Ruskin's later years were troubled – not, however, by women. He wrote an intemperate criticism of the rising American artist James Whistler, who had settled in London. Whistler sued for libel. Though he got only a farthing damages – that is, 'contemptuous' damages, expressing the court's view that the action should never have been brought – he would not leave the subject alone.

Health, too, was a problem. Ruskin was beginning to have bad dreams, even delusions. He gave more lectures at Oxford, but his platform manner grew erratic, and occasionally a chairman had to stop him. Yet he still managed to produce a fragment of autobiography, characteristically entitled *Praeterita*. A new Oxford college for trade unionists was named after him, Ruskin College. It made a significant contribution to Labour politics. Still, the old man's mental condition continued slowly to deteriorate until, in January 1900, he died. Today Ruskin Park, near by the old family home in Denmark Hill, commemorates him. And, of course, his works survived – thirty-nine volumes – and so did his influence, more effectively in some respects than the writers of obituaries cared to admit.

9

Morris

By the latter part of the nineteenth century, the French Revolution was a lifetime away, and the reaction against its bloodier aspects had dwindled. However, Carlyle's account of the Terror kept the memory of it alive, and *A Tale of Two Cities* planted it in the minds of Dickens's millions of readers.

The French, moreover, had a habit of never settling down. In 1871, after defeat in the Franco-Prussian War, Paris virtually seceded and set up a civic organisation of its own. The Paris Commune lasted for several weeks and succumbed finally in an appalling struggle with government troops. The ferocity of repression reflected the shock of a new and alarming phenomenon. The Commune was formed and largely dominated by leaders of the Parisian working class. It was the first proletarian regime anywhere.

Marx and Engels, in England, saluted what they saw as a fulfilment of their predictions. Actually, the Commune was not particularly Marxist, and it did not survive long enough to put through various intended reforms; its achievement was that it existed at all. In subsequent Marxist tradition, Paris's heroic time was looked back upon as a 'brief shining moment'. Forty-six years later Lenin danced in the snow when his government had lasted one day longer.

In England this violent episode helped to revive anti-revolutionary feelings. During the early 1880s, Marx was quietly undermining capitalism, and Engels was giving their system a new dimension. A recognisable Left was beginning to appear, and socialism was beginning to be talked about. Few, however, were following Marx's path, or even knew that it existed. For the vast majority, any revolution at all was still alien and unthinkable.

In time to come, economists were to treat *Das Kapital* with respect, and militants were to echo the Communist Manifesto and urge the world's workers to unite. For now, England produced one Marxist of historic stature – but only one. William Morris was a younger contemporary of Engels, and it was quite in keeping with Offbeat antecedents that Engels failed to appreciate him. The left-wing historian E. P. Thompson said of him that although he could be 'assimilated' to Marxism, the assimilation was possible only by way of self-criticism and reordering within Marxism itself. While Morris was committed to Marxist ideals, there was far more to him than that. He was, in Thompson's words, 'one of those men whom history will never overtake'.

*

William Morris was born in 1834. The family home was at Walthamstow, then a village in Essex, now absorbed into London and a terminus of the Underground. His father was a successful business man, and William never lacked for money, but he escaped from dependency and became a unique entrepreneur himself.

After a childhood that included an unusual amount of reading – notably the novels of Scott – he was sent to school at Marlborough College in Wiltshire. He did not learn much, but there were extra-curricular influences. In the grounds of the school was a curious terraced mound, today called Merlin's Mount, formerly said to be the enchanter's grave. The town's old name, Maerlebi, was reputed (wrongly) to be derived from his. Not far away were the prehistoric monuments of Silbury and Avebury. Morris studied them with fascination, and also Avebury's ancient church.

From Marlborough he went to Oxford: Exeter College. There he formed a friendship with the artist Edward Burne-Jones, which would have sweeping consequences. Burne-Jones introduced him to Dante Gabriel Rossetti and other artists of the Pre-Raphaelite group. They were not likely to dispose him towards a conventional career, and in fact they did not. Thanks to the family fortune, there was no urgent need for one. The only open door was already closing. The Church had been considered, and an affluent young man with an Oxford education could enter the Anglican ministry with good prospects and no very positive divine call. But, with Burne-Jones's encouragement, Morris turned away from religion. In his maturity he always retained a love of old churches, and opposed misguided attempts to 'restore' them, but he loved them under the spell of Ruskin, as Gothic works of collective art, not as places of worship. Besides being indifferent to religion, he was indifferent to anti-religion. He never became involved with Bradlaugh's secularism or the shriller type of 'freethought' that grew from it.

His first career move was to article himself to G. E. Street, the architect who designed the Law Courts. But Burne-Jones, Rossetti and their artistic colleagues drew him firmly into the Pre-Raphaelite milieu. He was not in the first rank of painters, but he was fully able to hold his own among them. This phase of his life was the first proof of his versatility, and more than versatility: he was not only capable of doing a variety of things, he was capable of doing them well. Like himself, the Pre-Raphaelites were all under Ruskin's influence, and like himself, they had strong medieval interests – especially in the Arthurian legends, which Tennyson was reviving. Today it is hard to realise that a poet could ever have been truly popular, a national bestseller; yet

Tennyson was. Huge numbers of readers enjoyed his Arthurian evocations, and some, Morris included, were moved to explore the great fifteenth-century original, Sir Thomas Malory's *Morte d'Arthur*.

In 1857 Morris joined several of the Pre-Raphaelites in a team project commissioned by the Oxford Union, to paint murals in the Union's new building. The subjects were to be Arthurian. By that November, Morris alone had stayed with his job and finished it. New painters had to be taken on. The murals were unsatisfactory in any case, being in a position where the light from several large windows made it difficult to see them properly. Also, the wall had not been protected against damp. Morris noted the artists' lack of practical forethought, and in due course, when deterioration set in, the experience he had gained in another field suggested a practical remedy they would never have hit on.

During the Union project and after, he was writing poetry: that was another of the things he did well. Here too the first inspiration was medieval and Arthurian. But, like some other poets who responded to Tennyson, he showed – even in the act of responding – that he did not share Tennyson's moralistic attitude. He went back to Malory to form his own ideas. His best-known early poem, *The Defence of Guenevere*, is a protest against the demonisation of the queen.

He married a model, Jane Burden; they had two daughters. Their home was the Red House at Bexley Heath in Kent, so named from its red brick construction. Here, in 1861, with some of his artistic friends, he launched a totally original partnership called 'The Firm'. Already established as a painter and poet, he was now on the way to a future in which he could describe himself as a designer. The Firm's declared aim was to give a new status to the 'Decorative Arts', attacking the ugliness, dullness and general clutter of mid-Victorian dwellings. Morris exhorted clients and potential clients to have nothing in their houses but what they believed to be beautiful or knew to be useful. The scope of the Firm's activities extended beyond houses to churches, museums, and other public buildings. The partners offered the public striking murals, imaginative wallpapers, stained-glass windows, colourful fabrics, vivid tapestries. One of them, Philip Webb, created original furniture including functional chairs that were attractive to look at and (this was the real novelty) had some regard for the person who sat in them.

Families and friends helped, and men who were brought in from outside were trained as craftsmen, not employed merely as hired hands. Morris inspired loyalty, not least because he learned the techniques himself. He became an expert weaver and dyer: he never compartmentalised. In a much-quoted observation – perhaps a shade hyperbolic, but not much so – he said: 'If a chap can't compose an epic poem while he's weaving tapestry, he had better shut up'. When the unfortunate Oxford murals decayed to a point at which the Union Committee thought something had to be done, he suggested covering them with wallpaper.

He reorganised the Firm under his own name as Morris & Co., and consolidated most of the production at Merton Abbey south of London. The buildings were long and low, with a stream flowing between them, and a garden alongside. There were carpet looms in the spacious ground floor of one building, while printing was carried on above. Morris's enterprise had a long-term influence on interior decoration and furniture design, directly by way of its own achievements, indirectly by way of the Arts and Crafts movement that followed on from it.

All this time he was continuing to write poetry, copiously and with sustained power. *The Earthly Paradise*, published in 1868–70, is modelled on Chaucer's *Canterbury Tales*. After a prologue setting the scene in the fourteenth century comes a series of legends, classical and medieval, told by different narrators. The theme of a quest for the Earthly Paradise, 'where none grow old', is ultimately Irish. Morris inserts a personal reference:

> Dreamer of dreams, born out of my due time,
> Why should I strive to set the crooked straight?

He also describes himself as 'the idle singer of an empty day'. In view of the course he was to follow a few years later, the lines are ironic.

He visited Iceland and became enraptured with Norse sagas. They went into the making of some of his finest work, and help explain his notorious fondness for a plain 'Anglo-Saxon' vocabulary with a minimum of long words. And as if the Norse were not enough, he also translated the *Aeneid* and the *Odyssey*.

In 1871 Morris and Rossetti took up a joint tenancy of Kelmscott Manor, a noble seventeenth-century property by the Thames below Lechlade. It became a home for the Morrises for some of the time, and Rossetti for a great deal of the time, because he and Jane Morris had become lovers. Tension arose, but never reached the point of eruption. When Morris, in still another venture, founded his own publishing house, he called it the Kelmscott Press from love of the name only; it was not actually based there. He designed type, and learned to print himself, with close attention to layout. The Kelmscott Press produced a fine volume of Chaucer, and a bound edition of Morris's Utopian novel *News from Nowhere*, using a 'golden' type designed by himself, with a frontispiece depicting the main building of Kelmscott Manor. He printed Ruskin's famous chapter 'The Nature of Gothic' as a text by itself, and presented it to the author, who spoke of Morris as 'the ablest man of his time'.

*

In 1883 Morris became a Socialist.

It was an extraordinary step to take. Owenites had coined the word 'socialism', but they had given their own meaning to it, and in any case Owenism had long since faded out. When Morris adopted socialism as it was being re-invented, he was moving in the same direction as Annie Besant and a little ahead of her, and getting sketchy notions of Marx mediated through Henry Hyndman. He joined Hyndman's Social Democratic Federation. However, they were uneasy collaborators, and he was soon heading a separate Socialist League.

For Morris, socialism was a matter of attitude rather than doctrine. Ruskin was still very much with him, especially the Ruskin of *Unto This Last*, with his condemnation of amoral profit-seeking, and his conception of wealth consisting in human values and the quality of life, with an acceptance of planning to maintain justice.

Being an artist, Morris laid particular stress on Ruskin's view of art as a social activity. In a lecture at Oxford, he quoted him as recalling how art could once express joy in labour – cathedral-building, for instance. Morris argued that labour, in capitalism's mechanised industry, could never be joyful or produce an art expressive of joy: it could not be creative, it could not allow variety, it could not even give scope for physical skill, manual or otherwise.

Considerations like these led him to favour socialism in the belief that it stood for a society free from the deadly opposition of classes, those on top and those underneath, a society based instead on an 'equality of condition'. He reiterated his hatred of modern civilisation with its oppression, its stultification, its sheer ugliness. Only a revolution could put something better in its place, and only an organised working class could make the revolution; nobody else would. Morris did not dwell very much on such well-known socialist aims as the nationalisation of industry. That was implied, because the power of the capitalist owners must be destroyed, but it was not emphasised.

His leftward move looked quixotic. He had attached himself to a small sect of which few of his compatriots had even heard. As an enthusiastic convert, he wrote stirring verses about 'the people marching on'; but in practice the people were not. It was much to his credit that he had become so deeply aware of the evils of capitalism and commercialism; that he denounced a system which condemned millions to wear themselves out in factories and bring up families in slums; that he inveighed against the total unrewardingness of industrial work, and the unloveliness of its products. Yet a critic could object that most of his indignation was at second hand. He had always been comfortably off himself. And did he realise what he was campaigning for? Even if his proletarians did seize power, industry would still go on, doubtless benefiting employees rather than shareholders, but not shaping the different society which he said he wanted. People who had spent their days tending machines would not metamorphose into artists and craftworkers. Builders who had disfigured the landscape with industrial dwellings would not start covering it with Kelmscotts.

It could almost be said that, in 1883, Morris was making an honourable protest under the banner of socialism without knowing anything about it. However, he flung himself into speaking and writing for the cause – Ruskin chaired one of his lectures – and educated himself as he went along. His first attempt at self-education was courageous and daunting: he struggled with *Das Kapital* in a French translation. Yet his ardour survived that test and others, and he struck a chord with his audiences. He was not a born speaker, but his passion carried him along, though he had a tendency to lose his temper. One listener, Ernest Rhys, described him as short, sturdy, florid, with the air of a sea captain. At a later date, H. G. Wells observed the same sturdiness, praising his 'grand head, rough voice, sturdy figure, plain speech, lovable bearing'.

Morris attempted a definition:

> Whatever Socialism may lead to, our aim, to be always steadily kept in view, is, to obtain for the whole people, duly organised, the possession and control of all the means of production and exchange, destroying at the same time all national rivalries.†

Two points are significant here. One is that he speaks of 'whatever socialism may lead to'. It is not a final goal but a transitional one; he glimpses a 'beyond', a perspective that will be crucial for his future thinking. The second point is that he designates 'the whole people' as the beneficiaries, though supposedly the revolution will be proletarian, an achievement of the working class. Marxism does in fact reconcile these positions, but the reconciliation has to be clarified and spelt out. Previous revolutions always put a minority on top – the capitalists, for instance. The proletarian revolution will put a majority on top, because the workers *are* the majority. They will be able to eliminate the remnants of capitalism, complete the takeover, and create a single-class society – 'the whole people'.

This theorising does not interest Morris as much as his reflections on details. Because of the profit system, he says, capitalistic manufacturing forces people into cities, and compels them to toil in congested and horrible factories. How would it be different under socialism? In the first place, a great deal of production could be transferred to 'quiet country homes' and industrial colleges – could, in fact, be handled by cottage industries. Where large-scale operations are unavoidable, factories could be made more spacious and attractive, and offer a fuller social life; they could be 'centres of intellectual activity'. No employed person should have to work

† Morris, William. *William Morris by Himself*, Time Warner Books, 2004, p. 157.

all the time on the same endless, deadening task. Jobs should be rotated and made more rewarding, and machinery put to better use. As for work of the 'rougher and more repulsive kind', the people who have to do it should work for the shortest spells; and maybe, in a happier atmosphere, volunteers would be forthcoming.[†] This is the closest that Morris gets to Fourier's garbage-gathering boys.

Clearly Morris's socialism has taken hints from his medieval interests. His cottage industry belongs to a world of craft-working. His idealised factory is not a rigid structure with one capitalist at the top, condemning every worker to do the job that pays best and nothing else. The co-operative organisation has something in common with the medieval guild system; and its multiplicity, in contrast with dictatorship by one individual, recalls Ruskin's 'Nature of Gothic'.

H. G. Wells pointed out what he saw as an inconsistency. Morris might prophesy about the revolution to come, and the better life it would bring. But even in these musings on industry, a bygone age was so evidently with him. He had a personal day-dream, said Wells, and it was 'not futurity but an illuminated past'. He could invoke the fourteenth-century Peasants' Revolt, but in the act of invoking it he showed the tenacity of his medieval link. Readers of *The Earthly Paradise* would hardly forget his wishful image of London in the same period as 'small, and white, and clean'. Small, perhaps, but white – no; and clean – most definitely not. An illuminated past it certainly was. Engels called Morris a political 'innocent', a 'settled sentimental socialist', who hardly counted as a socialist at all.

Marxism, however, had grown since 1848. As we saw, Engels himself had extended its historical scheme at both ends. Far back before all the tyrannies and class conflicts, he had discovered a

† Morris, William. *William Morris: Selected Writings*, ed. Asa Briggs (Penguin, 1962), pp. 131–4.

classless golden age of 'primitive communism'. The coming revolution would lead – eventually – to its rebirth on a higher level. After the reign of socialism, the State would wither away; there would be no classes, no domination of life by cash values and getting-and-spending; all people would receive according to their needs.

Into that remoter future, Morris could project his own ideals without inconsistency. He could picture the Revolution abolishing capitalism and commercialism, and setting up the kind of society which his fellow socialists wanted. But the expansion of Marxist theory allowed him to look beyond: the artists and craftworkers and all the creative people he cared about could come into their own under the aegis of an ever-less-obtrusive State, and grow into liberty with society recognising what they deserved, and supplying their needs. The good things in his 'illuminated past' could return, reilluminated. Their full realisation might be long in coming, but they would be developing all the time.

Whether or not he worked this out explicitly for himself, he arrived at it somehow, as he presently showed.

*

On 13 November 1887, Morris fancied for a wild moment that the Revolution was starting. It was a time of national unrest, due largely to economic depression and unemployment, and that Sunday large numbers of left-wing demonstrators converged on Trafalgar Square. Sir Charles Warren, the chief of the Metropolitan Police, forbade access; but many defied the ban and pressed on, talking of free speech. Police, aided by troops, blocked the approaches. Blows were struck and injuries were inflicted. However, few of the demonstrators showed much inclination to fight. Bernard Shaw, who had come with a rising reputation to join one group, simply advised them to disperse, and went home to tea.

Some, including Annie Besant, did reach the Square, and tried to hold on to positions in it. They were dislodged with more police brutality (to use a modern phrase) than England had witnessed for some time. The day became 'Bloody Sunday' in socialist tradition. However, the single fatality occurred a week later, in the course of another attempt to invade the Square. A clerical worker named Alfred Linnell died tragically, and almost accidentally, in the fracas. He was only an onlooker, but he was briefly promoted to martyrdom. Morris wrote a 'Death Song' to be read at his funeral. It had four stanzas, each ending with a refrain:

> Not one, not one, nor thousands must they slay,
> But one and all if they would dusk the day.

This was too dramatic: the Metropolitan Police were not Cossacks. In such a confrontation, they would never have killed deliberately, and Warren would have been in deep trouble if they had. Linnell's funeral was accompanied by a long procession, but the poetry reading was rain-drenched and anti-climactic, and his grave never became a left-wing shrine.

After this, Shaw, who had had lingering revolutionary notions, gave them up, judging that the futility of the demonstrations had refuted the would-be revolutionaries. He concentrated instead on working for the gradual development of socialism. Morris, by contrast, did not give up. In fact, he continued to think that a revolution would be necessary for change to occur. But he accepted that it could not happen at once, or even soon, and would have to wait until the workers attained more awareness of their situation. He recognised for the first time that Parliament might play a part in creating a socialist order. But he still insisted that it could not do everything; it could not handle the mighty task of 'building up the new society in the shell of the old one' (a phrase that has been applied to Robert Owen's activities, and to those of some later militants, which may have originated with Morris).

As the outlook grew blurred, it would have been understandable if he had decided to drop politics and stick to his neo-medievalism, crafts and poetry: not retracting his social criticism – he would never have done that – but no longer spending vast amounts of his time on campaigns that seemed to achieve nothing.

A blow from an unexpected quarter put an end to any hesitation he might have felt. A dreadful travesty of socialism seized public attention and demanded a retort. Morris was the right person to make the retort, and it was one of the best things he ever did.

*

Edward Bellamy, a novelist from Chicopee Falls, Massachusetts, had produced a bestselling Utopian romance called *Looking Backward, 2000-1887* (1888). It offered a social programme in fictional disguise. Many readers took it seriously, as they were meant to do. Bellamy first located his Utopia in the year 3000, then shifted the date because he thought it could be realised sooner, and his contemporaries should be encouraged to start working towards it.

The narrator of the story, a Bostonian named Julian West, wakes from a trance in the year 2000 and finds America transformed by a Religion of Solidarity. The Nation – with a capital N – is supreme and absolute, embodied in a single enormous corporation that owns everything and employs everybody. All citizens, male and female, are conscripted for long-term service in an industrial army. Its General-in-Chief is the President.

Each year, the gross national product is added up, a surplus is calculated, and every citizen gets a share. The shares are equal, because it is assumed that all workers do their best, and doing one's best is the same for all and doesn't allow gradations. Awkward characters who don't do their best are put in prison.

The lack of financial incentives means very little, because there is no money in the familiar sense. As a citizen you do your shopping by filling in a form in a sample-store where goods are displayed, and paying with a credit card, on which your national share is debited by the amount of your purchase. You can't take the goods with you, they are dispatched from a warehouse to your home through electric 'tubes'. You must spend your whole annual allowance in the course of the year. Anything left over at the year-end reckoning is confiscated by the Nation. Hence, it is no use trying to save. But then nobody wants to save, because the Nation provides housing, education, and social security.

Everybody eats in communal dining-rooms. Public kitchens and laundries take care of all the cooking and washing. Cultural needs are met by such contrivances as playing music over the telephone. Julian West, the observer from the past, extols telephonic concerts as 'the limit of human felicity'.

Morris read *Looking Backward*, and detested Bellamy's 'cockney paradise', as he rather oddly called it. There was more yet. In imagining the building of the new order, from 1887 on, Bellamy assigned no role whatever to working-class organisation. On the contrary, he dismissed it with contempt. He said that it was opposed to real working-class interests; that it wouldn't contribute to the making of his ideal society, that it would actually slow the process down. Despite this anathema, quite a number of socialists applauded the Bellamy Utopia. In a way, surely, it was socialist – was it not?

This would never do! Morris's spirits rose in a memorable riposte. He was well qualified to give it, being, after all, a much better writer. He too could speculate about the future. Furthermore, in doing so, he could draw his own convictions together. *News from Nowhere*, the fiction that resulted, was a classic, and it put him in a position which was all his own. If we care to use the term 'Offbeat' here, it was this work that made him so; but it did not isolate him.

Morris had founded a periodical called *Commonweal*, in which *News from Nowhere* was serialised before its publication in book form in 1890. The story is a retort – a considered, not a hasty one – to Bellamy's bestseller. It is not a refutation. The text never mentions *Looking Backward*, or even hints at it, except in a few impish echoes. But the relationship matters.

The word 'Nowhere' marks a contrast with Bellamy's local habitation. Moreover, the book has a secondary title, *An Epoch of Rest*. It has nothing to do with Bellamy's industrial regimentation and mechanised shopping. Morris has no intention of introducing his reader to the progressive world which many of his Socialist comrades might favour. He is looking beyond it.

The story is presented as a dream, albeit an impossibly long one. This literary device, whose pedigree extends at least as far back as Bunyan's *The Pilgrim's Progress*, shows Morris's readers that they are not required to believe in Nowhere's potential reality, as Bellamy's are required to believe in the Nation. But he does invite them to take the vision seriously as something worth meditating upon; and it is.

Morris's narrator wakes from oblivion, or seems to wake, in his house by the Thames. When he goes outside, he finds everything altered. There are no factories, and the buildings are smaller. He meets people who are all good-looking and good-humoured and colourfully dressed, unlike Morris's sober-suited real-life contemporaries. A remark by one of them reveals that the year is later than 2003, but doesn't indicate how much later. This friendly acquaintance takes the narrator on a horse-drawn tour of London, now a wholly beautiful city. Commercialism has faded out, and the ugliness of commercial architecture has faded with it.

As in Bellamy, there is no such thing as money, but Morris's moneyless society is quite different. Cash has not been replaced by credit cards and elaborate accounting, it has really and truly vanished. People produce goods, not because they are paid or compelled to, but because they want to. The goods, attractive and skilfully crafted, are displayed as in Bellamy's sample-stores, but customers don't fill in order forms: they simply take what they need and no one takes more. Courtesy is universal, or nearly so.

Religion has disappeared: the narrator visits a church, but it has been turned into a community centre. Government has disappeared too: the Palace of Westminster, where Parliament met in the nineteenth century, now houses a storehouse of manure. Collective decisions, usually on local issues, are made by small groups. Education is a learn-as-you-please activity. Sexual partnerships are formed and dissolved by mutual consent. Women, however, are not emancipated. The narrator finds them youthful-looking and attractive, and flirts in a harmless way.

He accounts for his ignorance by posing as a visitor from a distant country. His new friends call him 'Guest' (Bellamy's narrator is 'West'). The device is awkward, and it is almost abandoned in a long conversation with an old man who tells him how 'the Change' happened, or, at least, how it got under way. Here Morris tries, sometimes perceptively, to sketch a credible future beginning from his own time. He imagines the working-class revolution as breaking out at long last in 1952, followed by two years of civil war, ending in victory for the workers and their sympathisers. The revolution is nothing like the French bloodbath; there is no liquidation of opponents. In any case, the main story is not about the revolution but about its remote consequences: the current year is 2100 or thereabouts, as we finally learn. There have been no more major upheavals. Society has evolved into its present sanity and balance.

Towards the book's end, Guest's friends take him on a leisurely boat trip up the Thames. They row through a peaceful countryside to a place where voluntary haymaking is going on, and visit Kelmscott, which is still there. At last, the dream vision dissolves in a church that has ceased to be a church. It is in fact the one close to the Manor, where Morris is buried.

It might seem easy to ridicule this future England as a fairyland constructed with no serious thought behind it; but that would be wrong. Even a casual reading should dispose of the allegation – though some critics have made it – that England has merely gone back to the fourteenth century, or a romanticised version of it. True, Morris's neo-medievalism is a pervasive presence, and, to some extent, an inspiration. But this imagined society with no monarch, no nobility, no Church, no castles, and no money is hardly a reconstitution of the Middle Ages.

What then? This happy state of affairs may seem, at first, to consist in everyone having a sense of responsibility and being nice to everyone else. Mastery has vanished in all its forms and fellowship has taken its place. A reader mindful of Joachim of Fiore might suggest that this is the Age of the Holy Spirit without the Holy Spirit. Ordinary living has not been transcended, but it has been raised to a higher quality. And, in reality, ideas from previous radical thinkers are interwoven, so subtly that their adoption is not noticed.

Robert Owen, for instance, is in the background, with his implication that an ideally ordered society might well condition its members to behave like this. Again, reflection on the economics of Nowhere will point to a source for some of its features. There is admittedly a gap here. All the work that is described is craft or agricultural work. England's population still seems considerable, and a reader may wonder how these millions are supported. Machinery exists, but is barely mentioned. Even when a power-driven boat goes by – called a force-barge – we are not told what propels it. However, human labour (though 'labour' is an inappropriate word) has one very specific quality.

All these people do work that they enjoy doing, and find fulfilment in. Society is so constituted that they can, and further incentives are unnecessary. No, we are not in fairyland: we are in Fourier-land. Nowhere has achieved his aim of making work loveable. There is none of his ingenious community planning, which is not in Morris's style. The narrator doesn't see boys revelling in garbage collection. But the affinity is plain, and it is all the plainer because Morris's people not only do work they enjoy, but are free to switch to other activities when they feel inclined. Fourier's 'passion papillonne' is provided for.

More important than any of this is the unobtrusive harmony with Marxism as developed in Morris's time. Critics have dismissed *News from Nowhere* as a failed prophecy because they have read it carelessly, and assumed that it is meant to portray the short-term result of the Revolution. Morris makes it lucidly clear that the perspective is much longer. One hundred and fifty years have passed. The Revolution is ancient history, and most people know very little about it. Society has attained this 'epoch of rest' by getting past the transitional stage of socialism, and it has all happened strictly on Marxist lines. Authority has withered away; the world of cash values and getting-and-spending has dissolved; and people don't receive according to the work they do, they receive according to their needs. Engels' golden age of true 'communism' has reappeared as predicted, on a higher level. Morris has reformulated the Joachimist quantum leap. The quantum leap in his 1952 Revolution is not portrayed as, in itself, the dawn of a transfigured society. Rather, it is a turning of the corner. He undoubtedly believed that once the corner was turned, progress towards the golden age would follow; however, he recognised that it would take a long time.

A friend once told me, before I read *News from Nowhere*, that it was 'the only *possible* Utopia'; and he was an old-style communist, who knew where his ideology was supposed to lead. Morris did not live to see what happened in Russia, where the revolutionary corner was turned in 1917, but the subsequent transitional phase froze into dictatorship and the promised sequel never materialised.

*

He was right to be distressed about *Looking Backward*. Besides selling prodigiously at home, it was widely translated, appearing in Russian, Bulgarian, and Arabic, among other languages. It even inspired a Nationalist Movement in America, devoted to its realisation. This petered out, but Bellamy's Utopia continued to attract some left-wingers well into the twentieth century.

After *News from Nowhere* Morris continued to write and lecture. He remained impenitently subversive, though with variations of emphasis. Engels accused him of speculating too much about abolishing government (which, of course, Marxist theory wouldn't allow just yet) and becoming a stooge of anarchists. That did not prevent him from being a popular speaker at the Hammersmith Socialist Society, where other well-known figures appeared on the platform, including Bernard Shaw and the miners' leader Keir Hardie.

When Tennyson died, Morris was spoken of as a possible new Poet Laureate. Predictably, he made it clear that he would refuse the honour, and by that time he would have been a politically impossible choice. His unavailability left a gap which remained open for several years. It was filled at last by the appointment of Alfred Austin, a safe conservative, who survives only in anthologies of bad verse.

In 1893 Morris acknowledged more explicitly that he had been wrong at first to talk about a sudden and speedy change. Late Victorian England was so far from being ready for it. But change could come in other ways. The following year he supported a parliamentary candidate, George Lansbury, who contested Walworth for the Social Democratic Federation. It was a wise endorsement. When the Labour Party was formed, Lansbury became an outstanding member, and in due course rose to its leadership. Morris died in 1896, having outlived Engels by a year. To Wells's criticism that he dwelt on an illuminated past, he could have replied by quoting from the great French socialist, Jean Jaurès: 'Take from the altars of the past the fire, not the ashes.'

DIFFUSION

10

Fabians and Non-Fabians

In 1884 a society was founded in London with vaguely uplifting aspirations. Soon, owing to an influx of outstanding recruits, its aspirations became more concrete. It was called the Fabian Society and it invented a British form of socialism. One might say that it invented *the* British form of socialism.

The Society's name was meant to make a point by recalling the Roman general Fabius, who resisted the invading Carthaginian leader Hannibal. He did not do so by fighting. Fabius avoided battle, manoeuvred endlessly, and wore the Carthaginians down until they were forced to leave Italy, and Rome could recover. In that spirit Fabian socialism rejected violence, class war, and revolution. Its socialism was gradual and constitutional. So, in due course, was the socialism of the old Labour Party which Fabian thinking did much to shape.

Under Fabianism, the State was to take over industries piecemeal, as might seem proper in the interests of better organisation and better conditions for the work force. Public utilities were to be owned and run by local authorities. Social insurance (as yet, no one spoke of a Welfare State) was to guarantee against hardship and the worst miseries of unemployment. These changes would come through fairly painless political action, simply because they would be seen to be desirable. Fabian ideas would 'permeate' society, and make converts who were in a position to implement them. And some would just happen without intervention, simply because economic logic and practical considerations made it inevitable.

Fabians, in fact, believed that modern society had an in-built trend towards collectivism, which had already gone some distance and could not be reversed. Politically conscious people had the job of helping it along, and making its effects as smooth and constructive as possible. On this basis socialism could, for the first time, become respectable. There would be no moment of transition, no equivalent of a revolution, but a time would come when you could look around and say that Britain had ceased to be individualistic and had become collective.

The Society's principal manifesto was a volume of *Fabian Essays* (1889) written by several of its members. The members best known in the early days were Sidney Webb, George Bernard Shaw, and Annie Besant. Webb carried out exhaustive researches into various aspects of society, and founded the London School of Economics. He married Beatrice Potter, whose contribution was also impressive. Shaw, tall and bearded, an Irishman and a vegetarian, was known as a music critic – not yet as a dramatist – and a witty public speaker. He debated with William Morris, and good-humouredly goaded him until he showed signs of losing his composure; they were very different, and Morris's loss of hope for an early revolution had not made him a gradualist. As for Annie Besant, Shaw, as a friend, had been instrumental in bringing her into the Society after her conversion to socialism. She had shown more courage than him on Bloody Sunday, and had organised a successful strike by women employed in the manufacture of matches. Her own Fabian essay argued for decentralisation. Publicly owned enterprises should be run as far as possible by municipalities and co-operatives.

The Fabians believed in progress. They believed in the British Empire, then approaching its zenith. But they seldom concerned themselves with the Empire's subject populations, which were not, in their sense, progressive, or anywhere near to being ready for self-government.

*

One evening in 1888, a Fabian audience assembled to hear a guest lecturer. By the time he sat down, most of them were furious. He had said something that did not suit them at all.

His name was Edward Carpenter. He was a former clergyman and a protester against established society, but not in a style with much appeal for anyone who talked about progress. His lecture encapsulated the first of several papers, grouped under the provocative title *Civilisation: its Cause and Cure*. This one was published soon afterwards, and the others followed.

Carpenter was an admirer of Morris, and a supporter of the Arts and Crafts movement. Before his Fabian collision, he did something that Morris never did: he went to America. There he heard of Henry David Thoreau, who had become famous by living in a hermitage in a wood and writing about it. Carpenter also made the acquaintance of Walt Whitman. The outspoken old poet of *Leaves of Grass* had been stirring up readers in England for a long time. Tennyson spoke of him – rather acutely – as 'a great big something', and corresponded with him admiringly. Swinburne subjected him to adulation followed by vilification. But Carpenter was interested in Whitman's outlook and ideas. His attention was caught by two lines in the poet's 'Song of Myself':

> The friendly and flowing savage, who is he?
> Is he waiting for civilisation, or past it and mastering it?
>
> (36: 976–77)

Whitman was enthusiastic for America as it actually was, and here the 'savage' seems to be a prototype for backwoodsmen in various parts of the country, of whom he thought highly. Carpenter, however, took the lines in isolation and pursued the thought along his own path. Might it be possible to cure the ills of civilisation, not by trying to reform it or even revolutionise it, but by getting past it like Whitman's savage and recovering a goodness which it had lost?

For Carpenter, civilisation is a disease which many nations have contracted and from which none have recovered. Like Lewis Morgan and Engels, he believes in an early primitive communism. He doesn't call it that, but he means much the same thing: a long-ago golden age which the march of civilisation has effaced.

What are civilisation's 'plus' points, in the eyes of those who favour it? Advances in medicine and sanitation are obvious candidates. But, Carpenter argues, the mere absence of sickness is not health. He cites the testimony of early explorers, such as Captain Cook, as proving that Polynesians and New Zealanders were healthy before they were colonised and drawn into civilisation's orbit. Health is 'wholeness'; but western medical science is not about that, it is about disease. Of course the Polynesians and other peoples succumbed tragically to the white man's plagues when contact was established. But Carpenter, a latter-day Rousseau, has idyllic notions of what the Noble Savages were like before, and he extrapolates freely.

He enumerates three things that society needs in order to be healthy. First, it should be closer to nature. Second, science should be not purely 'of the brain', but part of actual life. Finally, morality should express 'the vital and organic unity of man with his fellows'.

Carpenter's cure for civilisation is another echo of Blake's 'fall into division and resurrection to unity'. It doesn't involve Luddite machine-smashing or anything like that; it is more about living differently. Clothing should be simpler and less restrictive. Carpenter made sandals himself, and popularised them. In the western world, sandal-wearing (outside religious orders) is one of his lasting legacies. Closeness to nature does not imply naturism, in the sense of wearing no clothes at all, but rather just wearing less, so that the body can commune with the sun – another of his legacies. He advocates vegetarianism, but not dogmatically. Meat may have its uses for special purposes, but, in general, the best diet consists mainly of fruit and nuts. Milk, butter, cheese and berries are acceptable, so long as there is no injury to living creatures.

In Carpenter's post-civilisation Utopia, people are healthy and beautiful and equal, with no accumulation of private wealth. Rules of conduct are few. Situational ethics govern society, taking the place of moral codes. All adults work at whatever they like working at. Here Carpenter is echoing Fourier, who also denounced civilisation, and he might seem to be echoing Morris too; but in fact he was annoying the Fabians with his lectures and articles before the publication of *News from Nowhere*.

It is none too clear how the abolition of civilisation is going to happen, or why its abolition should bring such happy results. Carpenter has no political agenda. He says democracy doesn't exist at present, and true democracy has yet to come, presumably after the overthrow of civilisation, not as a means to that end. The great change will have to be in minds and hearts, in the attainment of a 'higher order of consciousness'. Once civilisation has been rejected, existing religions will disappear, but the 'old Nature religion' will revive. When it does, interestingly, he expects nature-worship to bring back goddess-worship. Carpenter names Astarte, Diana, Isis. He also names the Virgin Mary, without explaining how Mary is to be worshipped if the ecclesiastical system in which she figures has vanished.

*

Carpenter's programme ruled him out of regular politics. However, he did go to Trafalgar Square on Bloody Sunday, and he wrote a rousing poem beginning 'England arise', which was set to music as a left-wing marching song; Shaw brought it into a play, *On the Rocks*. But Carpenter had the largest share in fomenting an upper-middle-class dissidence that was astir through the closing years of the nineteenth century, sometimes paralleling socialism, but never blending with it.

This was the time when the slogan 'The Simple Life' came into its own, drawing a contrast with the usual kind. It does not cover all the manifestations of dissidence, but it covers several. The most conspicuous was vegetarianism. The foundations had been laid during the 1880s. The chief advocate was Henry Stephens Salt, an authority on Shelley. Salt laid new stress on this neglected aspect of the poet's passion for reform. In a pamphlet, *A Plea for Vegetarianism*, Salt condemned the raising of animals for their flesh as cruel, degrading, and unhealthy; human beings, he claimed, are more akin to fruit-eating apes than to carnivores. He fitted his teaching about food reform into a wider context of social reform in general. As his pamphlet became well known in the atmosphere he had created, he kept open house at a vegetarian restaurant in London, where like-minded people gathered for discussion and tea-parties.

Another contributor to the fashion was Anna Kingsford, a doctor, who wrote *The Perfect Way in Diet* and carried the same thinking to extremes. 'Man,' she declared, 'is the master of the world... and working with God and Nature, he may reconvert it into Paradise.' T. R. Allinson, another doctor, enlarged vegetarianism into a whole way of life, with ideological baths and exercise and fresh air.

Simple-life thinking, in Carpenter, had included notions about clothing, and some of them were taken up. His home-made sandals began to find their way on to feet. Bicycles were becoming increasingly popular, and as women in long skirts were apt to be impeded, queries were raised about the feasibility of shorter ones and a 'rational' costume.

On sexual issues the dissidents differed among themselves, except in agreeing that respectable Victorian wedlock, blighted by money and male ascendancy, was wrong. Some elected for free love or at least Shelleyan emancipation; some wanted a new cult of celibacy and restraint; some talked about birth control. As for religion, there were atheists who rejected it, and others who groped behind the churches for a 'real teaching of Christ'. Here too there was a common enemy, established Christianity.

Besides Shelley, the dissidents read Ruskin – for his attacks on capitalistic society, rather than for his art criticism. They also read Tolstoy – not so much for his novels as for his later puritanical musings, when he condemned civilisation, in his own way, more vehemently even than Carpenter, and reduced Christianity to absolute pacifism.

Opinions overlapped, and some of the dissidents even joined the Fabian Society in its lower echelons, encouraged by the vegetarianism of Bernard Shaw. However, the Fabian Society remained resolutely itself. G. K. Chesterton's brother Cecil joined it because Fabianism allowed him to be a socialist strictly and solely, not entangled with vegetarians, freethinkers, or any others whom he regarded as cranks.

One who did drift into the dissident milieu via the Central Vegetarian Restaurant in Farringdon Street was no crank. Gandhi – Mohandas Karamchand Gandhi, still far from Mahatmaship – was, from 1888 to 1891, an insignificant law student in London. Hindu dietary laws, in a country that did not recognise them, had condemned him to very dull meals. At last he discovered the restaurant.† Besides leaving the table satisfied for the first time, he

† Sherlock Holmes passed this restaurant (*The Red-Headed League*). It was lunch-time, but Holmes and Watson went somewhere else to eat. If they had gone in, what would Holmes have deduced about the Indian student he might have noticed at one of the tables?

found Salt's *Plea for Vegetarianism* in a display case, and bought it. He was profoundly impressed by the way in which Salt offered a reasoned argument for what Hinduism merely laid down as dogma. He met Salt and members of his circle, and picked up a little of their recommended reading – Shelley, Ruskin, Tolstoy. These authors, even skimmed or at second hand (he read them properly later), gave him new ideas about social justice and non-violence which were to play an important role in his thinking when he began to develop neglected features of his own Hinduism, with momentous results. While remaining entirely and loyally Indian, he found support and clarification in what he learned from Europeans.

In January 1891 Charles Bradlaugh, the champion of secularism and the friend of India, died. Gandhi was among the numerous London Indians who attended their well-wisher's funeral in Woking. Gandhi was an Indian learning from western dissidents, but some of the dissidents were learning from India. Sir Edwin Arnold's narrative poem *The Light of Asia*, telling the story of Buddha, had found many readers besides Annie Besant. Arnold also translated – or rather paraphrased – the principal Hindu sacred text, the *Bhagavad Gita* or Song of the Blessed Lord, that is, Krishna. His writings were familiar to the seekers and reformers whom Gandhi met. Anna Kingsford, the author of *The Perfect Way in Diet*, and Carpenter himself, studied the *Gita*.

However, the interest aroused by Arnold's work was also exploited by a grotesquely different person, whose success was symptomatic of a widespread longing for a religion – or an acceptable substitute for religion – to replace Christianity. She was responsible, indirectly, for a phenomenon that extended far into the twentieth century. Whether it counts as another form of Offbeat Radicalism is a matter of opinion. It certainly began with a Fabian's rejection of Fabianism; and the ex-Fabian, in effect, revived the vision of Joachim of Fiore, prophesying a non-

Christian equivalent of his Age of the Holy Spirit. Morris had already imagined this in *News from Nowhere*, but on the assumption that religion would vanish altogether. The new prophecy would be something else again.

*

The central figure at the origin of this development was Helena Petrovna Blavatsky: 'Madame Blavatsky' or 'HPB', the founder of Theosophy. The word 'Theosophy', meaning divine wisdom, had a perfectly legitimate pedigree, but in the late 1880s and 90s it stood for a specific movement, of which she was the self-appointed high priestess. This was the movement that Annie Besant had heard about at a distance, and puzzled over, hoping that it would not seduce freethinkers.

Born in 1831, Madame Blavatsky was a ponderous, blue-eyed, cigarette-smoking Russian. She combined chaotic erudition with charlatanism. According to her own story she visited Tibet, then an isolated and mysterious country, and learned occult wisdom from a guru living in a cave. She also studied ancient writings concealed from outsiders. In fact, she probably never went to Tibet, but she did go to New York. A contemporary American vogue for spiritualism left her unmoved; but she made an exception for one spiritualist, a lawyer named Henry Steel Olcott. In 1875, with a few like-minded friends, the pair launched the Theosophical Society.

Madame Blavatsky was the dominant partner. To reach a wider public she wrote *Isis Unveiled*, a strange book mingling mythology, alleged esoteric lore, and argumentation. Among much else it started the modern interest in the supposed lost continent of Atlantis. Atlantis's major populariser was the amateur prehistorian Ignatius Donnelly, but Madame Blavatsky, to do her justice, came first.

Her Society's aims were proclaimed as follows:

1. To form a nucleus of a universal brotherhood of humanity, without distinction of race, creed, sex, caste or colour.

2. To study comparative religion, philosophy and science.
3. To investigate the unexplained laws of nature and the psychical powers latent in man.

Theosophy had a motto: 'There is no religion higher than truth'. All systems of belief were regarded as valid within their own terms of reference, imperfectly expressing the same deeper reality. Thus far it all sounded enlightened and comprehensive enough to exert a powerful appeal, in the atmosphere of the late nineteenth century. But it had a sub-agenda that gave it an extra allure for all who had come under the influence of secularism, like Annie Besant. Madame Blavatsky anathematised Christianity as a pack of lies. Though all religions were equal, some, to adapt Orwell's phrase, were less equal than others.

Theosophy also had a bias on the positive side, which was destined to be crucial, and to open up a fresh vista for its adherents. Hinduism seemed to say much of what Blavatsky was saying – about reincarnation, for instance – and she was drawn towards a rapprochement with it, a rapprochement that would help her to find a footing on ground prepared by authors like Edwin Arnold.

Under foreign rule, India's majority religion had long been at a low ebb, practised as ever, but reduced to little more than ritual and formality. Recently, however, a learned authority on its scriptures, Dayananda Saraswati, had formed an organisation aimed at restoring essential Hinduism, free from the corruptions and superstitions that had crept in over the centuries. Interested, Madame Blavatsky and Henry Olcott sailed from New York and arrived in India in February 1879.

At first the Hindu reformers made them welcome. Indians could be pleased that westerners were treating their culture with respect, and wanting to learn from them. The honeymoon, alas, was brief. Dayananda decided that he could not work with the Theosophists, and they were presented with a bill for their own entertainment. However, the Society acquired a seaside estate at Adyar, a suburb of Madras, which became its headquarters.

Madame Blavatsky was building up a personality cult centred on herself. In her name Theosophy grew more bizarre, yet, paradoxically, more attractive. She claimed that she was in touch with a hierarchy of superior beings known as 'Masters' or 'Mahatmas', the latter term meaning 'great soul'. (In its later application to Gandhi, it had a different meaning.) Two who took a special interest in the Society were Kuthumi, 'the Master KH', and Morya, 'the Master M'. They communicated with her telepathically and sometimes in writing. Their letters did not normally come through the post: they were precipitated, falling out of nowhere. At Adyar she excited her disciples with miracles – rather feeble ones, as H. G. Wells presently remarked – and apparitions of the Masters.

Pseudo-magic was not Madame Blavatsky's strong suit. The letters were suspect in the last degree, and the two Masters were mythified versions of identifiable Indians. A barrage of accusations charged her with using not only forged writings but trick doors and cabinets, even dummies. In 1885 she left India and settled in London. She survived the crisis, and so did Theosophy. Future Indian leaders, such as Motilal Nehru, the father of India's first prime minister, were to take an interest in it. Her London circle included W. B. Yeats, who described her as 'a sort of old Irish peasant woman with an air of humour and audacious power'.

In 1888, after a long literary gestation, she produced her magnum opus, *The Secret Doctrine*. Theosophy was beginning to gain ground, as part of the general ferment of the time. The book is about – well, what it is about? It embraces cosmic law, reincarnation, the nature of life, and other portentous matters. The custodians of the Secret Doctrine are Masters of Wisdom who live in remote retreats or outside the material world, and dole out portions of the doctrine to humanity. All religions, even

Christianity, have been based on it. Myths contain occult 'keys' that unlock hidden meanings, and initiates have been taught some of the keys. The Renaissance polymath Paracelsus was one, and so, of course, was Madame Blavatsky.

The Secret Doctrine is prolix, pretentious, muddled, and very hard going. A great deal of it can be dismissed, on grounds of plagiarism or fabrication, or, indeed, sheer incomprehensibility; but not quite all. Madame Blavatsky had her insights. In her views on mythology, for instance, she was ahead of the fashionable scholarship of her time, stressing historical factors which scholars tended to ignore. And Theosophy, as expounded here and elsewhere, had aspects that could appeal to contemporary minds. Its conception of evolution had a spiritual dimension lacking in Darwinism. It proposed that the actions and thoughts of individuals in this life determine what they will be in the next. As the tendency, on the whole, is progressive, human beings are passing through many lives that move generally upwards, on the way to greater enlightenment, higher morality, and ultimate liberation, in union with the Absolute.

Theosophy had a special appeal for troubled Christians and former Christians. It allowed new developments. Christianity did not: its long-awaited Christ had already come, and now nothing more would happen until he returned at the end of the world. Joachim's prophecy of the third age was almost unknown. As the Secular Society had revealed, many saw Christianity as small, cramped, mean-spirited. Theosophy not only rejected it in its approved forms, but flung open the door to Hinduism, and Hinduism envisaged immense cosmic epochs that contrasted sharply with the few thousand years the Bible allowed, if you took it at face value. This was a potent asset when science was manifestly favouring the scale of Hindu chronology rather than the biblical.

Theosophy gave humanity a history with a vast duration. It

told of a succession of 'root-races' and sub-races, some of the earliest not at all like present-day humans, and some living in long-vanished homelands such as Atlantis. This panorama had possibilities for science fiction and fantasy, and imaginative writers were to make use of it. Madame Blavatsky was again ahead of her time in spreading her humans and pre-humans over millions of years. However, only convinced Theosophists could believe in the system as a whole. For that reason among others, the hoped-for universal brotherhood was never likely to be much more than a network of devotees. Still, Blavatsky's Society did expand after her time, with an eventual membership of about forty thousand, scattered through Europe, the United States, India and Australia.

When *The Secret Doctrine* was published, in two volumes, she was ill and prematurely ageing. But the book brought her a prodigious success. A review copy was sent to a leading newspaper, the *Pall Mall Gazette*. Its enterprising editor, W. T. Stead, invited Annie Besant to write the review. Theosophy was sufficiently in the news to justify treatment by a celebrity. Stead could not understand what Madame Blavatsky was driving at, but he hoped Annie could.

Against all rational probability, *The Secret Doctrine* bowled her over. In March 1889 she visited the author, who said, 'Oh, my dear Mrs Besant, if you could only come among us!' Meeting the author of an admired book can be a disappointment, but in this case it was not. Annie quickly succumbed. After her years of secularism and socialism, she was in need of something spiritually positive. Not only was Theosophy positive, it was positive without pretending to rehabilitate the Christianity she detested. Madame Blavatsky boldly showed her an account of the accusations of fraud in India; Annie was easily persuaded that the account itself was fraudulent. She joined the Theosophical Society, and began writing and speaking in support of it.

This was Annie's second great transition. Apparently she thought she could still remain in both the National Secular Society and the Fabian Society, at least nominally. Bradlaugh, in one of his last authoritative pronouncements, annihilated the former notion, all the more firmly and even sadly because she had again failed to keep him informed. Among the Fabians, Shaw was totally bewildered, and the others concurred if less emphatically. Annie resigned from both organisations, giving up secularism and socialism together.

Shaw decided that the key to her character was psychological. She was a born actress with a wonderful voice. She stepped into different roles and immersed herself in each. The constant and consistent thing was that she was always aspiring to be a sort of priestess. Shaw's assessment was at least partly true, and her second transition led to her becoming a priestess indeed.

*

The inconspicuous Gandhi was no celebrity, but he too came under pressure. Two brothers[†], Theosophists both, introduced him to Edwin Arnold's paraphrase of the *Gita*. Expecting illuminating comments from a real Hindu, they were disillusioned to learn that he had never read it in any form. However, they persuaded him to study Blavatsky and Besant, and took him to meet both women. He respectfully declined to commit himself to the Society, beyond an associate membership, and soon resigned from that. Later in life, he derided Theosophy as humbug. Later still, with pleasant memories of friends, he said he had found 'Hinduism at its best' in that setting – but no more.

As for Annie, since Theosophy attracted few people of comparable calibre, she stood out among her new colleagues. She soon learned everything further that she needed to learn, and was enrolled in Theosophy's Esoteric Section, an inner ring that

† Unnamed, in Gandhi's account of the incident.

included Yeats. Madame Blavatsky died in 1891. Some of her associates had suspected that she was a man in disguise, but it finally became clear that she was not. Her co-founder Henry Olcott hung on to the Society's presidency through fifteen years of declining health. At last, on the orders (so he said) of the Masters M and KH, he appointed Annie as his successor. Not all the members trusted the revelation, or approved the choice, but when he died in February 1907 she was elected president, and soon began to prepare for an astonishing step.

11

Joachimism Re-Echoing

During the early decades of the twentieth century, the Fabians pressed on with the gradual evolution of their brand of socialism, and began to mould the ideas of the rising Labour Party. Yet, of the five Fabians who had been most widely publicised, only two were firmly and consistently gradualist. Sidney and Beatrice Webb did not waver. The three others did. The word 'waver', in fact, came to be an understatement. In one way and another, all three proved the tenacity of Joachim's way of thinking. All three conceived a quantum leap: one of them fictionally, one speculatively, and one prophetically.

*

H. G. Wells was a late-comer to the Society. He joined it in 1903 with an established fame as an author of scientific romances. He was also beginning to produce fiction that was more orthodox, and more relevant to Fabian concerns. In retrospect, with knowledge of Wells's later career, it is easy to think of him as an optimistic Utopian, voicing grandiose hopes of social emancipation, technological advance, and world unity; but in fact the optimistic utopianism was a development. In his earliest writing his projections of the future were sombre. His joining a society that was supposed to be dedicated to feasible progress was entirely logical.

His first important story, *The Time Machine*, was thoroughly pessimistic. It came about almost by accident. Having written a popular philosophical article for the *Fortnightly Review*, he followed it up with a discussion of time as a fourth dimension. The editor, Frank Harris of dubious memory, rejected it with ridicule. Wells recast the main idea in fictional form. His Time Traveller (not named) explains his theory to some sceptical guests. He tells them that he has made a machine for actually travelling in time – and proceeds to use it. In a vivid passage, Wells imagines what rushing into the future would be like, and brings the machine to a bumpy halt in the year 802,701.

The picture of society in that remote future is depressing. Wells is making a wry comment on the evils of his own day – evils that socialists deplored, and proposed to cure. The gap between the Haves and the Have-nots, the rich and the poor, has never narrowed, and humanity has split into two distinct species. The descendants of the Haves – the leisure class – are the Eloi, a race of small, pretty, vacuous people, leading a futile existence on the bounty of nature. The descendants of the Have-nots – the workers – are the Morlocks, pallid beings who live underground, and emerge on dark nights to carry off Eloi and eat them. (In another comparatively early story, *When the Sleeper Wakes*, Wells imagines a much nearer future, in a commercial and technocratic metropolis with a ruling oligarchy and a stultified populace: the future is none too cheerful here either.)

As a Fabian recruit, temporarily hopeful, Wells wrote a little about the potentialities of socialism. But he never took kindly to the Fabians' gradualist approach. He thought they would only be effective if they took their programme more seriously, and became an active revolutionary elite, rather as the Communist Party did in

Russia. He had the outlandish notion of calling his hypothetical leaders 'Samuraï'. This was not acceptable to the Fabians. When he addressed a meeting about his ideas, Bernard Shaw scored off him in the discussion and swung the majority against him. In 1908, he left the Society.

He had already been turning away from gradualism in 1906, as his writings showed. Another novel, *In the Days of the Comet*, presents a quantum leap in a science-fiction form, not as something that might actually happen, but as an image of something that ought to.

A prologue introduces an elderly man in a tower room, writing. The time is future, but not very far off. He is working on a personal history of 'the Change' – Wells adopts that word from Morris – and his first-person narrative constitutes the novel. He begins early in the twentieth century with himself at the age of twenty-one, a fairly ordinary youth in an unlovely industrial town. A friend with an interest in astronomy draws his attention to a new comet, still far away, but on course to come close to Earth and even collide. He is not interested himself; he is more concerned – much more, as the plot develops – with a frustrated love. In an eventual frenzy of jealousy, he plans to kill his rival. Meanwhile, in the greater world, society's own madness is pushing Britain into war.

By this time the comet is near, a vast green portent in the night sky, and is expected to hit Earth. Before the narrator has perpetrated his crime, it does so, engulfing the planet in green vapours which cause all human beings to lose consciousness. When they wake, the vapours have dispersed, and everything is subtly different. Soon it appears that the comet has worked a psychological transformation. People everywhere have seen through their illusions and prejudices, their hates and obsessions, and entered a kind of spiritual sunlight, ready to make a fresh start. Consciously or otherwise, Wells is inventing a modern version of Shelley's benign apocalypse in *Prometheus Unbound*: when Jupiter has fallen, his earthly manifestations have disappeared, the 'painted veil' of pseudo-reality no longer deceives, and a liberated world becomes what it is meant to be.

In the Days of the Comet ends with an epilogue that gives a glimpse of a 'dreamland city' in the post-comet era, 'its galleries and open spaces, its trees of golden fruit and crystal waters, its music and rejoicing, love and beauty without ceasing flowing through its varied and intricate streets'; and its people, exalted themselves, and changed 'as a woman is changed in the eyes of her lover'. Fabian gradualism could hardly be expected to have that result.

Possibly encouraged by his own vision, Wells moved on into his more hopeful phase. It was still un-Fabian, but it was not apocalyptic either. He thought he had a special gift for detecting tendencies. The all-too-memorable phrase 'the war to end war' originated with Wells: the war that was going to do it was the one that began in 1914. He sustained his optimism, more or less, until near the end of his life, but lapsed finally into despair because of the Second World War and the atomic bomb; he wrote *Mind at the End of Its Tether*.

Bernard Shaw remained a Fabian socialist in his own way, but still deviated, and along essentially the same line. He lectured tirelessly; wrote brilliant and successful plays, some of them on serious topics; and arrived at his version of a necessary leap. He decided that the world would never make any real progress until human life was greatly prolonged, getting rid of the restrictions of ageing and imminent death. At present, he said, people may often know what is good, but they don't live long enough to find out how to make it happen. Shaw did not picture the change as a gradual consequence of medical advances or any other comprehensible cause. If it happened at all, it would begin quite suddenly and with no visible reason, as a sort of mutation. A few people would begin, unobtrusively, to live for his ideal period of three hundred years, and the number of 'long-livers' would increase until they were dominant.

Shaw believed in evolution, but not as a purely hit-or-miss Darwinian process. Species could change, he claimed, because of a deep-seated desire or need for change. If the need for long life was sufficiently implanted, long life would become a reality. Annexing phrases from the French philosopher Henri Bergson, he talked of 'Creative Evolution' and a 'Life Force' overriding individual wills. This was not simply a Shavian quirk. Bergsonism in various aspects was weaving spells with many contemporaries, among them Marcel Proust. However, Shaw was unique in his application of it.

All this went into a cycle of five plays under the title *Back to Methuselah*, completed in 1920, and published with one of Shaw's colossal prefaces. He described it as a 'Metabiological Pentateuch'. The first play, 'In the Beginning', opens with a scene in the Garden of Eden. Adam and Eve discuss mortality, with prompting from the Serpent. They are seen again many years later. They have descendants whose prospects are uncertain; the Life Force is experimenting.

The next play is 'The Gospel of the Brothers Barnabas'. This is set in the aftermath of the First World War. One of the two brothers, Conrad, is a biologist; the other, Franklyn, is an ex-clergyman. Together they have arrived at the Shavian vision of longevity. Two politicians – perceptive caricatures of two real ones, Asquith and Lloyd George – come to visit the Barnabases, and form the impression that they have discovered a life-prolonging elixir. All they can think of is that it might be exploited politically: hence the slogan 'Back to Methuselah'. When they learn that there is no elixir, their interest flags. In a key speech, Conrad, the biologist, voices Shaw's conception of the quantum leap:

> Nature always proceeds by jumps. She may spend twenty thousand years making up her mind to jump; but

> when she makes it up at last, the jump is big enough to take us into a new age.

The third play is entitled 'The Thing Happens'. The date is 2170. Politicians reappear, and are shocked to find that the thing *has* happened. A man and a woman, minor characters in the previous play, are still living and in good condition. The man is 283 years old and has become Archbishop of Canterbury. The woman, at 274, is a minister in the government. Dreadful prospects open up. What if they marry and produce long-lived offspring? What if there are other long-livers, undiscovered so far, who may get together and organise? The play ends on a note of consternation.

Next comes 'Tragedy of an Elderly Gentleman', set in the year 3000. War has greatly reduced the world's population. Ireland has a large community of long-lived people, classified by age as primaries, secondaries and tertiaries. Short-livers revere them, and travel a long way to consult them, as custodians of oracular wisdom. A vital decision is clearly going to be taken: some of the long-livers think they should confine themselves to the British Isles, others favour spreading out through the world. The 'elderly gentleman' of the title is a short-liver who can adapt to neither milieu, and sinks into a fatal 'discouragement', which is now the chronic affliction of short-lived people. After talking with him, one of the long-livers is inclined to think there shouldn't be any short-lived at all. The new breed of humans should replace the old entirely.

The last play, 'As Far as Thought Can Reach', is dated 30,000 years ahead. Only long-lived people exist, and apparently not many of them. They control biological processes and can take any shape they want. Humans are hatched from eggs and resemble sixteen-year-olds in our own time. After four years of 'infancy' devoted to art, sport and emotional delights, they put such matters behind them and grow up quickly. The mature figures of this world are the Ancients, living a purely intellectual life. They have no hair, no emotions and no sex, though they are still anatomically male and female.

If the Ancients are the best that the Life Force can offer after so many years of experimentation, the prospect does not seem very bright. Shaw, however, thinks it is, and indicates that there are more developments to come.

Back to Methuselah was staged in New York, but was never a commercial success. In book form, with its enormous preface, it sold well. It made Shaw's essential point, that short-lived humanity must stagnate or self-destruct, unless the Life Force pitches it forward into a fundamental expansion. He admitted, however, that in the last two plays he had set himself an impossible task. As a short-liver himself (he lived to be ninety-four, but not 300) he could not really imagine what long-livers would be like.

*

Another Fabian made a comparable turn in a non-Fabian direction, and surpassed the purely imaginative flights of Wells and Shaw.

Though Annie Besant left the Society when she embraced Theosophy, activities of a more or less Fabian kind went on. They went on, however, in India, which Theosophy had made an adopted country for her. She gave powerful support to Indian higher education, and when the movement for Indian self-rule began to stir, she supported that too. The Indian National Congress elected her to its presidency, an amazing honour for an English woman. Later, the leadership of Gandhi, no longer the timid student she had met in London, reduced her importance; but she remained loyal to the cause.

It was outside politics that she proclaimed a quantum leap of her own, in intention and expectation a real one, and very big indeed. Religious in character, it still had a certain appropriateness to her earlier secular career, and to her alliance with the pro-Indian Bradlaugh. An Indian revelation was to supersede Christianity, she announced; an Indian Messiah was to arise as a successor to Christ.

When Annie became President of the Theosophical Society, she was sixty years old, full of ideas and energy, and confident of approval on the higher spiritual planes. She managed to hold the movement together with its founders gone. Its destiny, she believed, was to do more than mark time. It was called to open the way for a world-transforming event. At first she did not know what this was, but Hinduism, predictably, supplied a hint. The *Bhagavad Gita* tells of divine intervention at critical junctures in history. Annie combined this theme with the Messianic traditions of Jews and Christians. Theosophy's pantheon included a being known as the World Teacher, who occasionally took control of a mortal, and acted through that 'vehicle' to enlighten humanity. Buddha and Christ were manifestations. Soon, Annie predicted, he would be manifested again, restoring truths which Christians had falsified, and going beyond. It might not be necessary to wait for an actual birth; the Teacher's new human vehicle might be living already, to be taken over when suitably prepared. Theosophists would have the task and the honour of preparing. In 1908 she began to publicise this prophecy, and claimed to have been encouraged by a revelation.

Now, however, a figure out of her past was looming ever larger, and his impact on her hopes would be crucial. Charles Webster Leadbeater was a former clergyman, born in 1854, who had listened to Annie's Secular preaching at a time when he was uneasy about his own clerical calling. Large and copiously bearded, with an overwhelming physical presence, he spun yarns about adventures in the Brazilian forests, and academic achievements, that were totally unsupported by evidence. Tamely employed as a Hampshire curate, he was well known locally for organising children's activities, a reputation that would later raise questions.

Leadbeater joined the Theosophical Society in 1883. Oscar Wilde was present at the ceremony. Madame Blavatsky visited London, and made disparaging remarks about clergymen, but accepted that a converted curate was a fairly prestigious catch. Leadbeater resigned his post in the Church and accompanied her when she returned to India. He stayed at the Society's Adyar headquarters for several months, believed in the Masters more and more confidently, became a channel of communication with them, and wrote articles that made him known among Theosophists.

From 1895 on, in England, Annie Besant treated him as a valued collaborator. He taught her a pseudo-science of his own invention called occult chemistry, and she closed her mind to rumours about his sexual proclivities. Early in 1909, when she was in the full flood of prophecy about the World Teacher, they agreed on a candidate for the role of his human vehicle. The Teacher, in his own good time, would take control of an eleven-year-old American boy named Hubert van Hook, the son of a rich Chicago Theosophist. Leadbeater praised Hubert's aura, though he may have had designs on the boy that were not purely spiritual. Mrs van Hook brought her son to India, expecting to see him launched on his Messianic career. But when she arrived she was told that a mistake had been made. Hubert wasn't the Messiah. Someone else was.

At this point, it would be easy to dismiss the whole business as absurd. Yet it is just now that it becomes seriously interesting, for a reason that would only become apparent many years later.

The true light had illuminated Leadbeater as far back as the spring of 1909; the message had not got through to Chicago, if indeed it was ever sent. The Theosophists' Adyar estate bordered on the sea, and male residents used to go to the beach and swim. One evening the beach party included a thirteen-year-old, Jiddu Krishnamurti, the son of a Brahmin Theosophist who lived at Adyar with the rest of his family. Krishnamurti did not swim, but watched his brother take to the water, then sat on the sand in a meditative silence, his large eyes staring into the distance.

He looked frail and undistinguished. Around him, however, Leadbeater saw an aura brighter than Hubert's, and decided that this time he had got it right. Krishnamurti would be the World Teacher's vehicle. Talks were initiated with that in view. The boy was religiously inclined, but with no settled ideas. Leadbeater was glad to see his mind as a virtual void that Theosophical teachings could fill. Annie met him and approved.

Leadbeater explored Krishnamurti's past by what might now be called hypnotic regression, and published his findings. In January 1910 he locked the two of them together in Annie's bedroom at Adyar, and conducted his pupil through a series of trance experiences. They met some of the Masters, and, climactically, the head of the occult hierarchy, the 'King of the World'. This astral encounter was said to have happened in Shambhala, a point of contact between Theosophy and authentic mythology. It may once have been a literal sacred place in the Altai Mountains. In Tibetan Buddhism it becomes a vaguely located spiritual power-centre that will some day have world importance. Shambhalic lore fascinated the Russian artist and anthropologist Nicholas Roerich, who supplied background material for Stravinsky's *Rite of Spring*. Theosophists, however, detached it from its real roots and planted it in the Gobi Desert as an invisible, impalpable meeting-place of the Masters and the King of the World.

After these experiments, Krishnamurti stepped forth from the revelatory bedroom with an air of spiritual intensity. Even his relatives were impressed. So were several outsiders who met him about this time; among them, Professor E. A. Wodehouse, a brother of P. G. Wodehouse (the future creator of Jeeves was not, however, drawn to Theosophy).

Annie continued to approve. She had astral contacts herself, and the King of the World gave her advice and encouragement. She adopted Krishnamurti legally after prolonged trouble with his father. Within the Society's framework she formed a new organisation, the Order of the Star in the East (OSE for short), to prepare for his epiphany as World Teacher. Many Theosophists looked askance at the growing personality cult. The educational pioneer Rudolf Steiner, who was then head of the German section, broke away and launched his own system, Anthroposophy. Undaunted by the protests, Annie brought her protégé to England, where he had his hair cut and failed to pass the entrance examinations for London University. As he matured, he made his mark in other quarters. One memorable conquest was Lady Emily Lutyens, the wife of the architect Edwin Lutyens, who designed the government buildings in New Delhi. She became the OSE's chief representative in England. She also gave up sex, with the result that her husband always resented Theosophy, Krishnamurti, and Annie Besant.

Krishnamurti's principal sponsors were not, of course, monomaniacs. While the World Teacher project was taking shape, Annie pursued her political activities on behalf of India. She never drifted off into mere otherworldliness, or lost sight of radical issues, though she favoured constitutional methods rather than the direct action of Gandhi. As for Leadbeater, he went to Australia and reverted to Christianity – a Theosophical Christianity that would have appalled Madame Blavatsky. Having received priestly ordination by a somewhat devious process – through the breakaway 'Old Catholic' group – he founded the Liberal Catholic Church, headed by himself as its chief bishop, with showy rituals and a very small membership. He reaffirmed his loyalty to the OSE by explaining that his church would give it support in ways not open to other bodies. Few were convinced. Further, he continued to be beset by accusations of sexual misconduct. He had assembled a group of boys – even some girls too – and (it was said) expounded a kind of mystical masturbation that was alleged to increase psychic energy. Hubert van Hook, the victim of his false start, reappeared and corroborated some of the scandal.

The faithful dismissed the charges, and Leadbeater was never convicted of breaking any law. But more Theosophists were echoing Steiner's complaint that the Order of the Star in the East was false to the Theosophy they knew, and had taken on a life of its own. There was even a 'Back to Blavatsky' movement. Annie viewed such disquiet with equanimity. The Society was not meant to sit motionless on its inheritance, like a Christian sect clinging to 'the Faith once delivered to the Saints'. It was to be an instrument of change, with the OSE as vanguard. It would continue to prepare for the Teacher and the new order he would inaugurate.

In the disillusionment following the First World War, her vision had a considerable appeal. The nature of the new order was not defined – after all, it would have been presumptuous to anticipate the Teacher's programme – but hints were dropped. It would be international, keeping peace better than the incomplete League of Nations which the War's victors had created. It would be anti-imperial: in particular, a free and resurgent India would carry weight politically as well as ideologically.

The first OSE conference was held in Paris in 1921, attended by 1,400 delegates from 39 countries. Then, thanks to a Dutch enthusiast, the Order was allowed to make use of Castle Eerde, a large house near Ommen in Holland. International Star Camps were held in the grounds. Krishnamurti himself, meanwhile, had adjusted to western ways, and was living comfortably on the generosity of friends. In 1922, while staying at Ojai in California, he underwent a psychological and physical crisis. He had sensations of burning; he felt an outside 'presence' and heard voices. The experience was so vivid that it left him, for the moment, more fully committed to his Theosophical destiny. Handsome, well-dressed, eloquent, he addressed audiences at Castle Eerde and they hung on his words. He talked about liberation: from systems in general, from orthodox religion in particular, from conventional marriage, and from other constraints on the divine in all of us.

Attendance at the Star Camps rose into the thousands. Dreams of a new day were in the air, with encouragement from people of deserved prestige. One supporter, at least for a time, was the explorer and humanitarian Fridtjof Nansen. Another was a future leader of the Labour Party, George Lansbury, who, it will be recalled, had begun in politics with Morris's blessing. Before the War he had been one of the few male activists in the 'Votes for Women' campaign. A militant leader in the same cause, Charlotte Pankhurst, was now flirting with the OSE. Glimpsed occasionally also were the conductor Leopold Stokowski and the actor John Barrymore, the 'Great Profile'. These seekers and sympathisers came nowhere near the commitment of Theosophists, but they did seek, they did sympathise, however peripherally. Even Bernard Shaw was favourably impressed, from a safe distance.

Krishnamurti spoke at Adyar in 1925, and his hearers noticed a change in his voice and manner, even in his vocabulary. They inferred that the World Teacher was beginning to take full possession of him. Annie agreed. Leadbeater, who had bounced back from threatened disgrace and was still involved as an adviser, was not so sure. All was not going as anticipated. Krishnamurti might be sounding different, but what was he actually saying? He was laying more and more stress on personal responsibility, less and less on external guidance and the Theosophical apparatus, which, in fact, was beginning to strike his followers as old-fashioned and needlessly complicated. Presently he confessed that he no longer believed in the Masters, and spoke slightingly of Theosophical 'jargon'. Annie was busy with her Indian activities, and not as close to the vehicle as she had been. She still fancied that he could be steered in the intended direction; but he had grown tired of being steered.

At Eerde in August 1929 the breaking point came. Krishnamurti dissolved the Order and relinquished the Messianic role. His decision showed notable integrity. The OSE was a ready-made organisation that could give him fame, wealth, publicity, influence; yet he turned his back on it. He could no longer believe in any organisation that constricted and codified the quest for truth.

While he had prepared his followers to a certain extent, he had not done it clearly enough, and many of them felt betrayed. They had poured out money and devotion, and now he rejected all of it. Emily Lutyens felt that she was 'dropping into nothingness'. Annie Besant herself sank under the blow. Yet her resilience did not quite desert her. In her eighties, radical to the last, she still clung to one of her dearest hopes, that she would live to see India independent. However, independence was not to be achieved yet, and she died four years later, in 1933.

The odd feature of this tragicomedy, which justifies viewing it as more than a pure delusion, is that in its inception a real insight was at work.

When Charles Leadbeater, on the beach at Adyar, picked out one boy among several as exceptional – a boy who was not in the least outstanding – there was no obvious reason for him to do so. His action was not frivolous; it was, for whatever reason, strongly motivated. Having previously named Hubert van Hook, he was now so convinced of the claim of an obscure Indian that he decided to drop Hubert and try again, even at the cost of losing wealthy support. When Mrs van Hook and her son made the voyage to India – a long one, since most of it was then by sea – he was prepared to confess that he had made a mistake. It was not a trivial admission: years later, in adult life, Hubert was still so embittered that he forbade his wife and children even to mention Theosophy.

Leadbeater had some reason for his choice, and the intuition that guided it was, after a fashion, correct, however we may interpret the fact. Krishnamurti actually did turn out to be exceptional.

He not only sustained the exacting role he was groomed to sustain, but went on after his abdication to become a public philosopher in his own right. Settling in California, he attracted a new set of interested seekers, among them Aldous Huxley, Christopher Isherwood, Igor Stravinsky, and several Hollywood celebrities, even Greta Garbo. His books, and, later, his taped lectures, had a respectable sale. He was going his own way, and in no sense carrying on his Theosophical phase, which he refused to discuss with anyone, asserting a selective amnesia. He lived until 1986.

12

The Last Offbeat Radical

The second play of Shaw's *Back to Methuselah* cycle, 'The Gospel of the Brothers Barnabas', originally included a long scene which he reconsidered and finally discarded. It can still be read, however, because he published it separately. It introduces a remarkable woman, Mrs Etteen. She turns out to have been the person who first put the longevity idea into Franklyn's head, and, indirectly, into Conrad's. Mrs Etteen has a long conversation with Franklyn's brother-in-law, whose name is Immenso Champernoon. 'Immenso' is a joke, understood as soon as the character enters, but he is much more than a joke.

Shaw's stage direction describes him as 'a man of colossal mould, with the head of a cherub and the body of a Falstaff'. With the brothers and (a little more soberly) with Mrs Etteen, Immenso is tremendously voluble, and full of wildly original humour; he zigzags from one serious topic to another and is hard to pin down. He is a caricature – an affectionate and deeply respectful caricature – of a public figure whom many of the audience, even in a pre-television age, would have known with amusement to be the original.

Shaw attached a note saying that he brought in this 'notable social philosopher of our day' for the mere fun of caricaturing him, but in the upshot he could only produce 'a manifestly inferior copy of a gorgeous original'. Yet it was worth trying:

> I think it possible that my thumbnail sketch, inadequate and libellous as it is, may give a hint or two to some future great biographer as to what the original of Immenso Champernoon was like in the first half of his career, when, in defiance of the very order of nature, he began . . . [by] deriding his own aspect, and in middle life slimmed into a Catholic saint.

The final phrase, to an unprepared reader, would have been startling.

Gilbert Keith Chesterton, the original of Immenso, was born in 1874 in a house on Campden Hill, Kensington. A brother who arrived subsequently, and played an important role in his life, was named Cecil. Gilbert went to St Paul's School, then in Hammersmith, where masters and other boys thought him absent-minded but intermittently brilliant. He chaired an unofficial debating society formed by a group of friends. After leaving St Paul's, not caring to join the family business as a house agent, he attended the Slade School of Art and then found a job with a publisher. He was already writing poems and articles and reviews, and he gradually became known. By 1900 he was a more or less established book critic and a published author. He was six feet two inches tall, and with the passage of time, he became extremely bulky and often made jokes about his size – hence the Immenso caricature. In journalism, as George Bernard Shaw was 'GBS', so Gilbert Keith Chesterton was 'GKC'. Shaw, though eighteen years older, was a lifelong friend, and their affection survived through many ideological differences. Gilbert married happily, but there were no children, to the disappointment of both partners; his wife Frances was found to be unable to have them, for physiological reasons. The couple lived in Battersea on the south side of the Thames.

Chesterton wrote on all kinds of topics, and produced fiction as well. The style varied appropriately. Except in plain narrative – and even that was apt to be not entirely plain – it was unique and distinctive. His prose could be rhetorical and ebullient, with a rhythm of its own that never slipped into unintentional verse. It could sparkle with wit and fancy; it could be serious and moving; and it could, on occasion, do both within the same paragraph. It was full of parallelisms, alliterations, internal echoes, even puns. He might be saying something quite obvious, or voicing plain common sense, yet he could do it so that what he said didn't sound like a platitude. He was notorious for his paradoxes. To make a point, he would say something surprising, unexpected, and apparently wrong, and then show how it was correct. He spoke of paradox as 'Truth standing on her head to attract attention'.

Chestertonian prose often seemed to invite parody, yet it is doubtful whether anyone ever managed this convincingly – even Max Beerbohm, who composed an ingenious pastiche. In the mass of Chesterton's writing, the style could become mechanical and tiresome, but right through to the end of his life, he maintained momentum and never declined like some of his contemporaries.

It is important to be aware of this output – thirty-five volumes in a collected edition – to get his Offbeat Radicalism into perspective. In a full account of his career, that part of it will be overshadowed by other things. Yet to pick out the Offbeat episodes alone may give them a disproportionate weight. It remains the only viable course; but, in tracing those episodes, one must bear in mind always that other things were happening at the same time – not only writing but lecturing, debating, travelling, social activities, and, as will appear, a personal quest.

*

There are foretastes of Chesterton's unique development in a book that he brought out in 1904. *The Napoleon of Notting Hill* is not a statement but a story. He wrote it in a hurry, to raise an advance from a publisher when he and Frances were penniless. It hints, however, at things to come. Also it has an accidental peculiarity: the story begins in 1984.

An introductory chapter explains why the author portrays the future as he does. After a characteristically Chestertonian opening – 'The human race, to which so many of my readers belong' – he reviews several contemporary trends: Wells's scientific progress, Carpenter's apostolate of the Simple Life, the Fabians' systematising and stereotyping, and so on. He invents anecdotes that carry each trend further to a *reductio ad absurdum*. Vegetarianism, for instance, culminates in vegetarians proposing to live on salt, and a pamphlet asking indignantly why salt should suffer. The general notion is that none of the trends will go where their exponents imagine.

At the end of Chapter One, 'eighty years after the present date', all these progressive, rational tendencies have passed into oblivion without fundamentally changing anything. England is much the same, only duller. Government is carried on by a bureaucracy that is in control because no one sees any point in protest. There is a head of state called the king, with a few minor prerogatives, but kings are picked from a list as jurors are, because it makes no difference who reigns.

Then a newly-chosen king, Auberon Quin, *is* different. Reputedly, this character is modelled on Beerbohm. He has an impish sense of humour, and tries to liven things up with what might today, in America, be called 'creative anachronism'. He gives the London boroughs medieval-style charters, and insists on officials having titles like Lord High Provost and wearing ceremonial costume. The masquerade is resented at first, then tolerated as the king's eccentricity, and the system absorbs it.

But now something actually happens. Developers plan to drive a new highway through western London. Properties are bought up and demolished without resistance. However, the shopkeepers of one small street in Notting Hill (near Chesterton's birthplace) are unwilling to sell out, and their Provost, Adam Wayne, gives them his backing. He is a young and charismatic leader with no sense of humour, and he has taken the royal programme seriously – to King Auberon's consternation. He stands on what he assumes to be his rights, and says he would 'die for the sacred mountain, even if it were ringed with all the armies of Bayswater'.

Attempts to dispossess him fail, and his resourceful defence of Notting Hill awakens a new national spirit. Local patriotism, local customs, local imagination and independence revive. London becomes a cluster of free city-states, each with its own character. For twenty years this transformation endures. Then Notting Hill, in the pride of precedence, becomes imperialist and tries to dictate to the rest of London. Adam Wayne is still Provost, and knows that this betrayal of the small-scale will be disastrous. However, his councillors overrule him. And Bayswater does march against Notting Hill; and so do North Kensington and Shepherds Bush. Adam makes a hopeless personal stand, and the old king rallies to his support. Both are killed – representatives of two aspects of human nature, reconciled.

The Napoleon of Notting Hill may or may not count as a novel, but vital ideas are embedded in the fantasy. Its romanticisation of violence may be held against it. Still, this is less objectionable in a story written before 1914, and Adam wins his guerrilla war against the developers by a stratagem that inflicts no casualties at all.

Chesterton is making two real points, both of which anticipate his later thinking. The first is that vague 'progress' and social evolution, in whatever form, will not bring fundamental change. Different versions merely blend and cancel each other. Change for the better can only happen through firm and definite conviction: even conviction like Adam Wayne's, which the progressive mind will dismiss as irrational.

The second point is that the watchword for a better society must be – to adopt the slogan of E. F. Schumacher – 'Small is Beautiful'. While Chesterton's focus in the story is on local patriotism, he relates this to the rights of small nationalities. *The Napoleon of Notting Hill* was a favourite book of Michael Collins, the Irish nationalist leader who negotiated with Lloyd George about independence. Chesterton will be saying 'Small is Beautiful', or something like it, in other connections too.

He followed *The Napoleon of Notting Hill* with a volume of essays, *Heretics*. In this he expanded the novel's opening chapter by looking at several contemporary authors in the same spirit, still with considerable humour, but with serious intent. Some of them were more popular than himself, and better established. He included his friend Bernard Shaw, and Wells (again), and Kipling, and Ibsen. The word 'heretic' was a curious choice. It would normally have implied an orthodoxy from which these authors dissented, but Chesterton's writing carried no such implication – not yet. Like Lewis Carroll's Humpty Dumpty, he made the word mean what he wanted. He defined a heretic as 'a man whose philosophy is quite solid, quite coherent, and quite wrong'. The subjects of his treatment, he argued, brilliant as some of them were, all propagated philosophies which were at best only partial, therefore misguided, and which pulled in different directions. The result, as the *Napoleon* introduction had suggested, would be confusion and intellectual deadlock, not the freedom and progress which most of them, in one way or another, professed to stand for.

Naturally *Heretics* roused antagonism. Its author could hardly have hoped to get away with criticism of all these respected figures, even though he declared his own respect for them. One contemporary writer, G. S. Street, remarked that it was all very well for Chesterton to talk like this about everybody else's philosophy; but, said Street, 'I will begin to worry about my philosophy when Mr Chesterton has given us his.'

Street's challenge was taken up, though not at once. Chesterton was in no hurry; he was busy with a book on Dickens (one of his best literary studies) and his reply to Street took shape after that, and would not appear until 1908. An attentive reader of his work could have foreseen that it would be, in some Chestertonian fashion, about Christianity; but not a conventional apologia. A few years previously, Chesterton had plunged into a newspaper controversy with a well-known agnostic socialist, Robert Blatchford, and defended some aspects of Christian belief and practice, eliciting the complaint that you couldn't pin him down. He had not then been notably successful in persuading readers.

It was not the only time he was reproached for an apparent evasiveness. In his *Autobiography*, Chesterton recalls a socialist dinner at which he sat next to a 'very refined and rather academic gentleman from Cambridge':

> He said suddenly, with abrupt civility: 'Excuse my asking, Mr Chesterton, of course I shall quite understand if you prefer not to answer, and I shan't think any the worse of it, you know, even if it's true. But I suppose I'm right in thinking you don't really believe in those things you're defending against Blatchford?' I informed him with adamantine gravity that I did most definitely believe in those things. . . . He went on eating his (probably vegetarian) meal. But I was sure that for the rest of the evening, despite his calm, he felt as if he were sitting next to a fabulous griffin.

In 1908 the fabulous griffin spoke again, much more eloquently, and with a much broader range. The book was called, appropriately, *Orthodoxy*. One immediate result was that when it reached Russia, the Tsar's censors banned it unread, assuming that it must be about the Orthodox Church, and that anything about the Orthodox Church must be an attack on it. Elsewhere, it reached the public safely. Chesterton was now at a high point of reputation, through accumulated journalism, fiction, and literary criticism. His new book sold well and influenced many.

Orthodoxy is a *tour de force* which no contemporary, Christian or otherwise, could have equalled. In this case, the author undoubtedly is pinned down. In answer to Street's invitation, Chesterton offers a personal statement. He starts with some general topics, more or less foreshadowed in *Heretics*; then he goes on to explore Christian doctrine in relation to convictions and intuitions of his own. He has found that Christianity makes sense of them and, so to speak, holds everything together. One emphatic testimony follows another. He tells how fairy tales taught him the true logic of the universe; how he saw the inadequacy and restrictiveness of a purely 'rational' point of view; how he saw through philosophical muddles over cause and effect; how he realised that 'freethinkers' in the Bradlaugh style were anything but free; how he realised that people must be treated as individuals, not bits of a shapeless humanity or a Theosophical fudge. And in every case traditional Christian teaching confirmed and clarified the answers he had arrived at himself.

There is no hint of fundamentalism, and while the tone is often exuberant, there is no mindless zeal about being 'saved'. Chesterton's Christian enthusiasm, though infectious, is very far from the emotionalism of the evangelist. Nor is there any sectarian propaganda. Several of his points are easier to grasp on Catholic assumptions than on Protestant ones. But the notion some of his readers have formed – that after *Orthodoxy* he should logically have become a Catholic – is mistaken. *Orthodoxy* does not present any direct arguments for Catholic teaching being true. It does present, sometimes exhilaratingly, a series of considerations that Chesterton found impressive. But they were not impressive enough to make him go to church. In one biography, this hard and simple fact of his non-attendance is attested briefly; in others it is ignored, and a reader, aware of his pro-Christian stance, is left to assume that he must have gone – but he didn't, until, fourteen years later, he accepted an obligation to do so.

With his hugely successful detective stories – the Father Brown saga began in 1911 – the chronology implies nothing different. In these he achieved the feat, difficult at that time, of inventing a detective who should not be like Sherlock Holmes. A devoted reader of *Orthodoxy*, Dorothy L. Sayers, presently invented another one, but Father Brown's début came long before Lord Peter Wimsey's. His creator exploited the notion that a priest who had heard numerous confessions might be exceptionally well equipped to solve crimes. Father Brown is based on a real priest, Father John O'Connor, who surprised Chesterton with his knowledge of evil behind a façade of innocence. But the first Father Brown stories are the work of a sympathetic outsider, not a member of Brown's communion.

In *The Napoleon of Notting Hill*, *Orthodoxy*, and other writings, Chesterton deployed several of his major beliefs and interests. They would grow more explicit, and converge in his ideology of distributism. Not quite yet, however.

*

Chesterton was a patriot, but, as might be inferred from *The Napoleon of Notting Hill*, he was not enthusiastic about the British Empire. During the Boer War he was one of a small group that opposed the war. In September 1909 he made his sole contribution to imperial politics, and it was quite in character. He sparked off a train of events that eventually posed a major challenge to British rule in India. Yet he was not trying to do this, and he probably never knew that he had done it.

He was a regular contributor to the *Illustrated London News*, and there on 19 September he discussed the demand for Indian self-rule – *swaraj* or *swarajya* – which some in the sub-continent were beginning to voice. He could respect them, he said, if they were genuinely Indian. The western civilisation which the British had been trying to impose on their country might well be regarded as a blight. But the more articulate nationalists didn't want to eliminate the blight so that India could go its own way; they wanted to push on further into westernisation, to have parliamentary democracy and modern industry, to ape the English and call it freedom.

> When young Indians talk of independence for India, I get a feeling that they do not understand what they are talking about. I admit that they who demand *swarajya* are fine fellows; most young idealists are fine fellows. I do not doubt that many of our officials are stupid and oppressive. Most such officials are stupid and oppressive. But when I see the actual papers and know the views of Indian nationalists, I get bored and feel dubious about them. What they want is not very Indian and not very national. They talk about Herbert Spencer's philosophy and other similar matters. What is the good of the Indian national spirit if they cannot protect themselves from Herbert Spencer? . . .
>
> One of their papers is called *The Indian Sociologist*. Do the Indian youths want to pollute their ancient villages and poison their kindly homes by introducing Spencer's philosophy into them?

At this time Gandhi was living in South Africa, practising as a lawyer, campaigning for civil rights for the Indian minority, and publishing a weekly paper, *Indian Opinion*. He had long since digested the ideas of his western mentors such as Ruskin and Tolstoy, and worked out his own interpretations. In an amazing moment of synchronicity, or coincidence, he happened to be visiting England on business when the *Illustrated London News* came out. Chesterton's reputation was potent enough to attract his attention. Gandhi read the article and it burst on him like a revelation. He translated it into Gujarati (what became of Chesterton's prose in that language?) and sent it home for publication in *Indian Opinion*. On the return voyage he composed a pamphlet, *Hind Swaraj*, sketching a new, Chesterton-prompted patriotism that denounced the features of Britain which Indian politicians wanted to imitate. Those politicians were horrified; but when he returned to India, his conception gave him unequalled strength.

Gandhi developed the loss-and-recovery syndrome on a vast scale. He discovered a 'true India' long ago, in a legendary epoch of heroes and sages and village communes, before Muslim and British conquests trampled Hindu society. The present imperial regime was the worst affliction of all. Anybody could see, for instance, how England's machine-made textiles had ruined India's cottage industry, and condemned millions to life-destroying seasonal unemployment. Gandhi's constructive programme, as he called it, meant self-reliance, the revival of hand-spinning and hand-weaving, local democracy. A 'Small is Beautiful' policy would enable the submerged true India to revive. If British power could be turned back by creating an alternative society, the British themselves could be converted. *Satyagraha*, the non-violence that Shelley had first conceived, could further the process. Gandhi recognised that it had to include a moral regeneration. Hindus, for instance, must end one of the worst corruptions of their own religion, Untouchability, which reduced its victims to a sub-human state.

An account of Chesterton is not the place to assess the effectiveness of Gandhi's programme, but two facts stand out. One is that it mobilised the Indian masses as the westernised politicians failed to do. The other is that it was by no means unlike what Chesterton arrived at himself – certainly without imitation.

*

When the Indian article appeared, the Chestertons were settling in at a new home in Beaconsfield. Frances may have initiated the move. She was deeply saddened by her inability – now medically confirmed – to have children, and the London environment was depressing for her. Also she feared that as a Fleet Street character, Gilbert was spending too much time on his work and drinking too much. At any rate, he acquiesced. Beaconsfield distanced him from the immediate pressures of journalism, but some of the journalism went on, as in the *Illustrated London News*, and their new home was reasonably close to the capital – their friends did not drift out of touch.

Gilbert produced a book on one of the best of them, Bernard Shaw. He began assembling the Father Brown saga, and he also wrote two long poems, *The Ballad of the White Horse* and *Lepanto*. The *Ballad* is a condensed epic about Alfred the Great and his struggle against the heathen Danes: at a grim moment in the Second World War, *The Times* quoted two stanzas at the head of the leader page. As for *Lepanto*, this too has the theme of Christian resistance to conquerors. It is about as far from political correctness as it could possibly be. The trouble is that it is magnificent. An obtuse critic once described it as a mere 'noise-poem'; it is in fact an extremely erudite poem, requiring dozens of notes for the full understanding of its allusions. Chesterton's achievement is that the reader can follow it without any notes, enjoying its headlong sweep and its dazzling imagery. Even the most obscure of the allusions don't slow it down.

For all this, though, there is nothing yet to justify Shaw's description, in his note on the Immenso caricature, of the original as a 'notable social philosopher of our day'. Shaw is thinking of later developments, well known by the time he wrote the scene; the phrase, applied to Chesterton, would not have been apt before about 1910.

At that time there was a renewed quest for something radical, even revolutionary like socialism, that would not actually *be* socialism – at any rate as Fabians understood it. The Blakean phrase 'New Age' reappeared more publicly as the title of a weekly review in which 'Guild Socialism' emerged as an alternative. Its advocates, with Ruskin and Morris in mind, were recalling the craft guilds and merchant guilds of a pre-capitalist era. Industries, instead of being annexed by the State, were to be owned and run by corporations representing the people who worked in them. Some labour activists welcomed this idea, seeing existing trade-unions as potential guilds. *The New Age* had an excellent if eccentric editor, A. R. Orage, who succeeded in attracting a cluster of star contributors. One was G. D. H. Cole, later a distinguished left-wing economist,† who began his career as a young and brash guild socialist. However, no leader emerged, Orage wandered off on paths of his own, and the movement petered out.

In its phase of growth Chesterton was attracted to guild socialism, and offered suggestions, but did not see it as a serious political force. His own incipient Offbeat Radicalism went a different way. Instrumental in the process was his younger brother. Cecil was an ex-Fabian, decidedly 'ex', but still, after his fashion, a socialist. He worked for *The New Age*, and became assistant editor of a more polemical weekly, the *Eye Witness*, later becoming editor-in-chief when it was reconstructed as the *New Witness*. His journalism reflected disillusionment, Gilbert's as well as his own, with the Liberal government. The Liberal Party had come to power

† Cole wrote, among other books, a history of British working-class movements, and the principal biographies of Robert Owen and William Cobbett.

in 1906 with a huge majority, talking about reforms; but it had achieved only limited success, being hindered and blocked by the House of Lords. The Budget introduced by Lloyd George as Chancellor caused a crisis and two further elections, and more complications followed. Cecil could be merciless in his criticisms; Gilbert, who thought the Party was manipulated by its financial backers, and not concerned with liberty, stopped contributing to a Liberal paper.

Worse followed when Cecil exposed insider dealings on the stock market by Government ministers, including Lloyd George himself – the 'Marconi Scandal'. Cecil overstated the case, and the ministers more or less rebutted the charges, but they were manifestly not innocent. Gilbert drew an interesting conclusion about Fabianism. What was the point in looking for progress by way of more and more government, if government was ineffectual and – even to the extent revealed by the scandal – corrupt?

While he loved and admired his brother, a more portentous figure was beginning to impinge on his life, the friend to whom he had dedicated *The Napoleon of Notting Hill*. Hilaire Belloc edited the *Eye Witness*, and handed it over to Cecil when it became the *New Witness*. In the current literary scene he was almost as ubiquitous as G. K Chesterton himself. He was half French by parentage and had served in the French army, but his mother Bessie Parkes was English and a friend of George Eliot. At Balliol College he achieved distinction both as a student and as a debater in the Union. A 'cradle Catholic' – and sometimes a pugnacious one – he believed that he had been denied an Oxford fellowship by religious prejudice, and kept up a prolonged feud against professional scholars. The result was that they seldom recognised his claim to be a scholar himself, though sometimes he deserved recognition.

He had an American wife and five children, and maintained his household precariously by freelance writing and lecturing. His misfortune today is that he is remembered chiefly for books of comic verse, such as *The Bad Child's Book of Beasts* and *Cautionary Tales*. But he wrote serious poetry, travel books, essays, fiction, biographies and histories, and some of his productions in every genre were good. He entered Parliament as a Liberal in the landslide of 1906, then became disenchanted like the Chestertons, and did not stand again in the second election of 1910. His departure from politics resulted in two important books; Cecil collaborated on the first. Both were crucial in Offbeat development.

The first, published in 1911, was *The Party System*. Belloc had decided, largely on the basis of his own experience, that the Liberal-Conservative conflict was a sham fight. The country's real rulers – the still-powerful aristocracy, the magnates of industry and finance – constituted a bloc that governed all the time, tolerating a change of faces on the front benches every so often, but not genuinely divided. Elections made no real difference. Belloc supported his thesis by observing that all the upper-class folk mingled socially, got together in business, and intermarried, without hostility. This was truer at the time of writing than it became a year or two later, when feelings ran so high about the arguments over the House of Lords that the parties really were opposed, and the upper-class folk didn't mingle as freely as heretofore. Nevertheless Belloc made a case, and Liberals and Tories did govern in coalition during the Great War and for four years after it.

His other important book at this juncture was *The Servile State* (1912), which is still occasionally reprinted, and not merely as a museum piece – it impressed George Orwell. It is a refutation of the whole idea of replacing capitalism with socialism by constitutional means – the Fabian or social-democratic idea. Belloc shows reason why this can never happen. A few years later, numerous left-wingers would be saying the same, and calling for violent revolution.

Belloc's is a more subtle point, which is the explanation of the title. Lloyd George's Liberals, he remarks, are bringing in 'welfare' measures – unemployment benefit, old age pensions, and so forth – with the approval of the infant Labour Party. But all such measures to benefit the workers define them *as* workers, and exclude their becoming anything else. Call this Fabianism or social democracy or whatever you like. The logical result of such legislation, if carried far enough, will be a society with a very similar privileged class on top, unopposed, and most of the people planned and classified, cut down and coerced, in the name of welfare: slavery by status, perhaps even a gentle and defensible slavery, but slavery all the same and with no escape route. If you are tied to a bench or a machine, you will go on being tied to it, and the law will say in effect, 'That's where you belong.'

Does Belloc propose an alternative? Not by pressing further along the same line, and not exactly by putting the clock back: rather, by getting another clock and effecting a general alteration of status. Guilds or whatever may have their place, but for him the key word is 'property', meaning small property, not vast agglomerations. Here he is taking his cue from Pope Leo XIII, whose encyclical *Rerum Novarum* (1891) deplored the wage-slavery of the proletariat, and called for government policies to spread small-scale ownership. Belloc's view is that if more and more employees cease to be employees at all and become owners instead – in full possession of their houses, their means of livelihood, their small farms or orchards or vegetable plots – this can be the beginning of a truly free society delivered from poverty and dependence. He is perfectly aware that there is no popular demand for such a change, but he believes that it is the only one that actually would change anything.[†]

† When staying in the country, Belloc named two favourite pigs Carlyle and Ruskin. I am not sure of the implications.

Besides his political dissent from almost everyone, Belloc held controversial opinions on English history, and his ideas about the past were closely related to his ideas about the present. In particular, he elaborated a view of the Tudor period that defied conventional notions and normal school teaching. It was not, he said, chiefly a time of liberation or national growth: it was a time of profiteering, when the rich got out of control. They began displacing peasants and enclosing the common lands, so that they could make money by sheep-farming – and as enclosures went on and on, land privatisation created bigger and bigger private domains. When Henry VIII broke with Rome and seized the wealth of the monasteries, rapacious courtiers and other entrepreneurs exploited his economic difficulties to make him disgorge most of the loot and hand it over to them, free of charge or at bargain prices. Families grew rich on the spoils. When the Industrial Revolution dawned, the luckier ones found coal and iron on their estates, grew richer still, and discovered lucrative methods of investing the proceeds. Hence, ultimately, the structure of wealth and power known to Belloc.

This was a minority view of things, but it was not entirely original to him. The radical William Cobbett had expressed it almost a century before. But Cobbett himself took material from the Catholic historian Lingard, and in Belloc's hands the religious aspect came to the fore again, the sufferings of the victims were given prominence, and the Reformation, seen as rationalisation of the great pillage, showed an unacceptable face.

Chesterton accepted most of what Belloc had to say, and distributism, the programme based on it, began to take shape. The two had been echoing each other so often that Shaw joked about a new quadruped which had come into being, the Chesterbelloc. Then the time for jokes ended abruptly.

*

In the summer of 1914 the Great War broke out. British public opinion was at first dubious about getting involved, but when Imperial Germany invaded neutral Belgium everything changed almost overnight. This was an atrocity that could not be tolerated. Today, after nearly a century of other atrocities, the appalling impact of this one may be hard to realise, but appalling it was, and British entry into the war was generally supported.

Cecil Chesterton was under forty, and was accepted for the army. Belloc, who was regarded as a military expert on the strength of various writings, acquired a job commenting on current events in a publication called *Land and Water*, which followed the activities of the armies and navies. Gilbert wrote on the general situation, as Shaw, Wells and others did. However, he was out of action for six months owing to illness; for a time there were fears for his life.

His most important book in the aftermath was *A Short History of England*. It endorsed Belloc's view of the Reformation and its consequences, but that was only an episode in a narrative covering the whole Christian era. Some of it, like the Bellocian part, opposed academic orthodoxies, and, like much of Chesterton's work, combined glaring errors of fact and interpretation with insights that put academics in the shade. He exemplified a rule that should be borne in mind when exploring history, and indeed other fields: *There is a wrongness that can lead to rightness more effectively than rightness itself.*

Near the beginning of *A Short History*, there is a chapter on 'The Age of Legends' that brings in the traditions of Arthur and Glastonbury. Even as an account of the legends it is inaccurate. Yet at least Chesterton brings them in, whereas historians have ignored them or dismissed them as fables – virtually always in his time, and too often since. Of course they are not literally true, but it has become clear that reflection on them in the light of archaeological and other researches is far from being a waste of time. Readers of

Chesterton's chapter have gone on to make discoveries that might not have been made otherwise.

Besides taking the Arthurian legend seriously, he opposes the Victorian myth propagated by John Richard Green† – that the people of England are all descended from Anglo-Saxon settlers in the fifth century, warriors from Schleswig-Holstein who blotted out Romano-British society; so that the English are culturally and genetically pure Anglo-Saxons, therefore Germanic, and all their achievements are Germanic achievements.

> It is perhaps permissible to disagree with the historian Green when he says that no spot should be more sacred to modern Englishmen than the neighbourhood of Ramsgate, where the Schleswig people are supposed to have landed.

Again:

> The orthodox historian, notably Green, remarks on the singularity of Britain in being alone of all Roman provinces wholly cleared and repeopled by a Germanic race. He does not entertain, as an escape from the singularity of this event, the possibility that it never happened.

Today, while events in post-Roman Britain are much disputed, Chesterton is closer to scholarly opinion than Green is. The total clearance and repeopling never did happen.

When Chesterton comes to the Middle Ages, he is not as naively wishful as might be expected. He does not idealise the period as Ruskin and Morris sometimes do. He says it would have been a good thing if the Peasants' Revolt had succeeded; but he

† Author of the immensely popular *A Short History of the English People* (1874), on which much of the teaching of English history in schools used largely to be based.

acknowledges that it didn't. Still, medieval England had the potential for going right. It had some of the right attitudes, and some wise institutions (the guilds, for instance) to put them into practice; and above all it had the Catholic faith. The *History* goes on to the sixteenth-century upheavals anatomised by Belloc, the wrecking of medieval England by the rich in alliance with Protestantism, and after that the rise of the new aristocracy and the rural squirearchy, and the enormous expansion since – the whole of it presented characteristically, with penetrating comments and massive yet luminous mistakes.

A feature of the book which has historical interest, and sheds light on Chesterton himself, is an onslaught near the end on a phenomenon which had been, in his time, a real and disturbing issue: the enthusiasm of the English intelligentsia for Germany. They admired its efficiency, its philosophy, its scholarship, its technology and its social services – all linked, of course, with the myth of the Anglo-Saxons, the virile (and apparently genocidal) ancestors, whose heirs the English were.

Chesterton remarks on the prevalence of this kind of thinking in schools and universities. They were teaching, he said:

> That England was but a little branch on a large Teutonic tree; that an unfathomable spiritual sympathy, all-encircling like the sea, had always made us the natural allies of the great folk by the flowing Rhine; that all light came from Luther and Lutheran Germany, whose science was still purging Christianity of its Greek and Roman accretions; that Germany was a forest fated to grow; that France was a dung-heap fated to rot.

And then, after the litany of abasement before the idolised German, Chesterton brings us to the revelation of 1914.

> He in whose honour all had been said and sung stirred,
> and stepped across the border of Belgium.

It comes with a crash, almost epigrammatically. The atrocity blows away the rest.

*

Chesterton's two great concerns, the social and the religious, were intertwining. He might logically have raised the question of conversion, though his mentor Belloc doubted that he would take the final step, and continued to doubt until he actually took it. During 1919 and 1920, the Chestertons were travelling: to Palestine (detached from Turkey and under British control), to Italy, and to America. Back home at last, Gilbert still hesitated, because he was worried about the effect his conversion would have on Frances. She said, however, that she would be relieved when he stopped fretting and went ahead. So he did.

On 30 July 1922, in Beaconsfield, Chesterton was received into the Catholic Church. Shaw was almost as deeply shocked as he had been by Annie Besant's plunge into Theosophy. This conversion, however, was much less of a surprise. There had been plenty of indications, not in *Orthodoxy* alone, of the direction Gilbert was taking. Friends such as H. G. Wells, who disagreed heartily with his decision, remained friends. He was not easy to quarrel with. Frances shed tears, but acquiesced; she would find her own way into the Church later. Her husband was deluged with letters about his action, many from strangers, and replied personally and courteously. He was not an exhibitionist convert, and he said little for public consumption. When asked 'Why?' he gave a brief and curiously old-fashioned answer – 'To get rid of my sins.' To the cliché accusation of having been seduced by ritual and music and beautiful surroundings, he replied, truthfully, 'I was received in a tin shed at the back of a railway hotel.' He wrote a moving sonnet, 'The Convert', and left the matter there, as far as possible.

Opponents charged him with forsaking radicalism to become a 'common Catholic propagandist' and waste his talents on the lives of saints. Nothing could have made him a 'common' propagandist for anything. As for saints, he wrote small books on two: Francis, who founded the Franciscans, and the philosopher Thomas Aquinas, both of whom had an interest ranging far beyond Catholic piety. Even the agnostic Bertrand Russell, in his *History of Western Philosophy*, gave them fifteen pages (he gave only nine to Marx) and added: 'If I had to choose between Thomas Aquinas and Rousseau, I should unhesitatingly choose the saint.'

However, the principal book in Chesterton's later years was *The Everlasting Man* (1925), a highly individual survey of the whole human past that reacts against Wells's best-selling *Outline of History*. This narrative does not even touch on Catholicism until near the end, though when it does, it makes a powerful and original case for the faith, arising out of the entire story. One reader on whom its impact was overwhelming was C. S. Lewis. He certainly did not feel that it was narrowly 'Roman' or that he was being proselytised.

Through journalism and lecturing Chesterton gave the ancient Faith a new effulgence for millions. His writing on the subject was not clerical hack-work; it was, at its best, as able as his writing on any subject. However, it had the defects of its qualities. His style was apt to be so flamboyant and idiosyncratic that it could give the uninitiated a biased notion of what Catholicism was actually like; and he sometimes presented a forceful argument with verbal acrobatics that could entertain but gave a 'too-clever-by-half' impression, so that his point was less effective than it would have been if stated in plain language. It was a good thing, perhaps, that he came to be associated with a weekly paper, and a movement in which others besides himself could make themselves heard.

His brother Cecil had managed to survive the War, only to die most tragically in 1918. Cecil's investigative journal, the *New Witness*, went into a decline. Gilbert, from a sense of fraternal duty, took on the editorship and allowed it to reappear in 1925, restyled and renamed with his own initials, as *G. K.'s Weekly*. Too much of it was written by himself, but it drew in some valued contributors, and could stand comparison with 'quality' reviews such as the *New Statesman*. Very soon it became the voice of an ideology called distributism.

On 17 September 1926, Chesterton presided over the launch of the Distributist League, offering his Bellocian alternative to both capitalism and socialism. The inaugural meeting was held at the Essex Hall off the Strand. He was reluctant to coin another 'ism' word, and several other names were suggested, such as the Luddite league, and the League of Small Property. Someone proposed (not too seriously) the League of the Little People, which would have established a standing joke in view of Chesterton's own dimensions. But the term 'distributist' had already been coined, and it made the essential point about 'distributing' property. At the first committee meeting the following week, he was elected president, and branches were soon formed in several cities besides London. The price of *G. K.'s Weekly* was reduced, and its circulation rose to 8,000.

Chesterton wrote a manifesto for the movement, called *The Outline of Sanity*. He acknowledged his debt to Belloc and, before Belloc, to Pope Leo XIII. These antecedents helped to encourage Catholic interest. Informal distributist gatherings in public houses were noted for their vociferous quotations from Thomas Aquinas, an uncommon feature in normal pub conversation. But a fellow-Dominican of St Thomas whom Chesterton admired, Father Vincent McNabb, pointed out that if distributists meant what they said, they ought to be working, not arguing in pubs; they ought to be building the new society themselves.

It was the challenge Ruskin had tried to meet with his Guild of St George. Some, indeed, were doing what Father McNabb urged. The ex-Fabian sculptor Eric Gill formed a distributist-inspired commune at Ditchling in Sussex, and became art editor of *G. K.'s Weekly*. But while a few did make a modest start with back-to-the-land activities, the League tended to attract more self-proclaimed activists of exactly the wrong sort. One of the paper's staff, Desmond Gleeson, reminisced long afterwards:

> There was a certain kind of person who drifted to Distributist meetings; possibly because he had outstayed his welcome elsewhere. Knowing little enough of the matter, he was instantly anxious that something should be done.... He had always just left a job; he never seemed to be in a job.... Now it was this type which had never held down a decent job long enough to learn what the job really was that was eternally urging the League to quit talking and get doing.

Gleeson added that when a few such enthusiasts did acquire a plot of land, they were apt to start trying to build a chapel instead of digging, if they did anything at all.

In fact, there never was much effective action. The Distributist League reached an apex of public interest in October 1927 when Chesterton (speaking for the League) and Shaw (speaking for socialism) discussed economic fundamentals, with Belloc in the chair, and the debate was broadcast live. After this, the League began to decline, with internal dissent splitting it over questions like the proper use and ownership of machinery. Chesterton at least tried to tackle that issue with suggestions about co-operatives. Many members evaded it. The paper declined alongside.

The record shows one unexpected name. In December 1928, *G. K.'s Weekly* was the first publication in England to carry a contribution by George Orwell. It was an article on misuse of the press for propaganda. While he retained his independence of mind, Orwell told a friend, as late as 1935, that 'what England needed was to follow the kind of policies in Chesterton's *G. K.'s Weekly*.' He seems to have been an unspoken distributist before he was a socialist.

Distributism had been a quixotic cause from the start. In the 1920s, adherents of the Right and the Left had their entrenched beliefs, and very few were looking for an alternative. The movement had some effect in overseas parts of the British Commonwealth. In Nova Scotia, for instance, St Francis Xavier University organised a co-operative movement to combat the Depression. But British distributism had a flaw in its own nature: its most vocal and visible exponents were Catholics. Some besides Chesterton himself were persons of high calibre, but the impression of sectarianism, especially the sectarianism of what was then an unpopular minority sect, remained a handicap.

Gilbert managed to keep his habitual aplomb, but his rejection of both capitalism and socialism laid him open to a political hazard. While in Rome to collect material for a book, he met the Italian dictator Mussolini, who astutely led him to think that Fascism was a 'third thing' and therefore of interest to distributists. Happily, Gilbert's resulting half-sympathy never extended to Nazism, which he detested utterly, and attacked again and again before it was fashionable to do so.

After his death in 1936, the remnants of distributism became largely right wing in outlook, and lost the plot altogether. Belloc faded into the background; he died in 1953. His son-in-law Reginald Jebb continued to give lectures, and welcomed Conservative sloganising about a 'property-owning democracy'.

For a variety of reasons, G. K. Chesterton remains a marvellous literary figure, inspiring and invigorating as few of his contemporaries were. Whether distributism could ever revive is another matter. The difficulty is not so much that its aims cannot be achieved as that some have been achieved without bringing the fundamental difference for which the League hoped. The premiership of Mrs Thatcher made it clear that there need not be anything revolutionary, or even subversive, about enabling people to own houses. To achieve more, distributism required a shift in attitudes, a shift in the psychological bias of society. Its failure to materialise consigned the movement to nullity.

With the end of distributism, we come to the end – for the present, anyhow – of Offbeat Radicalism.

Epilogue

The Russian Revolution, like the French, attracted ardent support outside, and sympathisers were still numerous in the Stalin era. But sympathy dwindled as the nature of the Russian regime became clear, and died with its collapse; after that, there was nothing left to sympathise with. In this case, the Revolution never provoked an Offbeat Radical retort. Later, in the junior ferment of the Sixties, people talked of an alternative society, but not coherently or effectively. They seldom went beyond minor experiments in communal living.

There was, however, a related phenomenon. The Age of the Holy Spirit reappeared in one of its recurrent disguises when Pop culture embraced the Age of Aquarius. The notion that the Earth passes through astrological phases arises from the fact that it oscillates in its orbit. The theory is that history falls into equal periods, determined by the oscillations and ruled by whichever sign of the Zodiac the sun is in at the spring equinox. The Age of Pisces is said to be near its end, or, indeed, to have ended already. The world is passing or about to pass into the Age of Aquarius. The 'dawning of the Age of Aquarius' became an orthodoxy from the late Sixties on. This was to be a time of harmony, understanding, and spiritual growth. It is not clear whether it has started yet.

Such speculations helped to foster a new interest in William Blake and his vision of a new age – an interest that leads back to the beginning of the Offbeat story; even to a geographic beginning. As we saw, a popular interpretation of Blake's 'Jerusalem' poem fastened on the supposed allusion to Glastonbury. The Sixties' ferment brought a revival of interest in that legend-haunted place in its Isle of Avalon. Glastonbury began to attract a stream of seekers and neo-mystics. They seldom showed much interest in its real history and mythology. They preferred modern theories – for instance, that signs of the Zodiac are marked out on the surrounding landscape; or that ancient Glastonbury was the chief British sanctuary of a Goddess who presided over a golden age, which an appropriate religious change might restore.

Glastonbury rose to national and international prominence in that much-publicised time to which the Blakean term 'New Age' came to be applied. It became a centre for astrology and witchcraft, clairvoyance and reincarnation, alternative therapies, 'Earth Magic' and the like. Some of this was a legacy of Theosophy, latent for a spell, now made manifest. That strange temporary ally of Offbeat Radicalism was inspiring science fiction and fantasy long ago, and in the New Age it has advanced with rapid strides, while maintaining anonymity.

It has inspired belief in books of Ancient Wisdom which only initiates are allowed to see; in mysterious wire-pulling by unseen groups; in the esoteric symbolism of familiar myths; in secret history known only to a privileged few; in 'real' Christian origins suppressed or perverted by the Church. All who favour such notions are in fact spiritual heirs of Madame Blavatsky. Indirectly, she has been supplying material for bestselling fiction as well as much that purports to be factual. Offbeat Radicalism may have reached its end, but the Theosophical ally from which it freed itself has made a surprising return. To use a more appropriate word, it has been reincarnated, in a medley of disguises.

However, let us recapitulate. Offbeat Radicalism, as examined in this book, was a British – mainly English – phenomenon, that arose from a certain historical situation. It signified protest, sometimes extreme protest, coupled with dissent from the political forms of protest, and a search for alternatives. William Morris was a partial exception and did endorse Marxist revolution; but even he saw it as the way to a society embodying his own ideals, in a distant 'epoch of rest' which Marxists allowed him to imagine, but seldom mentioned in practice.

The Offbeat Radicals are linked in various ways, and form a kind of succession. But had they any characteristics in common? How do they compare with each other under such headings as class, circumstances, financial status? Was an Offbeat Radical a recognisable type of person?

Let us pass them in review. Blake was a skilful and inventive engraver who made very little money. Shelley was a university-educated scion of landed gentry, who never worked at a regular job, and lived in debt and confusion until an inheritance rescued him. Owen was a self-made industrialist with a working-class background, who rose to affluence by his own abilities. The two most eminent women, George Eliot and Annie Besant, were outstanding writers in different ways – George Eliot, one of the greatest. Ruskin was born into a prosperous commercial family, hung on to his privileges, and was fairly successful as a part-time academic. Morris was a poet, and a supremely gifted entrepreneur in such fields as interior decoration and book production. Carpenter was an eccentric ex-clergyman. Shaw (if we include him despite his socialism, as being decidedly Offbeat in his conception of it) came from an Irish family with musical pretensions, was supported by his mother for years, and eventually became rich and famous as a dramatist. Chesterton, the son of a London house-agent, was a journalist and a poet and much more.

They were plainly very different. They all talked and wrote, but they were not simply theorists, and two of them, Owen and Morris, were publicly and practically successful. No stereotype emerges.

But if we turn to religious and anti-religious attitudes, while we also find variations, we do find a common factor – a negative one from which a positive conclusion emerges. The common factor was rejection of one of the greatest Victorian institutions, the established Church of England. That is obvious with the unbelievers, but it applies also (for example) to Annie Besant, who began her adult life as the wife of a vicar, but broke with her clerical husband, and remained utterly estranged from him and all that he stood for. It applies also to Chesterton, who never went to church as a nominal Anglican, and was taken by his conversion into a minority body which, in pre-ecumenical days, was sharply distinct from the established Church, and often at odds with it.

This common factor is more than a coincidence, it is a clue. The Church of England – as a conservative institution closely associated with the monarchy and the aristocracy, dominating most of the educational system, and, during the Darwin controversy, seen as obscurantist – was an entrenched obstacle to a certain kind of change, not political or economic, but human. All Offbeat Radicals desired, in various forms and degrees, what the Church prevented: *human* change, a transformation in attitudes, in thinking, in lifestyles, leading to a fundamentally different society.

The wished-for step, however conceived, was unambiguously a step forward. The Radical might draw inspiration from the past, and hope for the recovery of something lost, but was never a reactionary. And the idea of a step forward recalls a motif that occurs often enough to be interesting: the quantum leap. Several Offbeat Radicals were unwilling to see humanity as merely travelling, even in the right direction. For real change there would need to be, at the very least, a definite turning of the corner and perhaps more: in terms of Blake's myth, an awakening of Albion. People might start building Jerusalem; or take to practising heroic non-violence; or attain a sudden Owenite enlightenment; or execute a Shavian biological change and live much longer; or find a new Messiah. H. G. Wells went against his own principles when he invented his transfiguring comet, but he was in good company.

Is the conception of a leap simply wishful thinking? Or does it express an insight into the human condition and human potentialities? It certainly has a long pedigree, going back to Joachim of Fiore, who foretold a transition to a changed world. Sometimes recognisably, sometimes incognito, he is a presence in the imaginings of Offbeat Radicals, and others as well. It would be pleasant to think that he was a true prophet, and that in some form at present unknowable, the best is yet to be.

Bibliography

Abse, Joan. *John Ruskin: The Passionate Moralist*. London, Quartet Books, 1980.

Ahlquist, Dale. *G. K. Chesterton: The Apostle of Common Sense*. San Francisco, Ignatius Press, 2003.

Ashe, Geoffrey. *The Book of Prophecy: From Ancient Greece to the Modern Day*. Revised edition, London, Orion, 2002.

—— *Camelot and the Vision of Albion*. London, Heinemann, 1971.

—— *Gandhi: A Study in Revolution*. London, Heinemann, 1968. New edition *Gandhi: A Biography*. New York: Cooper Square Press, 2000.

Ashton, Rosemary. *George Eliot: A Life*. London, Hamish Hamilton, 1996.

Belloc, Hilaire. *The Servile State*. Original publication London, T. N. Foulis, 1912. Reissue with new introductory material, Indianapolis, Liberty Fund, 1977.

Besant, Annie. *An Autobiography*. London, T. Fisher Unwin, 1893.

Blake, William. *Blake: Complete Writings*. Ed. Geoffrey Keynes. London, Oxford University Press, 1966.

Boris, Eileen. *Art and Labor: Ruskin, Morris, and the Craftsman Ideal in America*. Philadelphia, Temple University Press, 1986.

Borsche, Chris R. Vanden. *Carlyle and the Search for Authority*. Columbus, Ohio State University Press, 1991.

Carey, John, ed. *The Faber Book of Utopias*. London, Faber and Faber, 1999.

Carlyle, Thomas. *The French Revolution*. Original publication 1837. New York, Modern Library Classics, 2002.

—— *Latter-Day Pamphlets*. Original publication 1850. London, J. M. Dent, 1962.

—— *Past and Present*. Original publication 1843. London, J. M. Dent, 1962.

Carpenter, Edward. *Civilisation: Its Cause and Cure and Other Essays*. London, George Allen and Unwin Ltd, 1921.

Chesterton, G. K. *Autobiography*. Original publication 1937. Reissue, Sevenoaks, Fisher Press, 1992.

—— *Heretics*. London, John Lane, 1905. Numerous reprints.

—— *The Napoleon of Notting Hill*. London, John Lane, 1904. Numerous reprints.

—— *Orthodoxy*. London, John Lane, 1908. Numerous reprints.

—— *A Short History of England*. Original publication, 1917. Re-issue, Sevenoaks, Fisher Press, 1994.

Clubbe, John, ed. *Carlyle and His Contemporaries: Essays in Honour of Charles Richard Sanders*. Durham, North Carolina, Duke University Press, 1976.

Cohn, Norman. *The Pursuit of the Millennium*. London, Secker and Warburg, 1957. Revised edition, Granada, 1970.

Cole, G. D. H. *The Life of Robert Owen*. London, Macmillan, 1930.

Dangerfield, George. *The Strange Death of Liberal England*. Original publication 1935. Reissue, London, Serif, in association with Stanford University Press, 1997.

Drake, Jane. *William Morris: An Illustrated Life*. Norwich, Pitkin Guides, 1996.

Eliot, George. *Romola* (1963). Vol. 6 in William Blackwood edition of her novels.

Faulkner, Peter. *Against the Age: An Introduction to William Morris*. London, George Allen and Unwin, 1980.

Foot, Michael. *The Politics of Paradise: A Vindication of Byron*. London, Collins, 1988.

French, Patrick. *Younghusband: The Last Great Imperial Adventurer*. London, HarperCollins, 1994.

Fuller, Jean Overton. *Shelley: A Biography.* London, Jonathan Cape, 1968.

Godwin, William. *Enquiry Concerning Political Justice.* Original publication, 1793. London, Penguin Classics, 1985.

Gould, F. J. *Auguste Comte.* London, Watts and Co., 1920.

Gray, Alexander. *The Socialist Tradition: Moses to Lenin.* London, Longmans Green, 1946.

Heffer, Simon. *Moral Desperado: A Life of Thomas Carlyle.* London, Weidenfeld and Nicolson, 1995.

Holmes, Richard. *Shelley: The Pursuit.* New York, E.P. Dutton, 1975.

Holroyd, Michael. *Bernard Shaw.* 3 vols. London, Chatto & Windus, and New York, Random House, 1988–91.

McGinn, Bernard. *Visions of the End: Apocalyptic Traditions in the Middle Ages.* New York, Columbia University Press, 1979.

Mairet, Philip. *A. R. Orage.* Original publication 1936. Re-issue with new material, New York, University Books, 1966.

Martin, Wallace. *The 'New Age' under Orage: Chapters in English Cultural History.* New York, Barnes and Noble, 1967.

Mee, John. *Dangerous Enthusiasm: William Blake and the Culture of Radicalism in the 1790s.* Oxford, Clarendon Press, 1992.

Morris, William. *William Morris by Himself.* Ed. Gillian Naylor. Time Warner Books, UK, 2004.

—— *Selected Writings and Designs.* Ed. with introduction by Asa Briggs. London, Penguin, 1962.

Nethercot, Arthur H. *The First Five Lives of Annie Besant.* Chicago, University of Chicago Press, 1960.

—— *The Last Four Lives of Annie Besant.* London, Rupert Hart-Davis, 1963.

Pearce, Joseph. *Old Thunder: A Life of Hilaire Belloc.* London, HarperCollins, 2002.

—— *Wisdom and Innocence: A Life of G. K. Chesterton.* San Francisco, Ignatius Press, 1996.

Penty, Arthur J. *The Restoration of the Gild System.* London, Swan Sonnenschein, 1906.

Quennell, Peter. *John Ruskin: The Portrait of a Prophet.* London, Collins, 1949.

Reeves, Marjorie. *The Influence of Prophecy in the Later Middle Ages: A Study in Joachimism.* Oxford, Clarendon Press, 1969. Revised edition, Notre Dame, London, University of Notre Dame Press, 1993.

—— *Joachim of Fiore and the Prophetic Future.* London, SPCK, 1976; New York, Harper and Row, 1977.

—— *Prophetic Rome in the High Renaissance Period.* Oxford, Clarendon Press, 1992.

Ruskin, John. *The Stones of Venice.* Ed. Jan Morris. London, Faber and Faber, 1981. (Includes 'The Nature of Gothic'.)

—— *Unto This Last.* Ninth edition. London, George Allen, 1893.

Sewell, Brocard. *Cecil Chesterton.* Faversham, Saint Albert's Press, 1975.

Shaw, George Bernard. *Back to Methuselah.* Original publication 1921. Penguin edition, 1939. The discarded scene is in a separate volume of Shaw's *Collected Works.*

Shelley, Percy Bysshe. *The Complete Poems of Percy Bysshe Shelley.* New York, The Modern Library, 1994.

Todd, Ruthven. *Tracks in the Snow: Studies in English Science and Art.* London, The Grey Walls Press, 1946.

Tribe, David. *President Charles Bradlaugh, MP.* London, Elek Books, 1971.

Vernon, Roland. *Star in the East: Krishnamurti, the Invention of a Messiah.* London, Constable, 2000.

Ward, Maisie. *Gilbert Keith Chesterton.* London, Sheed and Ward, 1944.

—— *Return to Chesterton.* London, Sheed and Ward, 1952.

White, Newman Ivey. *Shelley.* 2 vols. New York, Knopf, 1940.

Wilson, A.N. *Hilaire Belloc.* London, Hamish Hamilton, 1984.

—— *The Victorians*. London, Arrow Books (Random House), 2003.
Wilson, Edmund. *To the Finland Station.* Original publication 1940. London, Fontana, 1960.
Wilson, Mona. *The Life of William Blake.* Revised edition, ed. Geoffrey Keynes. London, Oxford University Press, 1971.

Index